The Bowie Companion

Also edited by Elizabeth Thomson and David Gutman

The Lennon Companion
The Dylan Companion

The Bowie Companion

Edited by

ELIZABETH THOMSON and DAVID GUTMAN

MACMILLAN
LONDON

First published 1993 by Macmillan London

a division of Pan Macmillan Publishers Limited
Cavaye Place London SW10 9PG
and Basingstoke

Associated companies throughout the world

ISBN 0-333-52226-2

9 8 7 6 5 4 3 2 1

A CIP catalogue record for this book is available from
the British Library

Typeset by Cambridge Composing (UK) Limited, Cambridge
Printed and bound in Great Britain by
Mackays of Chatham PLC, Chatham, Kent

For Maureen, and for Stephen

Contents

Contents

Contents

Acknowledgements

Every effort has been made to trace copyright holders of the material included in this collection. The Editors extend their apologies to those whom it has not been possible to contact or to anyone who may have been inadvertently slighted. Redress will be made in any future editions. All lyrics are quoted for the purpose of study, review or critical analysis only, and may differ from those reproduced on lyric sheets. Picture research was undertaken by the Editors.

We are grateful for the help and enthusiasm of all those who contributed to *The Bowie Companion*; particular thanks are due to David Buckley, Gus Dudgeon, Deborah H. Holdstein, Pauline Kael, Lindsay Kemp, Wilfrid Mellers, Philip Norman, Anne Rice and Leslie Thomas.

In addition, we would like to thank a number of others who offered help or shared ideas: Brian Eno, Alan Franks, Helen Fraser, Nick Hedges, Andrea LaBate, Charles Shaar Murray, John Morthland, Timothy W. Ryback and Neil Sinyard.

We are indebted to the following institutions for their assistance in tracking down an extraordinary range of materials: Cambridge University Library, the Institute of Popular Music at Liverpool University, the British Library, the National Sound Archive, Middlesex University, the *Melody Maker* archives and the British Film Institute.

Thanks also to discographer Dave Carr, family, friends and colleagues. And to Roland Philipps, Hazel Orme and all at Macmillan.

Copyright permissions

Copyright permissions

Introduction

'The essence of pop stardom', wrote Anthony Burgess, 'is immaturity – a wretched little pseudo-musical gift, a development of the capacity to shock, a short-lived notoriety, extreme depression, a yielding to the suicidal impulse.'[1] In 1973, Ziggy Stardust 'died' on stage at London's Hammersmith Odeon. Twenty years later, David Bowie released an album that most critics agreed was his best for a decade: *Black Tie/White Noise*. Ziggy is dead. Long live Bowie!

Burgess was right about the capacity to shock, about the notoriety – though that outlived Ziggy – and about the depression, which led to a retreat to Berlin and three albums that were not properly appreciated at the time of their release. But 'a wretched little pseudo-musical gift'? Philip Glass's *Low Symphony* demonstrates the composer's 'genuine regard for the music'[2] of David Bowie, building developmental structures from what he has described as 'fairly complex pieces of music, masquerading as simple pieces'.[3] Glass is a professional musician, Burgess a sometime symphonist forced to live by what he has called his 'unwanted literary gift'. It is Glass's testimony that carries the most weight here, not least because Burgess's pontifications on the pop process were extrapolated from the circumstances of Boy George's fall from grace. He does have a point, though. Rock has never been simply about the music but rather about its *trappings*, the social and political dimension, the sound *and vision*, the totality of experience. The thirtysomething generation grew up with Bowie: Ziggy was the soundtrack for our early adolescence; the Berlin trilogy saw us through college; 'Ashes to ashes' played relentlessly on the Walkman. The heterosexualized heroics of *Let's Dance* widened the fan base, to the regret of a few. Only the pre-grunge sound of Tin Man was a real let-down for, as Tony Parsons commented, the man who epitomized the 1970s could never be just one of the boys in the band.

Introduction

> Meeting David Bowie for the first time in 1991 is like finally getting a date with the girl of your dreams and finding she has brought along her three ugly friends . . . If you want to talk to Bowie, you talk to the band.[4]

For a previous generation, the album *New Morning* was supposed to give us back the 'real' Bob Dylan, invoked by Bowie on *Hunky Dory*. Now *Black Tie/White Noise* brings us what looks like a 'real' David Bowie, a *mature* man whose life, if recent interviews are to be believed, has achieved a certain balance. The album examines 'the twists and turns of companionship',[5] something his many fans will surely relate to – like their mentor, the Bowie Boys and Girls have long grown up. But who among them will not experience the ambient glow of nostalgia as they head to the nearest record store, debiting the plastic for a shiny aluminium disc where once they would have counted out their pocket-money for twelve inches of black vinyl? As sociologist Simon Frith has written:

> The experience of pop music is an experience of placing: in responding to a song, we are drawn, haphazardly, into affective emotional alliances with the performer and with the performer's other fans . . . Other cultural forms – painting, literature, design – can articulate and show off shared values and pride, but only music can make you *feel* them.[6]

Like Dylan and The Beatles, Bowie inspired a host of imitators whose small stars burned only briefly and then died. Bowie's has repeatedly metamorphosed but shows no sign of falling to earth. He topped the singles charts with Mick Jagger in the Live Aid cover of 'Dancing in the street' and he's topping the album charts as we write. It is therefore not unreasonable to ask why he remains the object of so much fascination. Granted a cursory audience some years previously, Adam Sweeting felt let down by the 1990 Sound + Vision 'golden oldies' tour:

> With much of his mystique peeled away, David Bowie seems like a good-looking bloke who can act a bit and write a few songs, and is making the best of what he's got while the going is good.[7]

Needless to say, that is not quite how Bowie sees it. Interviewing him for *Life*, Jim Jerome asked if he was surprised to have proved so durable. 'No,' Bowie replied,

> I deserve to be here. I'm a very good writer. I've gone my own way and been very stubborn. That's the only reason for my existence, and the rest be damned, you know. My saving grace is that I won't do things the way everybody around me wants. That's always given me the friction I've needed to keep writing with a certain freshness.[8]

Even if the original Ziggy generation tires of Bowie's new-found domesticity (and their hero's celebration of parenthood and marital bliss has yet to produce music as anodyne as John Lennon's *Double Fantasy*), teenagers and twentysomethings are discovering him anew. As they stomp through what looks like a seventies revival, young bands such as Suede, Blur, and The Auteurs have emerged to be greeted as the true heirs of Bowie and Ray Davies, locally inflected pop avatars whom Julie Burchill regards as 'singularly English', writing songs that are 'extensions of our "eccentricity"'.[9] With The Kinks, The Beatles, Roxy Music and a small handful of others, Bowie exemplifies 'a specifically English genius . . . that made little England so all-conquering and the big, "important" countries of Europe so pathetically clueless when it came to producing great pop.'[10]

Suede's debut album was swept into the charts on a tide of throwback pop journalism. In *New Musical Express*, editor Steve Sutherland, whose unfashionable Bowie interviews filled countless *Melody Maker* pages in 1989–90, even brought Brett Anderson and Bowie together for a long session of group therapy.[11] And, just as Bowie helped launch his career by posing in a dress, so twenty years later Anderson confessed to feelings of sexual ambiguity and strutted on stage revealing a bare midriff beneath a woman's blouse.

From the outset, Bowie gave journalists and future biographers plenty of good material. Yet, among the statements calculated simply to outrage can be discerned the thoughts of an ambitious young man with a multifaceted career already planned out. In 1972, with chart success still a novelty, Bowie told Michael Watts,

> I'm not content just to be a rock-and-roll star all my life. The reason I'm trying to be one at the moment is so that I can get off. Even now, I've got on to other things, great massive plans for the future . . . The aim of an artist is just to investigate. That's all I want to do: investigate and present the results.[12]

Ten years later, Bowie hadn't deviated from that position: '. . . when you are an artist, you can turn your hand to anything, in any style. Once you have the tools then all the art forms are the same in the end.'[13]

Such subtleties were lost on early biographers like the inevitable George Tremlett (1974), who took time off from GLC politics to riffle through the press clippings, or Vivian Claire (1977), who painted a fan's eye portrait. The ubiquitous Barry Miles combed his own files to come up with the *David Bowie Black Book* (1980), a steady seller that has since been updated by *Melody Maker*'s one-time 'man in New York', Chris Charlesworth; its pedestrian chronology was enlivened by good pictures and some modish packaging aimed at the fashion-conscious Bowie fan. Roy Carr and Charles Shaar Murray provided a more illuminating trawl through Bowie's life and work with their *David*

Introduction

Bowie: an illustrated record (1981), while Kevin Cann's scrupulous *David Bowie: a chronology* (1983) remains the only attempt to diarize Bowie's life and work along the lines of Tom Schultheiss's pioneering Beatles chronology, *A Day in the Life* (Pierian Press, 1980). American journalist Chet Flippo collaborated on *David Bowie: Serious Moonlight* (1984), a suitably elegant retrospective of the 1983 tour, and Dave Thompson followed up with *David Bowie: moonage daydream* (1987), a readable if unremarkable account. Dave Currie and Kerry Juby offered oral history, Currie bringing together highlights from his fanzine in *David Bowie: the Starzone interviews* (1985), while Juby based *In Other Words . . . David Bowie* (1986) on more than thirty interviews conducted for the radio series of the same name. Narrated by Angie Bowie, it drew on contributions from the likes of Brian Eno, Mick Ronson, Nic Roeg, Nile Rogers and Ken Pitt to examine Bowie's career through to 1985. Pitt himself had finally put pen to paper in *Bowie: the Pitt report* (1983), a valuable memoir of his years as Bowie's manager that also offered an intriguing glimpse into the cranky and often crooked workings of the music business.

Though there is currently a resurgence of biographical activity, with novelist and critic Michael Bracewell and former 'hip young gun-slinger' turned *Daily Telegraph* columnist Tony Parsons both apparently working on Bowie projects, the only genuinely investigative study published to date is *Alias David Bowie* (1986). Authors Peter Gillman, a former member of the *Sunday Times* Insight team, and his lecturer wife Leni, came to Bowie and the music world as self-confessed outsiders with a central thesis that Bowie's life and career had been largely shaped by a fear of madness, by the scary shadows cast by his schizophrenic half-brother Terry, the lad insane who committed suicide in January 1985, aged forty-seven. Less overtly sensational than Tony Zanetta and Henry Edwards's insider account, *Stardust: the life and times of David Bowie* (1986), their argument took pulp psychology to extremes, straining credibility in the attempt to force connections between 'David Bowie' and the real-life David Jones. For Bowie, who'd tried to keep his private life private, it was all too much, and, following early extracts in the *Sunday Times*, he attempted to obstruct the book, dashing the Gillmans' hopes of co-operation. Only on *Black Tie/White Noise* is Bowie able finally to write about Terry.[14] And, in one of the many interviews marking the album's release, Bowie admitted to Tony Parsons that, 'it scared me that my own sanity was in question at times but on the other hand I found it fascinating that my family had this streak of insanity . . .'[15] He continued,

> Terry . . . was manic depressive and schizophrenic. I often wondered at the time how near the line I was going and how far I should push myself.

I thought that I would be serving my mental health better if I was aware that insanity was a real possibility in my life.[16]

Ziggy, explained Bowie, had been 'a *doppelgänger* . . . an alternative ego that would take on everything that I was insecure about. [He] served my purpose because I found it easier to function through him', though by so doing Bowie was 'blurring the lines between sanity and an insane figure, and finally did break the lines down in the mid-seventies where I really couldn't perceive the difference between the stage persona and myself'.[17]

Having won over the critics as the innovative changeling of rock, Bowie spent the eighties perfecting a more conventional celebrity – at last recouping the sort of income generally supposed to go with the job. His distinctive reputation as rock's pre-eminent poseur, the doughty champion of artifice at the expense of authenticity, was compromised in the process, and the rather confused critical response mirrored the disillusion of die-hard fans.

The more 'together' Bowie photographed superbly but generated less compelling copy for the nationals and the music press, which had once devoted acres of small print to scrutinizing his every move. Charles Shaar Murray, subsequently of *New Musical Express*, first saw Bowie in 1970, taken to a performance at London's Roundhouse by Richard Neville, an *Oz* colleague. Shaar Murray was hooked, and some of his best criticism is collected in his anthology *Shots from the Hip* (1991). Though he didn't shy away from the more intimate aspects of Bowie's life, interviewing both Angie and Bowie's then estranged mother, he was nevertheless one of a handful of writers who took a more cerebral approach to the star. In November 1977, at the time of "*Heroes*", he noted,

> David Bowie is the one man in rock whose work will, I suspect, continue to fascinate me for the rest of my life, which I won't grow out of even if I stop listening to anything else in the rock field. Sometimes I'll love it and sometimes I'll hate it, sometimes I'll find it infuriating and sometimes exhilarating, sometimes riveting and sometimes incomprehensible, but I can think of no other rock artist whose *next* album is always the one I'm most looking forward to hearing.[18]

That view was shared by Chris Brazier, a winner in *Melody Maker*'s 1976 Student Essay Contest, who went on to contribute a series of earnest analytical articles to the paper. He saw Bowie as the inevitable antidote to all that sixties idealism:

> . . . rock was no longer about a bunch of working-class kids making good – they'd already made good, had been corrupted by luxury and now lived in a world of hangers-on. To a certain extent, Bowie simply painted an accurate picture of what he saw. In addition, the rock public helped to

determine the direction he took – we'd lived through relative prosperity and increasing liberalism and had found no answers, so decadence, the abandoning of the search for answers, was bound to appeal to us. As Bowie said, 'The performer is strictly a product of the public's imagination. We're just a reflection of what people want.'[19]

On this occasion, Brazier may have been right, but, as with so much pop journalism of the period, he rarely said in fifty words what might be said in five hundred and the result could be more dissipation than dissertation. Never mind pomp rock – what about pomp journalism? Even the more experienced Michael Watts was not immune, as his tripartite piece from February 1978 proves. Of course, such verbatim interviews could yield points of specific interest. Here, for example, they discuss Bowie's appropriation of the 'cut-up' technique:

> I still incorporate a lot of the [William] Burroughs ideas, and I still purposely fracture everything. Even if it's making too much sense. I now fracture more than I would've done in the past. But it's still a matter of taking my three or four statements and interrelating them. Not as literally as I used – I don't use the scissor method very much – but I'll write a sentence and then think of a nice juxtaposition to that sentence, and then do it in a methodical, longhand fashion. A lot of me goes into it now, whereas at one point it was getting very random. It was far more random on *Low*. On *"Heroes"* it was a bit more thought about. I wanted a phrase to give a particular feeling. But never a song as a whole – I never had an overall idea of the feeling. Each individual line I wanted to have a different atmosphere, so I would construct it in a Burroughs fashion. There are two or three themes in each song but they are interlinked in such a way as to produce a different atmosphere per line, and sometimes a whole batch of lines. But I didn't want to restrict myself with one process, so I would use straightforward narrative for maybe two lines and then go back to disorientation. '"Heroes"' was about the most narrative, about the Wall, on that album.[20]

When journalist Craig Copetas had the bright if whimsical idea of introducing Bowie and Burroughs in 1974, they seemed to enjoy swapping ideas, and his *Rolling Stone* report is as revealing as it is amusing.[21] One of several pieces which provide a snapshot of Bowie during various stages of what he later described as the 'nightmare time'[22] of the mid-1970s, it seems less laboured than those written from an avowedly British perspective. Perhaps American magazines could afford to cover an imported phenomenon with greater humour and detachment.

Given that the response to Bowie's music – indeed to any music – is intensely subjective, it makes sense to stand back and adopt an objective approach to the examination of his legacy. Even if the standard British rock biography no longer simply wraps a poster round a press release and calls itself a book, there have been plenty of bad books about David Bowie. Some lacquer the legend. Others knock it. As we have seen, few can be considered serious works. Suddenly, a change is in the air. The seventies are back in fashion, in the pop charts and the publishers' lists. In addition to those Bowie-centric projects cited earlier, there is a quasi-academic study in preparation from David Buckley. Clearly, these authors don't agree with Tony Visconti, who told us that there was nothing left to say about David Bowie: 'Contrary to what you say is the reason for putting your book together, I think far too much has been written about him already. Your words were . . . the "most under-researched figure in pop"; come on, what planet have you been living on for the past twenty years?'[23]

With no personal axe to grind and no lurid hypothesis to sustain, our aim is to present the best of thirty years' comment and commentary engendered by the man and his music. While *The Bowie Companion* looks at Bowie's career within a broadly chronological framework, we have sought to construct the biographical skeleton afresh. In so doing, we have been able to include, alongside such classic items as the 1972 Michael Watts interview, 'Oh you pretty thing', Dave Laing and Simon Frith's 'two views on the glitter prince of rock', and the crazed 1975 encounter with Bruno Stein, any number of lesser-known curios – Leslie Thomas on the length of young Davy Jones's hair, the Patti Smith 'review' of *"Heroes"*, and two assignations with the late Jean Rook which certainly shatter expectations. Since no similar Bowie anthology exists, we have been able to choose from a vast selection of material, though we have eschewed articles (including several by Shaar Murray) currently available in more general collections. In their place we have commissioned new critical work, written with the benefit of hindsight, from commentators who come at the subject from a multiplicity of angles: Buckley, whose Ph.D. thesis, 'Strange Fascination', is a study of Bowie and his art, examines Bowie's reinvention of self and, in a second piece, evaluates his various political statements. Wilfrid Mellers offers more strictly musicological food for thought. Lindsay Kemp, Bowie's 'living Pierrot', and Gus Dudgeon reminisce about their early Bowie collaborations. Tim Kindberg contributes a personal impression of Bowie as father figure and shaman. A recurring theme throughout the book is Bowie's 'place' in our shared past.

What we were trying to get across to Visconti was the dearth of *serious* comment. In particular, our researches showed that Bowie's career trajectory has posed a special problem for that newly fashionable breed of pop commentator, the full-time academic anxious to lend intellectual respectability to the unfathomable workings of popular culture. There has always been something pretty unsatisfactory about the value judgements of most contemporary writing on pop. As Clive James noted in 1974, its analytical procedures are 'damagingly tilted towards the descriptive',[24] reinforcing current perceptions rather than separating the wheat from the chaff, never questioning the 'silent mass receptivity'.[25] Could the academics at last get away from the widely held perception of rock journalism as a parasitic discharge, operating within shifting parameters of taste and commerce where each new fad requires a rewrite, a conscious re-evaluation of what has gone before? Or is this, in fact, the way modern society works?

The rise of pop may well be the most significant event in twentieth-century music, but the sociologizing academics have never agreed on a common approach to popular culture.

> Discussions have centred around the degree to which popular music can be regarded as a genuine grass-roots expression that responds to and fulfils emotional needs, or, alternatively, whether it should be recognized as a creation of corporate (or state) culture industries that exploit, manipulate or even create taste rather than respond to it. Does popular music rise from the people who constitute its audience, or is it superimposed upon them from above? Does it reflect and express their attitudes, tastes, aspirations and worldview, or does it serve to indoctrinate them, however imperceptibly, to the ideology of the class and gender which control the media? Does popular music enrich or alienate? Can popular music challenge a social order? Do listeners exercise a genuine choice among musics, or can they only passively select preferences from the styles proffered by the media?[26]

For every spokesperson who viewed 'mass' culture as a vital eruption from below, paralleling those pop journalists like Dave Marsh who prized the denim-clad authenticity of Bruce Springsteen, there were the 'high-cultural', post-Frankfurt School pessimists who sought to portray pop as an alien, 'pre-masticated' imposition (the Militant Tendency was famously opposed to pop as market-place capitalism in its purest form). Was its relative ephemerality an indubitably negative characteristic or could 'bad' art be as 'valuable' as 'good' in that it sent out more signals about the society in which we live? And who, in any case, decides?

Bowie's self-conscious manipulation of the pop process fits well with the view that finds cultural meanings all around us 'in a permanent state of contestation, in which dominant values are indeed at work in popular culture, but rarely without resistance or adaptation on the part of their audiences, while meanings which emerge more organically from popular life are always at risk of being appropriated and re-inflected by the ruling cultural order'.[27] The counter-culture may be dead, but while pop music is created within cultural industry systems that seek to maximize predictability of sales, only the novelty and innovation of the *un*predictable will really boost those sales. Within the anomalous production and reception of popular songs there is still space for something remarkable and indeed subversive to happen. Those who feel affronted that the radical possibilities and dreams of sixties pop have been co-opted as mere points of style in the post-modern culture factory should perhaps look again at the seventies: could Bowie have done it first?

No doubt our fascination with Bowie is in part a nostalgia for a generation's shared past – Michael Bracewell captures the peculiar, retroactive poignancy of the 'Ashes to ashes' video[28] – but, Bowie being Bowie, you do not forget that the images are consciously crafted with a view to allowing the appropriate reading.

In discussing the 'uncertain truths' of the music business in 1986, George H. Lewis showed how 'most stars have an *aura* of charisma built around them – through marketing and promotional techniques – rather than exhibiting the real thing.'[29] Whether or not Bowie has 'that certain something', what impresses is his ability to promote *himself* as the larger-than-life unattainable megastar, uniquely aware that 'without a certain amount of aloofness . . . the mystique of the manufactured charisma would break down, to the disappointment of both the star and the audience – both of whom are working hard to create and to maintain it'.[30] Dave Laing credits Bowie with

> . . . a deliberate strategy of reconstruction involving the explicit discussion of such issues as the nature of the stardom and the society in which he was embroiled. The key locus was . . . *The Rise and Fall of Ziggy Stardust*. This was a concept album (a rock notion) executed in three-minute songs (a pop form). On it, Bowie set out to tell the story of a type of superstar. The intention, on record and in live performance, was strictly dramatic: though dressed as Ziggy Stardust and singing his songs as well as those of the album's narrator, Bowie intended to *signify* Ziggy, not become him.[31]

Bowie's espousal of camp again permitted him to

> play with the distinction between first and third person. The artifice and exaggeration rendered ambiguous any simple recognition of Bowie as *in reality* a transvestite or bisexual. Through the artifice he was signalling that he was first of all *dressing* as such a person'.[32]

As early as 1973, American academic Michael Brown, addressing the annual meeting of the Midwest Political Science Association,[33] discerned a sea-change in youth attitudes. For sixties teenagers, lonely, aimless, affluent and looking for a sense of community and an escape from boredom, the options were radical political protest and the drug culture. Brown suggested that the movement had now 'cross-pollinated', with David Bowie doing for the ambisexual movement what The Rolling Stones and The Beatles had done for drugs.

Another way of looking at the relationship between Bowie and his audience was suggested by radical academicians committed to the study of subcultures, an approach which flourished in the UK in the 1970s. Pop music was then seen as at least potentially oppositional, garnering strength through its part in authentic, albeit mostly symbolic, cultures of resistance. In this context, Bowie's detached stance could not but be seen as some kind of cop-out. For Taylor and Wall, writing in 1976[34], the glam-rock cult represented an unholy synthesis of two dead or dying subcultures – specifically, the 'underground' and the skinheads – which risked delivering pop into the clutches of consumer capitalism. In particular, the authors seemed to hold Bowie responsible for 'emasculating' underground tradition:

> Bowie has in effect colluded in consumer capitalism's attempt to re-create a dependent adolescent class, involved as passive teenage consumers in the purchase of leisure prior to the assumption of 'adulthood' rather than being a youth culture of persons who question (from whatever class or cultural perspective) the value and meaning of adolescence and the transition to the adult world of work.[35]

For these committed ideologues, a song like Bowie's 'Changes' fails to challenge

> . . . the empty spirit and unbearable standards of bourgeois society . . . play[ing] back the alienation of youth on to itself, turning again and again the screws of a spiral of nihilism and meaninglessness on to a youth culture that could have offered an alternative.[36]

Even Dick Hebdidge, whose *Subculture: the meaning of style* (1979) was one of the first studies to take Bowie at all seriously as a cultural force, found him a disturbingly paradoxical figure, arraigning him at one point alongside Lou Reed and Roxy Music as an artist whose 'extreme foppishness, incipient élitism and morbid pretensions to art and intellect effectively precluded the growth of a larger mass audience'.[37] Elsewhere in the book, the analysis was more even-handed, with Bowie's novel agenda given its due. Were not the Bowie lookalikes also escaping from the 'notoriously pedestrian stereotypes conventionally available to working-class men and women'?[38]

> Bowie's meta-message was escape – from class, from sex, from personality, from obvious commitment – into a fantasy past (Isherwood's Berlin peopled by a ghostly cast of doomed bohemians) or a science fiction future. When the contemporary 'crisis' was addressed, it was done so obliquely, represented in transmogrified form as a dead world of humanoids ambiguously relished and reviled. As far as Bowie was concerned (and The Sex Pistols after him) there could be 'no future for you, no

future for me', and yet Bowie was responsible for opening up questions of sexual identity which had previously been repressed, ignored or merely hinted at in rock and youth culture . . . Although Bowie was by no means liberated in any mainstream radical sense, preferring disguise and dandyism – what Angela Carter . . . described as 'the ambivalent triumph of the oppressed' – to any 'genuine' transcendence of sexual role play, he and, by extension, those who copied his style, *did* 'question the value and meaning of adolescence and the transition to the adult world of work' (Taylor and Wall, 1976). And they did so in singular fashion, by artfully confounding the images of men and women through which the passage from childhood to maturity was traditionally accomplished.[39]

So, the Bowie-ites were rebels after all, by constructing 'an alternative identity which communicated a perceived difference: an Otherness. They were, in short, challenging at a symbolic level the "inevitability", the "naturalness" of class and gender stereotypes'.[40]

Some will find this analysis a bit profound for an era characterized by the sort of publicity which, in April 1974, encouraged fans to

Get Into David's Pants If You Win the Bowie Lookalike Contest . . . Remember the first kid on your block who had a Davy Crockett coonskin cap? Elvis Presley sideburns? Beatle haircut? Peter Fonda sunglasses? Mick Jagger lips? Well, this season it's David Bowie, and it seems that everywhere you turn there's another suburban streetcorner incarnation of that lunar prance.[41]

Leaving the arena of sexual politics, the old-style politicking of Bowie's career presents another conundrum. Despite the sexual rebelliousness of Ziggy, Bowie remained an essentially apolitical artiste in a way that John Lennon or Bob Dylan did not. Dylan's early friends and patrons valued his songs for their ability to propagate a particular social, political or philosophical line which accorded with their own clearly defined world view. Initially disinterested, Lennon allied himself with the New Left in the early seventies. By contrast, Bowie's dalliance with Fascist chic was no more than play-acting, another pose, easily cast off. And yet, embarrassingly, he remained an unlikely icon for many on the Far Right. 'Don't condemn pop', urged one *Spearhead* reader in April 1981:

It is this old 60s Flower Power music with its inclination to drugs etc. which more than anything constitutes the strong feelings many radical nationalists have against pop music in general. However, in the early 70s emerged David Bowie whose total rejection of this style of music is wonderfully indicative of his brand of Pop music coupling Stage mime, poetry and a ballad form of rock music. He became a breath of fresh air on the music scene – indeed, the influence of Friedrich Nietsche [*sic*] is plainly evident in Bowie's songs such as 'Starman', 'Changes' and the excellent 'Quicksands' [*sic*].[42]

Bulldog, the paper of the young National Front, discussed 'White European Dance Music' later the same year:

> Perhaps the anti-Communist backlash and the aspirations towards hero-ism by the Futurist movement has much to do with the imagery employed by the Big Daddy of Futurism, David Bowie. After all, it was Bowie who horrified the music establishment in the mid-seventies with his favourable comments about the NF [*sic*]. And it was Bowie who, on the album *Hunky Dory*, started the anti-Communist musical tradition which we now see flourishing amidst the new wave of Futurist bands.[43]

As David Buckley suggests, the socially 'responsible' stance of Tin Machine may have represented an attempt to come to terms with a dangerously mixed legacy.[44] In a series of interviews from the summer of 1975, Bowie proclaimed the death of rock-and-roll:

> 'It's a toothless old woman. It's really embarrassing.' So what's the next step? 'Dictatorship,' says Bowie. 'There'll be a political figure in the not too distant future who'll sweep this part of the world like early rock-and-roll did. You probably hope I'm not right. But I am. My predictions are very accurate . . . always.'[45]

Then, on 2 May 1976, Bowie was photographed wearing a black shirt and standing in the back of a black Mercedes, raising his right arm as if in Nazi salute.

Even so, Bowie was not Right enough for Steve and Jim Peters, ordained ministers of the Jesus People Fellowship in St Paul, Minne-sota, who, from 1979, organized anti-rock lectures and album-burning sessions throughout the United States. Bowie was included on their 'Ten Most Wanted List' along with Prince, Jagger and other less illustrious denizens of heavy metal:

> In hope that, through prayer and open dialogue, many of rock music's most notorious stars can come to know Christ and thus change their music and their motives, we have compiled a list of Ten Most Wanted. If you would like to change the future of rock music, and of one of America's most pervasive influences, please pray for the artists on this list on a daily basis. You might also consider writing to them. Tell them about Jesus and let them know you love them and are praying for them – but also that you cannot tolerate their behaviour and recorded material. Give them an opportunity to meet the Lord through you.[46]

In 1987 Bowie played an incidental role in unsettling East Germany's Honecker regime when the formerly quiescent rock fans of East Berlin fiercely asserted their right to be heroes – or at least to listen to Berlin's 750th anniversary celebration rock concerts taking place on the other side of the Wall and featuring Bowie, Phil Collins and the Eurhythmics.

> From June 6 to June 8 1987, several thousand East German rock fans gathered nightly on Unter den Linden near the Berlin Wall to hear the concerts. For the first two nights, East German security forces worked to disperse the crowds. On Monday night, June 8, scuffling erupted into open battle as an estimated four thousand rock fans clashed with police . . . Young people, screaming 'Police pigs!' and 'Tear down the Wall!' pelted the police with stones, bottles, and firecrackers. West German camera teams, on hand to cover the East German reaction to the concert, captured on film a bloody battle in which police armed with clubs and tear gas confronted mobs of angry fans. Before the confrontation ended, dozens of people were injured.[47]

Today, Bowie sees himself as a reconstructed Germanophile, no longer entranced by the grandoise symbols and statements of German *kultur* while hazy about the political baggage:

> I wasn't actually flirting with fascism *per se*. I was up to the neck in magick . . . a horrendous period . . . The irony is that I really didn't see any political implications in my interest in the Nazis. My interest in them was the fact that they supposedly came to England before the war to find the Holy Grail at Glastonbury and this whole Arthurian thought was running through my mind. So that's where all that came from. The idea that it was about putting Jews in concentration camps and the complete oppression of different races completely evaded my extraordinarily fucked-up nature at that particular time.[48]

Whatever the truth of the matter, one might expect there to have been more attention devoted to 'synthesizing' Bowie's work with the turbulent politics of the seventies. But, then, that decade has not had the irresistible allure of its predecessor. Until now . . .

Musicologists have also been hesitant about an artist whose music, though melodically and texturally adventurous, lacks the consistent tone and polish which makes The Beatles such a tempting target for formal exegesis. In the post-*Pepper* era, many students made a thesis out of a hobby. And professors with a taste for popular culture do sometimes like to turn their intellectual guns on the tunes they hear at student parties. Too often, this attention adds little to our general appreciation of the music. Just as the theorizers are apt to forget that popular music is there to be enjoyed, so the analysts are up against a perennial problem of rock music criticism: the absence of 'classical' music's full score. Empirically created yet definitive studio effects cannot be replicated in print. During the 1980s it was rare to find even pop practitioners prepared to defend Bowie's songwriting as such, though Roddy Frame of Aztec Camera was one obvious exception. On one level, songs like '"Heroes"', 'Let's dance' and 'Absolute beginners' invited derision: only Bowie would ever have attempted that cod-melodramatic delivery (though note the inverted commas). But look again at his song catalogue and, at the very least, you get a sense of glam rock's tribal simplicities mutating into the epic, emblematic hymnals of today's stadium rock.

In this anthology, producer Gus Dudgeon explains the collaborative process behind the definitive realization of a song like 'Space oddity', while Professor Wilfrid Mellers, a dogged and intensely personal practitioner of pop musicology, tackles Bowie's *Hunky Dory* from a more detached standpoint. The Mellers equation of song-as-perform-ance equals song-as-composition cannot allow for new and different versions of a song, but in Bowie's case the stadium rock of the eighties brought few worthwhile musical (as distinct from presentational) innovations to bear on older material. Of course, there is always the suspicion that Bowie's music means less than the packaging. For Simon Frith,

> The strength of his Ziggy music actually lay in its atmosphere. What Bowie captured was the unearthly desperation of consumer pleasures, the sense of discos, clubs and dance halls apart from 'real life' where people danced urgently because of their fears of what would happen when they stopped, where teenagers, in particular, invented their own transitory social order.[49]

Today, for the majority of listeners, the original recordings are the thing, remastered now but inviolable – particularly since Bowie's decision to abstain from live shows and rest his back catalogue for the time being. Like Philip Glass, most classically oriented commentators are happiest with the genre-quaking Berlin trilogy, examined here by Eric Tamm. In a milieu too often preoccupied with sign and surface, the search goes on for permanent critical values with which to assess an *oeuvre* which consciously jumped the signals.

Writers on Bowie's celluloid legacy have less of a problem – we do not expect film critics to encumber their discussions with the technical terminology of the film-maker. Bowie struck lucky with *The Man Who Fell to Earth* (1976). The movie may not have been a hit, but it traded on the public's established perception of him in a more subtle and effective manner than any straight, performance-related film. Pauline Kael, the doyenne of film critics, was not a great fan of the movie yet she immediately understood the Actor's strength in the part of Thomas Newton[50] – as did Bowie himself: images from the film adorn two consecutive album sleeves. Unexpectedly, his subsequent cinematic career has been something of a disappointment. His stage appearance in Bernard Pomerance's *The Elephant Man* was an unqualified critical success but Oshima's *Merry Christmas, Mr Lawrence* mystified commentators less broad-minded than Anne Rice.[51]

While exploring other media outlets, Bowie has continued to demonstrate his talent for theatrical innovation in the arena he knows best, rock-and-roll. Only the 1987 Glass Spider tour was critically panned: Bowie was thought to have overreached himself at last, breaching the boundaries of what can be done (or rather done comprehensibly) in the context of the stadium-rock event. Even here there were enthusiastic dissenters:

A translucent spider 40-feet in diameter, hovers ominously over the deck, which is strewn with sections of scaffold towers and band gear. A web of gold scaffolding ensnares the walls of speakers on either side . . . Sometimes it is bleak expressionism. Other times melodrama. Sometimes it is a circus. Other times grand opera. Sometimes it is even rock-and-roll. But, always, it is theatre.[52]

Bowie has released videos of certain live concerts, the traditional audio-visual presentation of rock. But there is more uniformity in the critical response to Bowie's promotional videos. These have often been artistically adventurous as well as commercially focused. There are (at least) two ways of looking at the form: either the pop video is merely the latest manifestation of the short promotional clip made by musicians from Duke Ellington on, or it represents a completely new way of experiencing music, symptomatic of an era of MTV-type musical consumption in which image is all. Instead of building over a career, the mythologizing, two-way relationship between 'pop star' and audience can be fabricated in two and a half minutes! Many such videos present little more than an artificial reconstruction of a 'live' performance, shot so as to heighten the sense of intimate contact with the musicians. But for Bowie, the trained mime, the medium offered him the chance to fuse his disparate skills as never before, sometimes winning the approval of mainstream music critics like the *New York Times*'s John Rockwell.[53]

Despite British broadcasting's traditional exclusion of anything smacking of sexual or political 'deviance', Bowie has often managed to smuggle through his provocative images. As we have seen, the androgynous image of masculinity projected by pop idols from Valentino to Michael Jackson achieved a peculiar intensity with Bowie who, in pointing up the lyrical ambiguities of 'Boys keep swinging', no doubt alienated some potential investors. 'China girl' included images open to a political reading, and the 'Let's dance' promo discussed here by Deborah Holdstein[54] added a vital layer of meaning to the generalized instruction to 'put on your red shoes and dance the blues'.

But Bowie is not in the business of tying himself down. Nor could he – working in a 'chaotic world of chance and ignorance run by people with little regard for or understanding of their audience',[55] even if we agree that the most interesting music videos tend to be made by the people with the time and money to work out their ideas. Bowie's appeal is not simply a question of good looks, though it was a factor impossible to ignore when Tina Brown, the journalist-turned-media-celebrity who successfully repackaged *herself* for the American market, interviewed him in 1975. 'Any story about David Bowie must begin with the way he looks,' she wrote in the *Sunday Times*.

> He has sold five million records but the discordant faces on the sleeves have done as much as the falsetto wheeze of his singing voice. As the cosmic yob – hair layered into an orange coxcomb over a painted face, Dietrich eyebrows raised in camp derision – he was aped by a generation of teenyboppers. They were slow to keep up with him. On his last American tour at the end of 1974 the concert halls were thronged with look-alikes of his last phase. They came expecting a Bowie who strutted and postured like a Moon-age Liberace. They found him as cool as a mint julep in a white suit and side parting.[56]

Frith, writing with Howard Horne in *Art into Pop* in 1987, understood what those look-alikes were looking for. 'What really mattered as an artist, then, was not what you did but what you were, and Bowie became a blank canvas on which consumers write their dreams, a media-made icon to whom art happened.'[57]

On to that blank canvas, countless dreams have been written and rewritten. In the worn grooves of those old albums, countless recollections are encoded. Each of us has our favourite Bowie, in whom is invested the crazy, hazy hopes of our fading youth. But, as *Arena* recently asked, who is David Bowie? For Tina Turner, simply 'an inspiration'.[58] For Adrian Belew, 'an original. Art on legs'.[59] 'I don't know,' mused Bono,

> and I doubt if he does: a Left Bank rightist, a Wilde colonial boy driven from England by his Englishness, an innovator on the cover of *Hello!* magazine? . . . I don't mind . . . But when he doesn't give in to art or pop, when these desires are equal as well as opposite, he is at his best and I am his biggest fan . . . The nicest fella from Mars I ever met.[60]

As John Landis, who directed Bowie in the film *Into the Night*, pointed out, 'David Bowie was one of the first rock-and-rollers to consciously approach music as art. At this point in his career he has nothing to prove, and yet I feel he will continue to surprise and amaze us.'[61]

Ten years separate *Black Tie/White Noise* from Bowie's last truly successful solo album, *Let's Dance*. Teamed up once more with producer Nile Rodgers, Bowie could easily have sat on tried-and-tested laurels and merely danced again. Yet referential as it is, recalling the stark, electronic Euro-funk of *Station to Station* and *Scary Monsters*, *Black Tie/White Noise* is also an album for the nineties – 'I'm the sound of tomorrow', he sings in 'You've been around' – skilfully blending dance, rock and jazz into a sound that is uniquely Bowie. A Bowie this time unmediated by any fictional third party. A Bowie who allows genuine emotion to displace dramatic irony. 'You've changed me . . . Ch-ch-ch-ch-ch-ch-changed me,' he tells us, and we believe him – at least for the duration of his song. For elsewhere Bowie admits that he is putting all of his eggs into the basket of post-modern song, still Mary Harron's 'master-puppeteer', the magician who understands the secret of eternal pop success, whose control of his own stardom is in some respect its own validation.[62]

No doubt the Starman has changed. And we've changed with him. *The Bowie Companion* chronicles those changes, rescuing Bowie from the brand of tabloid journalism which 'puts you there where things are hollow'.

Elizabeth Thomson and David Gutman
London, May 1993

Notes

1. Anthony Burgess, 'The killing of Boy George', *Daily Mail* (4 July 1986), pp. 20–1.

2. See James Delingpole, 'Half as musical as he used to be', *Daily Telegraph* (20 March 1993), p. xiv.

3. See David Patrick Stearns, 'Pop goes the composer', *BBC Music Magazine* (February 1993), p. 10.

4. Tony Parsons, 'The Tin Man', *Arena* (November 1991), p. 88.

5. See 'People', *Time* (18 January 1993), p. 48.

6. Simon Frith, 'Towards an aesthetic of popular music', in *Music and Society*, ed. Richard Leppert and Susan McClary (Cambridge, Cambridge University Press, 1987), pp. 139–40.

7. Adam Sweeting, 'The star who fell to earth', [Weekend] *Guardian* (3–4 March 1990), p. 6.

Introduction

8. Jim Jerome, 'A session with David Bowie', *Life* (1 December 1992), p. 92.

9. Julie Burchill, "'Ello Jon, got a new theory?', *Modern Review* (Autumn 1991), p. 18.

10. *Ibid.*

11. Published in two parts. See Steve Sutherland, 'One day son, all this could be yours . . .', *New Musical Express* (20 March 1993), pp. 28–31 and 'Alias Smiths and Jones', *New Musical Express* (27 March 1993), pp. 12–13.

12. See Michael Watts, 'The rise and rise of Ziggy Stardust', *Melody Maker* (19 August 1972), p. 8.

13. See David Thomas, 'David Bowie', *The Face* (May 1983), p. 17.

14. Sutherland, *op. cit.*

15. See Tony Parsons, 'Bowie by Bowie', *Arena* (May/June 1993), p. 68.

16. *Ibid.*

17. *Ibid.*

18. Charles Shaar Murray, 'David Bowie: who was that (un)masked man?', *New Musical Express* (12 November 1977); reprinted in *Shots from the Hip* (London, Penguin, 1991), pp. 237–8.

19. Chris Brazier, 'Bowie: beauty before outrage', *Melody Maker* (4 September 1976), p. 17.

20. See Michael Watts, 'Bowie on Bowie' in *Melody Maker Book of Bowie* [tour souvenir issue] (June 1978), p. 22.

21. See pp. 105–17.

22. See Parsons (May/June 1993), p. 66.

23. Tony Visconti, letter to the editors, 6 July 1992.

24. Clive James, 'Bringing some of it all back home', *Creem*; reprinted in *New Musical Express* (20 April 1974), pp. 10–12.

25. *Ibid.*

26. Peter Manuel, *Popular Musics of the Non-Western World* (Oxford, Oxford University Press, 1988), p. 8.

27. Terry Eagleton, 'Proust, punk or both', *Times Literary Supplement* (18 December 1992), p. 5.

28. See pp. 217–19.

29. George H. Lewis, 'Uncertain truths: the promotion of popular culture', *Journal of Popular Culture* 20/3 (Winter 1986), p. 36.

30. *Ibid.*

31. Dave Laing, *One Chord Wonders* (Milton Keynes, Open University Press, 1985), p. 24.

32. *Ibid.*, p. 25.

33. Michael Brown, 'Alienation among middle-class young: politics, drugs

and ambisexualism', cited in John Orman, *The Politics of Rock Music* (Chicago, Nelson-Hall, 1984), p. 37.

34. Ian Taylor and Dave Wall, 'Beyond the skinheads: comments on the emergence and significance of the glamrock cult', in *Working-Class Youth Culture*, ed. Geoff Mungham and Geoff Pearson (London, Routledge & Kegan Paul, 1976), pp. 105–23.

35. *Ibid.*, p. 117.

36. *Ibid.*, pp. 119–20.

37. Dick Hebdidge, *Subculture: the meaning of style* (London, Methuen, 1979), p. 62.

38. *Ibid.*, p. 60.

39. *Ibid.*, pp. 61–2.

40. *Ibid.*, p. 89.

41. *Creem* (April 1974), p. 33.

42. *Spearhead* 150 (April 1981).

43. *Bulldog* 25, (November/December 1981).

44. See pp. 207–13.

45. Anthony O'Grady, 'Dictatorship: the next step?', *New Musical Express* (23 August 1975), p. 5.

46. Jim and Dan Peters, *Why Knock Rock?* (Minneapolis, Bethany Fellowship, 1984); cited in Linda Martin and Kerry Segrave, *Anti-Rock* (Hamden, Connecticut, Archon Books, 1988), p. 287.

47. Timothy W. Ryback, *Rock Around the Bloc* (New York, Oxford University Press, 1990), p. 208.

48. Sutherland (20 March 1993), p. 30.

49. Simon Frith, 'Only Dancing: David Bowie flirts with the issues', *Mother Jones* (August 1983); reprinted in *Zoot Suits and Second-Hand Dresses*, ed. Angela McRobbie (London, Macmillan, 1989), p. 139.

50. See pp. 137–9.

51. See pp. 183–6.

52. Mark Loeffler, 'Designer remedies for Bowie's theatre bug', *Theatre Crafts* (November 1987), p. 39.

53. See pp. 169–70.

54. See pp. 190–2.

55. Mark Hustwitt, 'Sure feels like heaven to me: considerations on promotional videos', *IASPM Working Paper* 6 (IASPM, 1985), p. 41.

56. Tina Brown, 'The Bowie Odyssey', *The Sunday Times Magazine* (20 July 1975), p. 10.

57. Simon Frith and Howard Horne, *Art into Pop* (London, Methuen, 1987), p. 115.

58. See Parsons (May/June 1993), p. 73.

59. *Ibid.*

60. *Ibid.*, p. 72.

61. *Ibid.*, p. 74.

62. Mary Harron, 'McRock', in *Facing the Music*, ed. Simon Frith (London, Mandarin, 1990), p. 208.

ONE

Boy Keeps Swinging

DAVID BUCKLEY
Still pop's faker?

April 1992. The Freddie Mercury Tribute concert, Wembley Stadium. Bowie, a fit, tanned and confident figure in an implausibly loud lime-green suit, has just hammed it up effectively with Annie Lennox for 'Under pressure' and provided virtually inaudible sax for his seventies anthem 'All the young dudes'. After the obligatory '"Heroes"', Bowie cuts off, falls to his knees and recites the Lord's Prayer to a silent and, one would imagine, embarrassed audience. It was just about the most controversial thing he could have done.

Until Bowie's appearance, the concert had been the quintessential reaffirmation of traditional rock values, the bands vying with one another for the highest level of contact with the audience, spewing out laddish, guitar-based rock-and-roll musical clichés. Bowie's sudden departure into biblical drama of the most direct kind – putting aside his motives, honest or dishonest – can be best explained as a reminder of another view of pop and pop performance altogether, an aesthetic which Bowie championed in the seventies and which he still flirts with today: namely the triumph of artifice, of theatricality, of irony, over truth, authenticity and emotional verisimilitude.

If Bowie's career in the seventies has been crudely characterized as a musical and visual master plan executed with machiavellian, goblin-like glee, his pre-Ziggy career reads like a random and bizarre attempt to colonize as many different strands of popular culture as possible in search of an identity: commercial artist, jazz saxophonist, actor, mime artist, R & B singer, mod, hippie, Buddhist, cabaret singer, and at times a combination of two or three at once.[1] There was a desperate eclecticism on show here which was new to pop. Bowie was to comment in 1976:

3

> The only thing to do, if you want to contribute to culture, or politics, or music, or whatever, is to utilize your persona rather than just music. The best way to do this is to diversify and become a nuisance everywhere.[2]

When Bowie finally started making successful syntheses of pop and performance in the seventies, the breadth of his interests enabled him to draw upon a massive range of materials from both Western and Eastern culture and from disciplines which had been ignored for the most part by popular music. He occupied the same space throughout the seventies that The Beatles did very briefly in the sixties, as brilliant popularizers of the avant-garde.

As we all know, it was only with the construction of the famous alter ego Ziggy Stardust that Bowie hit upon the strategy that would make his career and, in so doing, revolutionize the way pop was encoded in popular culture. Fundamental to this redefinition was Bowie's assertion that he was *using* rock-and-roll, that he was pop's first self-avowed *poseur*, showing no allegiance to any one style of music or to any single visual presentation. As he argued in 1971:

> What the music says may be taken seriously, but as a medium it should not be questioned, analysed or taken so seriously. I think it should be tarted up, made into a prostitute, a parody of itself. It should be the clown, the Pierrot medium. The music is the mask the message wears – music is the Pierrot and I, the performer, am the message.[3]

Bowie, who in 1972 aptly described himself as a Xerox machine, tapped into the narcissism, the obsession with self, the self-conscious irony which was beginning to define itself against the communality of hippiedom. Two influences are striking. First, the influence of the Warhol scene:[4] in some respects Andy Warhol and David Bowie may be said to have shared many psychological states. Both were obsessed by fame and all its trappings. Both shared similar psychoses – a fear of violent death and a fear of flying. Most important, Warhol set himself up as a cypher. He was in many respects a non-person, blank, non-committal, and this had a huge effect on Bowie. Warhol constructed fame in the Factory, made 'talentless' people into celebrities and exploded the myth of 'organic' stardom. He codified a paradigm of posing that Bowie found irresistible.

Second, Bowie was slap-bang in the middle of what Susan Sontag defined as the sensibility of camp:

> Camp is a vision of the world in terms of style – but a particular kind of style. It is the love of the exaggerated, the 'off', of things-being-what-they-are-not.[5]

Sontag goes on to argue, 'Camp sees everything in quotation marks. It is not a lamp but a "lamp"'.[6] Or, in Bowie's case, it is '"Heroes"', not Heroes, implying an ironic distancing lost in its live power-pop renditions. Most important, Bowie's penchant for fabricating a personality, for seeing life in terms of theatre ('It was cold and it rained, so I felt like an actor' he sang in 'Five years', 1972) is prefigured in Sontag's argument that:

> To perceive camp in objects and persons is to understand Being-as-playing-a-Role. It is the farthest extension, in sensibility, of the metaphor of life as theatre.[7]

The emergence of theatricality as a strategy in pop around 1972, its ransacking of images and musical codes, was not just the sole preserve of Bowie. Roxy Music were, if anything, more radical in musical terms, though ultimately less successful at pop *bricolage*. Their rise to stardom was carefully stage-managed by Bryan Ferry, their look determinedly made up, from Ferry's gauche rock-and-roll quiff to Eno's strategic visual and electronic weirdness. For the rock establishment, both Bowie and Roxy Music were too much. BBC Television's *Old Grey Whistle Test* presenter, Bob Harris, felt sufficiently affronted by the prospect of Roxy's live appearance on the show to issue a specific disclaimer to the effect that he was totally against them performing at all![8]

Peter Gabriel, then lead singer with Genesis, incorporated a good deal of homespun theatricality into their shows, ostensibly to keep the audience's attention during the band's often laborious changeovers of instruments between songs. Gabriel took as his material the ironies and contradictions of 'Englishness' and represented them visually – with a music-hall-like flavour for 'Willow farm', dressed as a daffodil, and with a telling sense of theatre for the ageing sequence in 'Musical box' (for the 1973 tours). However, Gabriel was still to break through the confines of progressive rock, and his subsequent adoption of alter egos, most famously Rael for the Lamb Lies Down on Broadway tour of 1974, came over – as did Marc Bolan's half-baked Zinc Alloy project – as less successful recreations of the Ziggy phenomenon.

Ziggy was both a brilliant visual spectacle and a devastating critique of how stardom operated in pop. The question of how Bowie hit upon the character is open to some debate. Bowie has argued that the ultimate rock superstar was based, with suitable irony, on two failed pop stars, the manic Legendary Stardust Cowboy and the 'French Presley', Vince Taylor, whose last concert appearance saw him take the stage wearing a white sheet and proclaiming to the world he was Jesus Christ.[9] This messianic quality was also present in the Ziggy character and the album itself invites parallels between the rise and fall of both an archetypal rock star and Christ. Finally, Bowie tapped

5

into the then unutilized public fascination with science fiction and fantasy by incorporating a large dose of extraterrestrial references into both the music and the visuality of Ziggy.[10] Also crucial in this respect was the link between Bowie and that most saturnine of writers, William Burroughs, whom Bowie met in 1973* and whose visions of a future dystopia informed Bowie's own apocalyptic fantasies.

As Simon Frith put it, Bowie was the most photogenic pop star of all time.[11] No other pop star has proved visually malleable enough to successfully pull off the swingeing changes of style Bowie was able to achieve. The Ziggy persona remains his masterpiece. On stage, Bowie became the kabuki-rocker, appropriating the visual codes of Japanese drama for Western pop. Kabuki involves a mixture of music, dancing and acting. All parts, both male and female, are played by men, and the androgynous nature of kabuki was elevated by Bowie to a position of fundamental importance. It was the kabuki aesthetic of visual excess – its garish, though formal juxtaposition of colours – that attracted Bowie. Ziggy's heavily made-up red and gold lips, black eyeliner and red blusher, set against the whitened pallor of the rest of the face, echoed kabuki styles.

The constant changes of costume, so evident in the Ziggy and Aladdin Sane stage shows, also had their origins in kabuki. Bowie explained these costume changes as expressing new facets of the personality. While the number of changes he used does not appear to have any precedent in kabuki, the idea of costume signifying personality is deeply rooted. According to A. C. Scott:

> In *bukkaeri* [a kabuki form of dancing play] the actor takes his arms out of his sleeves from the inside and pushes down the upper portion of the garment to hang around the waist, revealing a completely different kimono beneath. Bukkaeri is used to convey the idea that the actor has now assumed a character and a personality which had formerly been concealed.[12]

Bowie brought a completely different look to rock shows, as *New Musical Express* noted in 1973:

> Study still photos of his performance and unless there happens to be a guitar or a microphone in the picture, then it's not really obvious that the shot was taken at a rock show.[13]

The intention was to *present* emotion, to signify Ziggy, to live out the thrills of rock performance vicariously. The experiment collapsed as both Bowie's audience and Bowie himself became unable to distinguish Ziggy from the real Bowie. The ever-narrowing gap between

* See p. 105.

alter ego and Bowie's own personality was apparent when Bowie paraded his aliases for public scrutiny in front of the media.

With hindsight, Bowie has said, many of the elements which made up Ziggy performances had a traditional music-hall quality which he didn't recognize at the time. Nevertheless, before Bowie nobody had put theatre at the very centre of things in the way he did. And certainly, nobody had ever before conceived of his or her career as the adoption of a succession of masks and alter egos.

Ziggy's final appearance at the Hammersmith Odeon on 3 July 1973 was caught for posterity on a rather grainy film by D. A. Pennebaker.[14] The incredible tension set up in these shows between Bowie's high-pitched, somehow disembodied vocal, his play with sexuality (including the famed mock-fellatio on Mick Ronson's guitar) and the driving proto-punk of The Spiders From Mars proved influential throughout the seventies and eighties, not just on punk but, as Jon Savage suggested, on the music of The Smiths and very early Pretenders too.[15]

Vocally, both Bowie and Ferry delivered a style which defined itself against the Americanized drawl of Mick Jagger or Rod Stewart. The indigenous twang of Elton John signified an allegiance to specifically English traditions, whereas the postures of Jagger exemplified the status quo, drawn from authentic R & B and the tradition of 'telling it how it is'. Bowie cut free from these vocal styles, paving the way for the caterwauling of Johnny Rotten and the stridently parochial timbres of punk.[16] Throughout the seventies, Bowie again showed that non-allegiance was his *métier*. From the crooning 'White hysteria' of the plastic soul phase and the icy, glacial blankness of the brilliant *Low* through to the richer timbres of today, Bowie showed and continues to show that he can reassemble a variety of different vocal styles for public consumption. There is no fixed centre even to his speaking voice: clipped and upper-middle class for the Serious Moonlight tour press conference in 1983, laddish, affected cockney for the launch of the Glass Spider extravaganza four years later.

The overall effect, both musically and visually, is one of irony. Once again, Susan Sontag put it so well:

> One is drawn to camp when one realizes that 'sincerity' is not enough. Sincerity can be simply philistinism, intellectual narrowness.[17]

When Ziggy sang 'Give me your hands, 'cos you're wonderful' ('Rock 'n' roll suicide', 1972) the words embodied not just the desperation and isolation felt by the rock star at the nadir of his career. They were also a telling critique of all those show business platitudes spouted in concert ('You've been a really wonderful audience tonight').[18] Bowie brilliantly turned upside down the whole idea of how songs are presented live. Before Bowie, it was considered essential that the link between performer and song remain intact, that the emotion of the song was portrayed as real to the audience. Singers were thus critically judged by how well they presented emotion. Bowie fundamentally challenged this notion, demonstrating the possibility that pop could be more about disengagement than about playing the game of emotional verisimilitude.

Bowie's performance aesthetic was codified with Ziggy. Of all his creations, it is Ziggy that has had the most lasting resonance within popular culture, but for Bowie it was just the starting point for different combinations of pop with performance. In April 1974, Bowie left Britain for the States and the Diamond Dogs tour, working with American choreographer Toni Basil. Playing in front of a façade of the collapsing city-scapes of the album's 'hunger city' and with the band hidden behind a screen, Bowie the doomster developed a series of theatrical set pieces, French kissing a skull in a sexual-Shakespearean 'Cracked actor', singing into a telephone while perched in an office chair suspended from a crane for 'Space oddity', and lassoed for 'Diamond dogs'. The show eventually disintegrated into acrimony after the recording of the *David Live* album (as befitted the story of a decaying city, Bowie later ruefully remarked) and was reassembled later in 1974 as the Philly Dogs tour, showcasing some of Bowie's new soul material.

The 1976 show was stripped of props and obvious theatrical conceits, working through the use of an almost Brechtian sense of estrangement and the appropriation of lighting techniques from German expressionist theatre of the twenties and thirties. A mood of both futurism and nostalgia was expertly evoked even before Bowie appeared on stage, with the use of clips from Salvador Dali and Luis Buñuel's 1928 surrealist film *Un Chien Andalou* and the 'motorik' of Kraftwerk's *Radioactivity*. Bowie took the stage dressed in white shirt and black waistcoat, hair slicked back and bathed in a dazzling wash of white light, the intensity of which unnerved the audience. Writer and broadcaster Paul Gambaccini called it the finest performance he had ever seen by a White artist outside America.[19]

All Bowie's tours in the seventies demonstrated an overriding need to theatricalize performance and a penchant for alienating (or at the very least confounding) audience expectations. This is not to say that his audience was disengaged from any feelings of empathy with Bowie. It is just that the bond was constructed in a very different way using very different strategies. All this takes us back to the Freddie Mercury concert and the ethos of communion in rock in general. Underpinning the majority of rock performance, this ethos derives from the antiphonal (call and response) techniques developed by R & B, blues and soul singers. Here the show's success depended on a process of reciprocity, not just between singer and audience ('Do you feel good?' – 'Yeh! Yeh!') but between lead singer and back-up singers and between musicians who would answer various musical phrases with related ones of their own.[20] This sense of communality became the bedrock where all else was shifting sand. In performance, everyone from Status Quo to Queen and The Rolling Stones based their techniques on reciprocity, leading to the clichéd spectacle of today's sea of glowing cigarette lighters during one of the slushier moments at a Chris de Burgh concert. Punk upset the code, replacing rehearsed appreciation with mutual mistrust where goading, gobbing and can-pelting became marks of appreciation,[21] but the bond remained, albeit redefined. Bowie sets up a confused dialectic between performer and audience and is at times self-consciously distant and cerebral, offering himself as an icon not for communal expression but for personal politics. It was Bowie who constructed an audience linked by an acute sense of their own individuality and a potent sense of *themselves* as stars which potentially tied in with the aesthetics of disco. On the dance floor *everyone* was a star. As Bowie continued to unearth different selves from within, he provided a model of psychic exploration for his fans. 'Bowie Boys' and 'Bowie Girls' became one of suburbia's bravest subcultures and a huge influence on punk in the mid-seventies.[22]

Perhaps the prime exponent of the ideology of communion in rock is Bruce Springsteen. In many ways, he is the ideal performer for the stadium rock spectacle of the nineties. His music is all broad, bold gestures. On stage he has constructed the persona of an honest Joe, a multimillionaire attired in shirt and jeans revving up the audience with the customary three hours of rock. Springsteen concerts invite admiration for his musical prowess, for his ability to power through a lengthy set, sweat cascading onto the mike-stand (and as Tony De Fries, Bowie's one-time manager commented, Bowie never sweats![23]), giving his audience demonstrable, *authentic* value for money. Yet in a sense, Springsteen is just as constructed as Bowie, his show of 'real emotion' reduced to the repetition of a few well-worn rock clichés. In any performance there is an element of self-re-creation. With Bowie, however, one is left with no illusions that it is *all* constructed and that performance is there for the exploration of visual ideas, not simply the replication of a formula. As Bowie put it in 1976:

> You can't go on stage and live – it's false all the way . . . I can't stand the premise of going on in jeans and a guitar and looking as real as you can in front of 18,000 people. I mean, it's not normal![24]

Bowie's career in the eighties and nineties has seen, paradoxically, a partial retreat from artifice and a confused attempt to reappropriate a less detached way of performing, more in touch with his new, less troubled psyche. The problem with the new besuited, heterosexualized Bowie is that the vast majority of his fans still yearn for that keen sense of emotional dispossession which oozed from every pore of the coked-out seventies version. The massive commercial success of *Let's Dance* in 1983 left Bowie in the uncomfortable position of trying to appease his new audience of thirtysomethings. His music since 1983 has been by turns unfocused and attractive, but his power as a pop icon faded as he became too left-field for his new audience and too showbiz for his often blinkered older fans. The post-Live Aid consensus which once again pushed guitar-based virtuosity and musical authenticity back to centre stage was absolutely the wrong climate for Bowie to work in.

These contradictions were worked out graphically on the road. The Glass Spider tour saw Bowie attempt to revive the theatricality of the Diamond Dogs era for his new stadium audience. The show drew inspiration from the contemporary dance styles of La La La Human Steps and set them against the power licks of the resurrected Peter Frampton. The mix failed, as Bowie is the first to admit. The show, featuring a mammoth spider, an acrobatic, abseiling Bowie[25] and a confused running commentary lip-synched by a cast of dancers through a less-than-perfect PA system, might have worked in the Hammersmith Odeon but it was far too fussy and diffuse to succeed in a stadium environment where most fans would have needed a stepladder and a telescope to get much out of it. It was Bowie at his most self-indulgent. Stadium rock requires a muscularity of perform-ance that the cerebral aesthete Bowie will never have. However, it was striking to see how much of the 'failed' material was then gobbled up by Prince and Madonna on subsequent tours.

The Sound + Vision tour of 1990 fared much better. In fact, it must have strong claims to being artistically the most successful Bowie show ever created. The key to its success was that Bowie solved the visibility problem of the Glass Spider tour by using interactive video techniques. A transparent sheeting was lowered at preprogrammed times, on to which were projected computer-generated images, developed in col-laboration with La La La Human Steps guru Edouard Lock. The result was often genuinely mesmerizing, as a sixty-foot pair of legs walked across the stage during 'Space Oddity', and a swirling, coked-out Major Tom lip-synched in time with Bowie's live vocal for 'Ashes to ashes'. This was a positively phantasmagorical display of thrilling proportions as these ghostly and disorienting images supposedly laid to rest the best back-catalogue in pop history.

For Bowie as solo artist, it looked as if theatricality was in. For Bowie as a member of a band, it was an aesthetic under attack. On the back of two unsuccessful albums (*Tonight* and *Never Let Me Down*) and a personally unhappy tour (Glass Spider), Bowie opted for drastic measures, a redefinition more fundamental than any of the many previous changes. Reacting to the criticism of over-theatricality and musical mediocrity, Bowie decided to strip down his look and his sound. Out went the scope and the intricacies so important to the success of his great albums. In came a tried and trusted blues-based rhythm section (Hunt and Tony Sales, with whom Bowie had worked in the seventies with Iggy Pop) and Reeves Gabrels' post-Hendrix avant-garde guitar freak-outs. All this worked well on the first Tin Machine album, but came over as oafish and dull live. Bowie had used hard rock in past musical lives, but always with ample doses of ironic detachment.

More damaging was the new set of values which this musical switch heralded. Out went the characters, the idea that Bowie was as important visually as he was musically. The new Bowie, 1989 style, was a bearded, chain-smoking rocker, gigging within the corporate identity of a band. Out went Bowie as the focus of attention. In came camaraderie. Out also went the idea that Bowie was pop's first and most important poseur, showing no allegiance to any one style or look. In 1971 Bowie was pop's 'faker' who in 'Changes' warned: 'Look out you rock and rollers'. In 1991 he could 'belong in rock-and-roll'[26] in a song with only a touch of irony, given its context.

It could be argued that Bowie is on the cusp between two opposed musical traditions, as we watch artifice and authenticity compete for his various musical selves. In the meantime, his influence continues, often unacknowledged by the antipathetic music press. The tradition of irony in performance has been embraced in recent years by the engaging Pet Shop Boys with their camp conceits, by Shakespear's Sister with their glam work-outs and, most surprisingly, by U2 on their Zoo TV tour. Out went the sloganizing of past U2 tours. In came an ample dose of irony as Bono postured and pranced on stage, singing 'Every poet is a thief'[27] in the 'false' glare of postmodernity. He borrowed the Bowie trick of filming the audience with a video camera, singing in front of a backdrop of television screens (evoking memories of Thomas Newton blissed out in front of his own wall of tellies in *The Man Who Fell to Earth*). He even gets the lads dressed up in drag for the 'withdrawn' video for 'One'. The artistic success of U2's conversion indicates that there is still mileage in faking it.

LESLIE THOMAS
For those beyond the fringe

Evening News and Star, 2 November 1964

Are you hairy? If so, are you proud of being hairy and want to remain hairy? And are you tired of people making fun of you? If so, join a new society formed just for you and other hirsute folk – the International League for the Preservation of Animal Filament.

'It's really for the protection of pop musicians, and those who wear their hair long,' explained the founder and president, David Jones, of Plaistow Grove, Bromley. 'Anyone who has the courage to wear hair down to his shoulders has to go through hell. It's time we united and stood up for our curls.'

David, who leads a professional pop group called The Manish Boys, is in the process of enrolling members.

'Screaming Lord Sutch, P. J. Proby, The Pretty Things and, of course, The Stones and The Beatles – we want them all as members. You've no idea the indignities you have to suffer just because you've got long hair,' said David, who gave up commercial art to go into the pop business. 'Dozens of times I've been politely told to clear out of the lounge bar at public houses. Everybody makes jokes about you on a bus, and if you go past navvies digging in the road, it's murder!'

The International League for the Preservation of Animal Filament will give long-haired lads a sense of belonging, he thinks. It will fight their causes and encourage them when too many people are poking fun.

A message to London from Dave

Melody Maker, 26 February 1966

Without doubt, David Bowie has talent. And also without doubt it will be exploited. For Mr Bowie, a 19-year-old Bromley boy, not only writes and arranges his own numbers, but he is also helping Tony Hatch to write a musical score and the numbers for a TV show. As if that wasn't enough, David also designs shirts and suits for John Stephen of the famed Carnaby Street clan.

And his ambition? 'I want to act,' says Bowie modestly, 'I'd like to do character parts. I think it takes a lot to become somebody else. It takes some doing.

'Also I want to go to Tibet. It's a fascinating place, you know. I'd like to take a holiday and have a look inside the monasteries. The Tibetan monks, lamas, bury themselves inside mountains for weeks and only eat every three days. They're ridiculous – and it's said they live for centuries.'

It should be stated that David is a well-read student of astrology and a believer in reincarnation . . .

'As far as I'm concerned the whole idea of Western life – that's the life we live now – is wrong. These are hard convictions to put into songs, though. At the moment I write nearly all of my songs round London. No. I should say the people who live in London – and the lack of real life they have. The majority just don't know what life is.'

Every number in Dave's stage act is an original that he has written. As he says, the theme is usually London kids and their lives. However, it leads to trouble.

'Several of the younger teenagers' programmes wouldn't play "Can't help thinking about me", because it is about leaving home. The number relates several incidents in every teenager's life – and leaving home is something which always comes up.

'Tony Hatch and I rather wanted to do another number I had written. It goes down very well in the stage act and lots of fans said I should have released it – but Tony and I thought the words were a bit strong.

'In what way? Well, it tells the story of life as some teenagers saw it – but we didn't think the lyrics were quite up many people's street. I do it on stage though, and we're probably keeping it for an EP or maybe an LP. Hope, hope! It's called "Now you've met the London boys", and mentions pills, and generally belittles the London night-life scene.

'I've lived in London and been brought up here, and I find it's a great subject to write songs about. And remember, with all original numbers the audiences are hearing numbers they've never heard before – so this makes for a varied stage act,' says David. 'It's risky, because the kids aren't familiar with the tunes, but I'm sure it makes their musical life more interesting.' He could be right.

The Bowie Companion

MARC BOLAN

Music-hall humorist

Melody Maker, 12 March 1977

David is a great singer . . . he can sing anything, almost. I remember him when he was in The Lower Third and he used to go to gigs in an ambulance. I used to think he was very professional. He was playing saxophone then, and singing. I suppose it was a blues band then, and he was produced by Shel Talmy. He did a record which I'm sure everybody has forgotten. It was pop art – your actual feedback. I can't remember what it was called.

After that he went to Decca around the time I was doing 'The wizard'. He was into bombardiers then. Don't you remember 'The little bombardier'? He was very cockney then. I used to go round to his place in Bromley and he always played Anthony Newley records. I haven't spoken to him about it, but I guess that was how he got into mime. Newley did mime in *Stop The World I Want To Get Off*. The funny thing is that 'The laughing gnome', which was later one of David's biggest singles here, came from that early period. It [was re-released] at the height of his supercool image. And that's very 'Strawberry fair' – 'the donkey's eaten all the strawberries!' That was his biggest single, so it just shows you it doesn't pay to be cool, man! 'Rock 'n' roll suicide' hit the dust and the laughing gnomes took over.

We were all looking for something to get into then. I wanted to be Bob Dylan, but I think David was looking into that music hall humour. It was the wrong time to do it, but all his songs were story songs, like 'The London boys'. They had a flavour, a very theatrical flavour, with very square backings. But in those days there weren't any groovy backings being laid down. I think if he played back those records now he'd smile at them, because he was an unformed talent then. He was putting together the nucleus of what he was eventually going to be.

When he had 'Space oddity' he was on tour with me in Tyrannosaurus Rex. He had a mime act and used to open up the show. He didn't sing at all but had a tape going and he'd act out a story about a Tibetan boy. It was quite good actually, and we did the Festival Hall with Roy Harper as well. I remember David playing me 'Space oddity' in his room and I loved it and said he needed a sound like The Bee Gees, who were very big then. The stylophones he used on that, I gave him. Tony Visconti turned me on to stylophones. The record was a sleeper for months before it became a hit, and I played on 'The prettiest star', you know. I thought it was a great song, and it flopped completely.

But I never got the feeling from David that he was ambitious. I remember he'd buy antiques if he had a hit, when he should have saved the money. David got his drive to be successful once I'd done it with the T Rex thing. At the beginning of the seventies it was the only way to go.

JOHNNY ROGAN

Ken Pitt

from *Starmakers and Svengalis*

Creative management effectively began for publicist Ken Pitt one Thursday afternoon in 1954. While working in the Albemarle Street office that he rented from bandleader Ted Heath, Pitt was distracted by the distant melodious sound of a ballad singer. When he investigated the commotion, his eyes feasted on a remarkable scene in the street below:

> There was this extremely attractive Mediterranean boy who sang through a megaphone and he had a one-legged 'bottler' who collected the money. This fellow was stomping around on a wooden leg like something out of *Treasure Island*. Another person was playing a French accordion. I was impressed by the effect that the singer had on the girls, who were hanging out of windows throwing money at him!

. . . By mid-1966 Pitt was determined to discover a new, original act with sufficient potential for achieving international stardom. Ever since the days of Danny Purches [Daniel Puccessi] he had dreamed of developing the career of a rough diamond, and in the wake of the beat boom there were innumerable young kids convinced that they were the new Bob Dylan or Elvis Presley. Pitt was adamant that a carefully tutored artiste could transcend the limitations of the fashion-conscious pop world and succeed in a number of related fields. In later years he was lampooned for suggesting that the time was right for the emergence of the new Tommy Steele, but that name expressed only a minimal aspect of Pitt's overall vision. What Pitt desired was an artiste of similar potential who was different enough to capture the public's imagination. The ideal applicant would be a charismatic singer, songwriter, actor and musician, capable of adopting a variety of roles and exploiting all areas of show business. Remarkably, the perfect candidate had been within Pitt's orbit for the previous nine months.

Pitt had first heard about David Bowie in September 1965, when a manager named Ralph Horton phoned his office requesting financial support. It transpired that Horton was Bowie's second manager, and the artiste had already cut three failed singles under the name David Jones. The singer hardly sounded like a world-beater but Ralph was convinced of his potential as a song-and-dance man. Pitt politely suggested that the name Jones should be dropped, and several weeks later he was informed that the boy had been rechristened David Bowie. Unfortunately, due to a bookful of commitments, Pitt was unable to pursue the Bowie case that year. Horton was too extravagant to wait patiently, so he temporarily abandoned Pitt in favour of other benefactors.

When Horton next contacted Ken Pitt in April 1966, his tone was as confident as ever. Bowie now had television experience, a chart hit[28] and a new record, 'Do anything you say', released only days before. In short, he was already on the threshold of stardom and all Horton required were the talents and business acumen of an established manager to provide that all-important final push. Pitt expressed enthusiasm and finally agreed to see this much-touted singing star play a Sunday afternoon concert at the Marquee. Ken recalls an amazing set of self-penned songs, R & B standards and, most surprisingly, a dramatic rendition of 'You'll never walk alone'. As the show reached its climax, the bespectacled entrepreneur closed his eyes and imagined the boy performing for a full house at one of the world's largest venues. He was transfixed.

During a subsequent meeting at Horton's Warwick Square flat, a verbal agreement was concluded between the two managers by which Ken agreed to take on the administrative workload, leaving Ralph free to concentrate on Bowie's gigging schedule. Rather uncharacteristically, Pitt neglected to commit these agreements to paper immediately, and this would cause some consternation in later months. Within days of allying himself to Horton, Ken discovered that his partner was an incurable spendthrift whose profligacy seemingly knew no bounds. Soon, Pitt was besieged by creditors ranging from the telephone company to car hire firms and even Bowie's own record company. Amazingly, Pye Records had obtained judgment against Horton for failing to pay for a small number of the artiste's records. Pitt immediately smoothed things over with Pye managing director Louis Benjamin, but these constant administrative and financial problems severely tested his patience.

The early summer of 1966 was not a particularly auspicious period in Bowie's history. Another Pye single, 'I dig everything', had failed and finances were tight. Ken had arranged for Maurice Hatton of Mithras Films to see Bowie at the Marquee in the hope of gaining him a part in a short musical film. Hatton was impressed and several ideas were thrashed out, but it was all pie in the sky. Undeterred by this disappointment, Pitt set about securing Bowie a new recording contract, this time with Deram, a subsidiary label of Decca that was about to be launched as a haven for promising young talent. In order to alleviate financial worries, Pitt also turned his attention to publishing. Negotiations commenced with David Platz of Essex Music who proffered an advance of £1000, a figure that Pitt felt could be bettered by an American publishing company.

On 8 November, Pitt embarked on an American/Australian tour with Crispian St Peters, and this allowed him sufficient time to negotiate with New York publishers and lawyers on behalf of Bowie. Following a series of meetings, Pitt finally secured a worldwide publishing deal offering a $10,000 advance, with a guarantee of a further $20,000 to be paid during the next three years. Ken neglected to cable Horton or Bowie about this piece of good fortune, preferring to wait until the contracts were actually in his hands. This was probably sound business sense since Pitt was in a dangerous position, having still not signed a management agreement with Horton. In the event of any dispute between the parties the lack of a written document would leave Pitt little hope of receiving full compensation for the time, effort and money he had already pumped into Bowie's career. Unfortunately, during Pitt's absence Horton had reassumed administrative control and made a disastrous decision that was to have far-reaching effects. Upon returning to England, Ken was shattered to learn that his partner had accepted an offer from Platz for an advance of £500, precisely half the figure previously negotiated. Poor Horton felt that he had made a sound decision at a time when hard cash was needed. For Pitt, the loss of the American publishing deal was a devastating blow and it would require all his tenacity to sustain David's livelihood during the next couple of years.

Ken Pitt's strategy for 1967 was to bury the mistakes of the previous year and start from scratch. David's Deram debut received a favourable response, though one perceptive reviewer felt obliged to point out the vocal similarities to Anthony Newley and added that the flip side, 'The London boys', was a stronger cut. All this was true, and much has been made of the contention that it was Ken Pitt who promoted the Newley image and suppressed the provocative flip side. In fact, it was the record company that made this decision, supported by Bowie himself, who evidently preferred 'Rubber band'. Contrary to popular belief, Pitt was actually concerned about the Newley comparisons, particularly as his wish was for Bowie to emerge as a unique and individual artiste.

Dismissing the Newley fixation as a passing phase, Pitt turned his attention to more pressing matters. Still smarting from the publishing fiasco and concerned about the lack of a binding management contract, he was forced to consider his future as Horton's partner. Conflicting loyalties, however, prevented decisive action. Eventually, it was Bowie who solved this political impasse:

> David phoned me one day and said, 'I'm very worried about Ralph'. He was concerned about the debts and felt that Ralph was a good friend and would tear up the contract that David had with him. He went to see him, and I think Ralph was rather relieved because the next day he phoned me and said, 'I'm going to finish with David'. To his credit, he's never bothered me since.

Indeed, Horton virtually disappeared from the music business overnight. In many respects, he was a classic example of the flamboyant but flawed manager – a breed that proliferated in the mid-sixties pop world. Horton had supported Bowie through some bad times, and his remarkable enthusiasm and braggadocio had extracted money from wealthy benefactors who really should have known better. He was also acutely aware of the importance of image and carefully groomed many of the musicians in his circle, not least Bowie himself. For all the bluster, however, Ralph could transform neither himself nor Bowie into the millionaire of his dreams. The price of his Epsteinian extravagance had been all too noticeable in the escalating debts that refused to subside.

It was not until 25 April 1967 that Pitt officially signed the contracts by which he was legally appointed David Bowie's manager. In the meantime, a second Deram single appeared in the form of 'The laughing gnome', an unashamed comedy work-out complete with Newley phraseology. It was certainly a dangerous move for Bowie and, had it charted, he would probably have been dismissed as a one-hit-wonder novelty singer in the vein of Napoleon XIV or Whistling Jack Smith. Surprisingly, Ken Pitt does not regard this embarrassing single as an error of judgment:

> Nothing he ever did was a mistake. This is late 1970s criticism . . . Nobody was aghast in 1967. You must put it in the context of the time. It was right for the time. David is a highly inventive writer and he does have a sense of humour. It was just another facet of David's personality.

The failure of 'The laughing gnome' at least enabled Pitt to push Bowie's debut album as a serious work worthy of critical attention.

Several good reviews were forthcoming, but without the back-up of a quality hit single, sales were negligible.

With Pitt providing food, money and shelter, Bowie was able to continue with his sometimes overambitious projects, but occasionally these extracurricular interests bore fruit. After enrolling in Lindsay Kemp's mime classes, for example, Bowie made a surprise appearance in several performances of *Pierrot in Turquoise*. This flirtation with mime contributed to his store of knowledge and would later encourage him to think in terms of fusing theatre and rock. In retrospect, one can see that Bowie was very much ahead of the pack in branching out from pop music. Had he been an established pop star, the publicity generated by his superficial involvements in theatre and film would have been invaluable. Unfortunately, Bowie was at best a cult figure and, until he achieved substantial commercial success, the music press would remain uninterested in his other activities. This was the major flaw in Pitt's plan of action. He had the power to influence and direct Bowie's butterfly mind, but there could be no immediate financial gain from such a policy without the elusive yet essential hit single which alone would focus attention on his artiste's many talents.

Pitt's commitment to Bowie was seemingly limitless, so perhaps it was not too surprising that the superstar-elect moved into his Manchester Street flat. This allowed Ken to spend even more time educating the singer and introducing him to cultural pursuits previously outside his experience.

Following the commercial failure of another promising single, 'Love you till Tuesday', Pitt engaged in a long war of attrition with Decca. He bombarded the record company with letters complaining about the lack of promotion on Bowie's discs, and even suggested that they drop him from the label rather than continue in a half-hearted fashion. When Bowie's next two singles were rejected as 'unsuitable', Pitt announced that he was taking his star elsewhere. Within hours he was knocking on the doors of Apple – The Beatles' enterprising record label for the development of new talent. Much to Bowie's disappointment, however, a terse rejection letter was all that Pitt received for his efforts. It would be over a year before another record contract was signed.

In spite of all his flop records, Bowie was still earning a reasonable working wage, and with support from an overprotective father and manager there was little chance of him starving. Nevertheless, Pitt was sufficiently concerned about his protégé's finances to suggest a stab at cabaret. For any serious young singer-songwriter such an artistic compromise would have been unthinkable, but Pitt's vision of Bowie as an all-round entertainer was broad enough to encompass

19

even this unlikely area. In the event, David's attitude remained ambivalent. Occasionally he was fired with enthusiasm for the idea, while at other times he seemed to regard it as demeaning. Pitt had the foresight to sweeten the pill by encouraging Bowie to perform a set consisting of a mixture of his own songs, sprinkled with a few Beatles covers. The cabaret concept reached the audition stage but went no further. It was probably just as well. According to Pitt, the well-known agent Harry Dawson was overwhelmed by Bowie's performance, and following the Astor Club audition he reputedly exclaimed, 'It's a marvellous act, but where can I book it? It's too good.' It is difficult to imagine how an act can possibly be 'too good' and when I finally found Harry, he was frank enough to admit that he had actually dismissed Bowie as a no-hoper:

> I turned around to Ken and said, 'Let him have a good day job – he's never going to get anywhere'. That was my judgment of David Bowie. Ken said, 'You're out of your mind. I'm going to make him an international star.' Bowie basically did impressions at the time. I couldn't see it.

Indeed, it suddenly seemed that the only person who was convinced of Bowie's talent was the ever-optimistic Kenneth Pitt.

It is difficult to determine precisely when Bowie began to lose faith in his manager, but the first signs of a possible change of heart occurred when he left the Manchester Street flat to move in with his girlfriend, Hermione Farthingale. Together they formed an acoustic group named Turquoise, which later became Feathers. It was an appropriate name, for their music was decidedly lightweight and their earnings were virtually non-existent. Bowie's adoption of a pseudo-hippie lifestyle was characteristically half-hearted, and when his money ran low he was more than willing to suffer the indignity of appearing in a Lyons Maid ice-cream commercial. Nevertheless, peer group pressure had placed the star-elect in an extremely uncomfortable position. He knew that Pitt represented security, order and direction in his life, but the new friends he was acquiring clearly disapproved of such a father figure. The hippie movement had been nurtured on the mid-sixties catchphrase 'never trust anyone over 30' and Pitt was not the kind of man who could lie about his age. Although Bowie was a long way from seriously considering the termination of his management contract with Pitt, the seeds of discontent had already been sown. Confused feelings about his possible career development seem to have thrust the singer into a series of ephemeral ventures. Feathers dissolved before it had time to develop and David's relationship with Hermione ended shortly afterwards. Suddenly, the singer seemed confused, dejected and unwilling to forge ahead with Pitt's carefully structured career plans.

Pitt wisely chose not to interfere in Bowie's artistic decisions, but voiced concern about the amount of time he was frittering away on counterculture pursuits. Ken had shared David's life long enough to understand the psychology of the performer, and realized that without a major long-term project to spark his interest there was always the danger of a descent into inertia:

> David had bouts of laziness and I would get a little sharp with him from time to time. Yet the moment he got interested in a particular scheme he outran everybody else. But he had to be turned on and fired with enthusiasm.

Clearly, Bowie no longer felt enthusiasm for the old ideal of becoming an accomplished all-round entertainer. However, the alternative life-style offered by hippie friends and folksingers seemed even less likely to enable him to achieve long-lasting success in the music business. Pitt decided that Bowie urgently needed to work on a major project before all momentum was permanently lost. In financing the projected television film *Love You Till Tuesday*, Pitt seemed to be proving beyond doubt that he was the major catalyst in Bowie's performing life. His investment was not only a magnanimous gesture, but a dangerous gamble involving several thousand pounds. Ultimately, his gesture of commitment proved only partly successful. The much hoped-for screening on a major network never took place and this prevented Bowie from ingratiating himself with television and film producers as Pitt had intended. On the credit side, the filming had encouraged Bowie to write several new songs, one of which, 'Space oddity', was particularly impressive.

For a time, Pitt remained firmly in the driving seat, but his power was gradually eroded by the intervention of two Americans – Calvin Mark Lee and Mary Angela Barnett. These latest acquaintances of Bowie had provided the connection through which Pitt negotiated a deal with Mercury Records. As the months passed their influence grew stronger, but Pitt still hoped that the old order could be restored if 'Space oddity' charted as a single. With the American moon launch imminent, the topical value of the single was undeniable and Pitt invested all his efforts in ensuring its success. He even employed the services of a chart-hyper, an uncharacteristic action, which underlined the extent of his desperation and determination. Weeks passed, but the expected chart breakthrough failed to materialize. Deflated by the poor sales, Bowie embarked on a Continental jaunt, appearing in two song festivals in Italy and Malta. Upon returning to England with his manager, Bowie received some disturbing news that made the fate of 'Space oddity' seem irrelevant by comparison.

Haywood Stenton Jones had always been a delicate figure, but his sudden death from a lung infection came as a terrible shock to his son. Jones had diligently guided David's career over the years, ensuring that he received the best professional advice and never fell into financial difficulties. His demise was also a serious blow to Pitt, who had established a close and trusting relationship with Bowie's family since signing the artiste in 1967. Without Jones's sobering influence it would prove increasingly difficult for Pitt to convince Bowie that he was acting in his best interests. Of course, Jones's death might have enabled Ken to adopt a more paternalistic role, but instead Bowie turned to his newer friends for moral support. In September, less than one month after his father's death, 'Space oddity' belatedly stormed the charts, peaking at number five. This long-awaited breakthrough would have been the cause of tumultuous celebration in earlier days, but Bowie was now an older, somewhat sadder figure. While the disc was scaling the charts he moved into a flat in Beckenham housed in a grand Edwardian building named Haddon Hall. There he lived with Angela Barnett, producer Tony Visconti and a host of visiting rock musicians and counterculture flag-wavers. Pitt was forced to watch from a distance as his rising star went through a tortuous period of reassessment:

> The disillusionment didn't really start until after the success of 'Space oddity' . . . I've always noted that artistes are nice people until they achieve their aims and become stars. David eventually got what he wanted, but it drove him to the depths of despair. A little bit of it was affectation, I admit. The putting down of the single and pretending he wasn't a pop star and hating all these people wanting to take his photograph. But you must remember he was living with this rather pseudo-hippie commune. They had a great influence on him; they were very anti-success, anti-hit record, anti-pop star. He'd go home at nights to that. It was a strange dichotomy.

For the final six months of his association with David Bowie, Pitt seems to have been singlehandedly fighting the inhabitants of Haddon Hall. He now admits, 'David became unmanageable. I was manager in name only.' The breakdown between artiste and manager resulted in organizational chaos. Prior to a prestigious Bowie concert at London's Purcell Room, Pitt was abruptly relieved of publicity duties by David's new aide, Calvin Mark Lee. The confusion caused the media to stay away in droves, and Bowie was incensed. After that concert Calvin was seldom seen in Bowie's circle, but Pitt did not particularly benefit from this turn of events. The second David Bowie album had

just been released and was largely ignored, much to the disappointment of its creator. While Pitt encouraged Bowie to take advantage of
his recent single success by working even harder, the disillusioned
star returned to his Haddon Hall sanctuary.

Pitt could have been forgiven for abandoning Bowie to his own
devices, but instead he pushed ahead with a number of new strategies.
The most intriguing of these was persuading Bowie to be interviewed
by the gay magazine *Jeremy*.[29] In 1969, it was an adventurous and
potentially dangerous move to ally an artiste with the gay movement,
but Pitt felt that Bowie's career prospects could be enhanced by tacitly
supporting such a cause:

> It was the turning point in the whole Bowie campaign. I probably put too
> much value on *Jeremy* and its readers. It wasn't a very good magazine,
> but one worked on the assumption that it was read by some very
> important people in the business. I didn't know what would happen,
> whether it would bring down on David all the calumny that the devil
> could muster . . . But it was important, especially when you consider
> what's happened since with Boy George, Frankie Goes To Hollywood
> and Marilyn.

Three years after the *Jeremy* interview, Pitt's pioneering publicity work
reached fruition when Bowie stunned the rock world by confessing to
Melody Maker that he was bisexual.[30] Surprisingly, Pitt could never
make up his mind about the nature of Bowie's sexuality:

> David had this aura. He would sometimes come into a room looking like
> a ravishingly beautiful girl then, ten minutes later, he'd be a 'Gor blimey'
> yobbo. He would turn the cockney persona on and off. He did a whole
> interview in cockney once. Of course, he was always surrounded by gay
> people and got on with them very well. But I really didn't know for
> certain until I read *Melody Maker*. Frankly, I wasn't quite sure then.

While Bowie remained in relative seclusion, Pitt continued with his
dream of establishing the artiste as a straight actor. There was talk of
casting David in an adaptation of Sir Walter Scott's *The Fair Maid of
Perth*, and plans were also under way for film director Tony Palmer to
produce a Bowie documentary. Strangely, the one area that remained
unexploited was the most obvious of all. As Christmas loomed the
patient public still awaited a follow-up to 'Space oddity'.

In many respects, the delay in releasing a new single was not
surprising. Deciding upon a successor to 'Space oddity' was no easy
task, and much was at stake. Eventually, almost six months after his
last single had charted, Bowie selected 'The prettiest star', a non-
gimmicky record that flopped. Although Pitt objected to its release, it
is debatable whether an alternative choice would have proven chart-
worthy. The problem lay in the nature of 'Space oddity', a self-

contained statement that offered little possibility of a follow-up along similar lines. Producer Tony Visconti had spotted the danger prior to its release and refused to be associated with the disc. In spite of its hit potential, 'Space oddity' had all the hallmarks of a one-off novelty record. The timing of its release persuaded many people that it had been written to cash in on the American moon launch. Significantly, one month before 'Space oddity' charted, an American duo, Zager and Evans, hit the top of the UK and US charts with the futuristic 'In the year 2525'. Thematically, there were superficial similarities between the songs, each dealing with possible future events and containing a pat moral. For Bowie to be placed alongside Zager and Evans in the public's consciousness was far from ideal. They were quintessential one-hit wonders, and following the enormous success of 'In the year 2525' they slipped back into the netherworld from which they had mysteriously emerged. In the autumn of 1969 it was by no means certain that Bowie would avoid the same fate. Even Pitt was forced to concede that in the public's eye, Bowie had been overshadowed by his own creation – the enigmatic Major Tom.

From Pitt's point of view, the ghosts of Haddon Hall remained the invisible force in Bowie's life, and any lingering hopes of winning back the impressionable star were irrevocably destroyed when he married his *âme damnée*, Mary Angela Barnett. David and Angela went on to become Beckenham's answer to John and Yoko, but even today Pitt sees the marriage as a form of artistic castration:

> Angela coming on the scene was the worst thing that ever happened to David Bowie. She would probably argue that she helped his career. In actual fact, she held it back. She turned out to be the division between David and me. I think she put him back at least two years. Her attitude towards life and other people didn't help him a great deal. I think she was the destroyer.

Following his marriage, Bowie became extremely capricious and seemingly unable to reconcile the Haddon Hall notions of artistic integrity with the common man's desire for an easy living. Pitt was unwittingly cast in the role of devil's advocate, and his willingness to procure Bowie steady work in television commercials was frowned upon. The fact that Bowie himself had requested such employment was apparently irrelevant. When Pitt booked a series of live performances Bowie again reversed previous instructions and complained that his manager was preventing the group from forging ahead with studio work. Given such inconsistencies, it was no great shock when the star phoned one afternoon to announce that he wanted to manage himself. Without fully articulating his fears, Bowie had evidently lost confidence in Pitt's managerial style and suddenly felt he needed a radically different approach. His disenchantment was probably a product of the times, for by the end of the sixties many artistes were searching for specialized business managers rather than the traditional Tin Pan Alley entrepreneurs who had often emerged as creative guiding forces in their clients' lives. Bowie took his problem to Olaf Wyper, General Manager of Philips, who swiftly washed his hands of the entire business but provided the artiste with the names of several lawyers, one of whom was willing to branch out into rock management.

Tony De Fries was the complete antithesis of Ken Pitt: arrogant, ruthless and aggressive in business dealings, he represented an attitude that was thoroughly distasteful to his quiet, urbane rival. Pitt recalls his feelings upon first meeting De Fries:

> I was most alarmed when he came to see me. He wasn't a manager. He was working as a litigation clerk at a firm of solicitors, one of whose clients was Olaf Wyper . . . He had no qualifications to manage anybody. David was still a close friend of mine and I wouldn't have taken him to court, but I didn't want this man cashing in on my investment. I'd seen the likes of Tony De Fries many a time. I tried to alert David to my worst fears but it didn't seem to sink in.

On the contrary, Bowie was evidently smitten by the idea of being represented by such a high-powered lawyer. In De Fries he had found his own version of Allen Klein, an alchemist who could apparently transform Mercury albums into gold.

Pitt's response to De Fries was to request £2000 compensation, an absurdly low figure in view of the work and money he had previously pumped into Bowie's career. Instead, De Fries fobbed him off with promises of a possible percentage of Bowie's future earnings. Pitt sat tight and strengthened his position by enforcing a clause in the Essex Music contract which ensured that any royalties due were payable initially to his company. De Fries later contested this arrangement, Essex froze the assets and a court case ensued. Pitt eventually settled with Bowie, but by that time De Fries was no longer managing the seventies superstar. Even from a distance, however, De Fries was an imposing figure whose influence could not be underestimated, as Pitt found to his cost:

> I was awarded £15,000 plus costs and De Fries tried to stop it. He said that David had no right to apportion any of the monies. But that couldn't work. It just delayed it for a long time. De Fries was fighting for his life. It would have gone on for ever if he'd had his way.

Tony De Fries has always been a controversial figure, so it is hardly surprising that his involvement in the Bowie saga still produces markedly ambivalent responses from different sources in the music business. His well-publicized achievements and dollar earnings during Bowie's RCA years have inevitably overshadowed Pitt's quiet industry and commitment during the late sixties. The extent to which De Fries profited from his predecessor's groundwork cannot be calculated, but Pitt clearly feels that his reputation was often hyped by the early-seventies music press:

> In *Melody Maker* there was a two-page article on De Fries where they used the cliché 'De Fries' masterstroke was taking Bowie away and not making him available to the press'. Bullshit! Do you know how many times that's been used during the past fifty years? Masterstroke?! It was an elementary stroke . . . Who do you think pointed Bowie into those somewhat 'unconventional' channels? He lived in my flat for two years and what eventually happened to David was all part of a plan that I had formed. The plan had nothing to do with Tony De Fries.

In spite of Pitt's objections, few would argue that De Fries was not responsible for breaking Bowie internationally. Yet the litigation clerk's entrepreneurial strategies are still derided by his older adversary:

> De Fries was a disaster. Is anybody better off for what De Fries has done? He managed *himself* very well. David didn't have money then. When *Hunky Dory* was in the charts and the name Bowie was quite big, he was living in Oakley Street. He and Angela came back one night and found the door padlocked. Things were so bad that Zowie had to go up to Aberdeen to his nanny's parents to ensure he got fed. He didn't take David Bowie over for the same reasons I did. Think about that and you've got the answer to the whole story.

Unfortunately, there are still several unanswered questions. Would Bowie have achieved megastardom without the consuming ambition of De Fries? Were De Fries' strategies devised to strengthen his position in anticipation of Bowie's eventual defection? Would their business relationship have improved if De Fries had given his artiste a larger slice of the cake? Since De Fries was exiled from Bowie's court such questions have continued to multiply and, as a result, his historical importance in terms of rock management has been reduced considerably. History has been kinder to Pitt, and in recent years his career has been placed in a clearer perspective. During the early seventies he was ridiculed as the manager who wanted to transform the embryonic Ziggy Stardust into a neo-Tommy Steele. Pitt's claim that Bowie was an all-round entertainer seemed an absurd conceit characteristic of a dinosaur mentality hopelessly entrenched in the outmoded philosophies of fifties rock-and-roll. However, Bowie's increasing involvement in film and theatre work in recent years has left the nagging suspicion that Pitt's vision may have been largely correct. Had he chosen a more radical analogy than Tommy Steele, mythologizing Bowie critics might have hailed him as a sage. Instead, his reputation remains that of a solicitous soul, strangely out of place in the rapacious rock music business.

The loss of Bowie at the end of the sixties effectively closed Pitt's career in pop management. Like many of his contemporaries, he became disillusioned with the American-style business manager favoured by many new artistes. He was also weary of young acts demanding financial support but refusing to accept advice on career development. Not wishing to become either a full-time accountant or a sugar daddy, Pitt gracefully bowed out. Before making that decision, however, he briefly represented Tony Dangerfield, one of the more durable performers of the previous decade. Ironically, Tony remembers Pitt not as the creative ideas man of the Bowie days but as a hard-nosed negotiator, eager to score points off cautious record companies:

> Ken was a very good organizer and highly efficient in negotiation, but I felt he could no longer see potential and break down walls. He was purely an office man; with a rock manager you need something more. I think he burnt himself out with David. He put so many ideas into him. He must have been disillusioned when he didn't get the cream. If I wanted advice on contracts today I'd go to Ken, but I wouldn't sign him as personal manager. Ken was too much of a gentleman, a pro. He couldn't stand inefficiency and the business is rife with it. It must have been difficult for Ken to deal with such people.

Pitt's old partner Dave Nicolson concurs with Dangerfield's viewpoint:

> Ken was honest, truthful and reliable. He was also very straight, in both the business sense and his attitude. I'm sure with Crispian St Peters he would have advised against making a statement like, 'I will be bigger than The Beatles'. He sobered up a lot of ideas I had which were quite crazy.

This emphasis on Pitt's sober and gentlemanly nature has often been made and may be the key to his lack of millionaire success. Bowie has seldom commented on Pitt, but one of his asides reiterates Dangerfield and Nicolson's main point: 'He is a very nice man. I like him very much, but that's not enough in this business.'

By his colleagues' reckoning, Pitt lacked the ruthlessness and aggression of an aspiring mogul. Even in the seventies he regarded diplomacy and integrity as the hallmarks of good management and refused to surrender to the demands of cynical young artistes. Instead, he acted as a consultant to visiting American and Continental stars, just as he had done twenty years before. Looking back over his career, he admits that his greatest weakness was a lack of effective communication with his acts:

27

Artistes always want to know what you're doing for them. If I'm guilty of anything it was sitting in my office being very busy while the artiste was at home biting his fingernails. This often happened. When they poured their hearts out, I listened but made no comment. They didn't realize I'd heard it all before, knew the problems and how to handle them. I knew David Bowie was going to be one of the biggest acts in the world, but I couldn't get it across to him with any emotion.

In analysing the strengths or weaknesses of Kenneth Pitt as a manager it is difficult to ignore an apparent streak of ill luck that runs through his career. Danny Purches, the untameable gypsy boy, could not control his urge to spend every penny he earned; Manfred Mann grew money-conscious; Crispian St Peters suffered psychological problems; Goldie fell victim to homesickness; Dangerfield arrived too late and, worst of all, David Bowie abandoned Pitt after achieving his first hit. Perhaps a more politically shrewd entrepreneur might have averted some of the above turns of fortune, but not all of them. Ultimately, one is left with the question, 'Was rock management the most suitable occupation for Pitt?' His younger contemporary, Simon Napier-Bell, clearly thinks not:

Ken Pitt was almost the epitome of the indulgent, all-on-the-side-of-the-artiste manager and Tony De Fries was the opposite. In both cases there you don't have what I would call the professional 'music business' manager. Neither has been substantially successful on a continuous basis with rock acts or continued with them. That isn't condemning them in terms of strengths or weaknesses. They just don't seem to have found their *métier* in rock management.

It should be added, however, that very few sixties managers were dedicated to rock management *per se*, and even fewer could sustain an interest over a long period. While admitting that no contemporary rock group would tolerate his ideas for more than a couple of hours, Pitt does not consider his unfulfilled dreams as evidence of failure. Indeed, he compares himself favourably with any of his multimillionaire contemporaries, and for his contribution to Bowie's career development alone, Pitt deserves a special place in the history of rock management.

LINDSAY KEMP
Pierrot in Turquoise

There have been so many accounts of how we met, not least the rather theatrical versions I invented – which were not intended to be *deliberately* untruthful, you understand, simply more impressive. I think what probably happened was that David and I were both represented at the time by [Brian Epstein's] NEMS Agency, and the girls in the office there had been raving on to each of us about how we should meet the other. They'd say to me, 'Oh Lindsay, there's this *wonderful* guy and he's written a song about a rubber band – you'd *adore* him.' Perhaps they actually gave me his first LP too, because I'd certainly heard the songs before I met him. And then I think someone from NEMS brought David to one of my shows at the Little Theatre in St Martin's Lane, and that's where we met for the first time – in the tiny, cramped backstage area. I adored him! A golden-haired swain with the voice of an angel! He began attending my classes at the Dance Centre straight away, and we collaborated on the show *Pierrot in Turquoise* – David suggested 'Turquoise' as it was the Buddhist symbol of everlastingness. He was very into Buddhism at the time and he had these beautiful Tibetan boots, I remember . . .

Pierrot in Turquoise was a variation on shows I'd been performing previously: *The Tinsel People* and *The Strange World of Pierrot Flour* were also concerned with the eternal triangle of Pierrot–Columbine–Harlequin. David played Cloud, a kind of protean narrator-figure, and sang 'When I live my dream' and 'Sell me a coat' from the first album, as well as new songs he'd composed especially for the show, such as 'Threepenny Pierrot', 'Columbine' and 'The mirror'. He was very prolific – always strumming away at his twelve-string guitar. I adored him because he adored *me*! He was the perfect audience for me – he thought I was so *witty* and so *wonderful*, and he encouraged me. He was Radiguet to my Cocteau! He also adored Jack Birkett, with whom I lived in Bateman Street and who played Harlequin in *Pierrot in Turquoise*. David thought Jack and I were like an old music hall double act – he loved it!

In class too, he would drink in my words and do exactly as I asked of him. And a few years later, when he invited me to stage Ziggy Stardust for him at the Rainbow, he was still a joy to direct. I would keep encouraging him to *simplify* his performance, which he did, and we never had any artistic disagreements. He was an ideal student.

DON CHAPMAN

Miming promise

Oxford Mail, 29 December 1967

After the master at the New Theatre, his disciple at the Playhouse. And the comparison is bound to be to the detriment of the younger man.

Even in those items he borrows from his repertoire – *The Lion Tamer* and *The Balloon Seller* – Lindsay Kemp cannot rival the great French mime's economy and eloquence of expression, and in his own mimes he only hints at universal truths Marcel Marceau somehow manages to express.

For all that he is an artist of great promise – as Marceau acknowledged when he saw him at the Edinburgh Festival – and *Pierrot in Turquoise*, the new show he gave members of the Young Playhouse Association a first glimpse of yesterday, has great promise too.

At the moment it is something of a pot-pourri. Mr Kemp – with the assistance of Craig San Roque – has devised a fetching pantomime through which Pierrot pursues his love of life, his Columbine, tricked by Harlequin and deceived by the ever-changing Cloud.

Natasha Kornilof has designed a beautiful backdrop and some gorgeous costumes. And David Bowie has composed some haunting songs, which he sings in a superb, dreamlike voice.

But beguilingly as he plays Cloud, and vigorously as Jack Birkett mimes Harlequin, the pantomime isn't a completely satisfactory framework for some of the items from his repertoire that Mr Kemp, who plays Pierrot, chooses to present.

His mime of the clown who sells his shirt to buy a flower for Columbine then, when Harlequin wins her from him with a bunch of flowers, exchanges the flower for a rope from which to hang himself, is perfect.

And with a little rearrangement *Butterflies*, *The Balloon Seller* and *Aimez Vous, Bach*? – an amusing number in which he snips open his inside, throws his heart away, and trips off using his intestines as a skipping rope – might be tailored to fit his chosen theme.

But *Lady Burlesque*, a satirical portrait of a bored striptease artist, *Adam and Eve*, a ribald retelling of the Bible story, and *Old Woman, Little Bird*, a sort of science fiction nightmare, have been shoved in without much forethought because they are mimes Mr Kemp performs extremely well.

No doubt these are shortcomings Mr Kemp will attend to before he presents *Pierrot in Turquoise* at the Prague Festival at the invitation of Marceau and Fialka next summer. No mean honour for an English mime troupe.

GUS DUDGEON
*Space oddity**

Decca's Deram label was an early underground label, specifically created for the younger acts and those that were seen as difficult to break because their music wasn't mainstream. I didn't know very much about Bowie when he first came in, though I was aware of songs like 'The London boys' and stuff he'd done with The Lower Third and The Buzz. From the minute I met him I thought he was the most amazing character. He didn't have an exotic entourage then, but he did tend to come in with weird line-ups – oboe and string bass and a drum kit or something strange – which was interesting from an engineering point of view. It was a challenge. I loved the way he broke all the rules. He wasn't concerned with the norms of making records.

The Anthony Newley thing really used to bother us though, Mike Vernon particularly. It was such a hang-up it was ridiculous. I can't remember if he ever said, 'Listen David, you just sound like Anthony Newley, we've got to cut this out.' I think the assumption was that this was the only way he *could* sound. Why did someone with such a unique ability to write songs, unusual songs for the time, sound like someone twice his age?

Mind you, he was an absolute doddle to work with, a really nice guy. One Christmas, he came round to my flat and we had a proper Christmas tree up, not a plastic job. He walked in – I made him a cup of coffee – and he went over to my Christmas tree, shook it by the hand, and all the bloody pine needles fell off. That was weird, but we had a lot of fun – and yes, I'm afraid I *am* a laughing gnome! For a brief period I enjoyed it, but then when the record came out and everyone said how awful it was I realized it *was* pretty terrible and I

* From discussions with the editors, February 1993.

got rather embarrassed by it. But I remember we sat around for ages, trying to come up with those ghastly jokes. I haven't had the courage to play the record at half-speed, because if I did I'd hear my actual voice. We had a good laugh, but I wasn't at all surprised that it didn't sell. He had a quirky way of putting his records together – nobody was writing songs quite like him – but sometimes that can work against you as much as for you.

Tony Visconti is a nice bloke but he doesn't half come out with some funny things sometimes. He said that Bowie only did 'Space oddity' to cash in on the moonshot – well, that's true. But as to whether it's a conscious attempt to sound like Simon and Garfunkel – that never crossed my mind. Maybe it's a result of a subsequent discussion Visconti had with Bowie. At the time, the subject never came up: let's make it sound like somebody else. Far from it – the whole idea was to make something that sounded like David Bowie. To say Bowie didn't believe in the song – well, he might have said that since. People do sometimes decide to slag off work they've done. It's like people who constantly retire from the stage and come back two months later when there're bills to pay.

I haven't got a clue why Visconti didn't like the song. The fact is, Mercury Records didn't have any major acts with the exception of Rod Stewart, who at that point wasn't a major act anyway; he was just lead singer with The Small Faces and wasn't selling bucket-loads of albums. As I understand it, they took Bowie on specifically because of 'Space oddity'. They'd heard the demo and in those days a gimmick was a big deal and people who had gimmicks were taken more seriously than those who hadn't. Bowie's was that he'd written a song about being in space at a time when the first American moonshot was about to take place. As far as I can remember, Visconti's line was that the song had to be recorded because it's what got him the deal with the record company. I listened to the demo and thought it was incredible. I couldn't believe that Tony didn't want to do it. I went over to see him – we had adjacent offices – and he said, 'That's great, you do that and the B-side, and I'll do the album.' I was only too pleased. I don't think it was like anything he'd ever done before. I guess in a way it wasn't like anything *anybody* had done before and that's why, today, the record is still a classic. I'm very proud to have been associated with it.

We used Herbie Flowers on bass – it was apparently his very first recording gig. I don't know how I found him. I think somebody mentioned him to me and he had such an incredible name – a bass player called Herbie Flowers. Wow – that has to be worth something! Let's get him in. That's how I remember it. We used Terry Cox, who was the drummer in Pentangle. Acoustic guitar, of course, was Bowie. Electric guitar was Mick Wayne, who was recommended to me by Visconti, who'd produced him in Mick's own band, Junior's Eyes. He did that great solo and the rocket take-off effect at the beginning. The famous one was Rick Wakeman, again suggested by Visconti. I'd heard this thing called the Mellotron and I really liked the sombre atmosphere it gave off. I asked Visconti if he knew a Mellotron player and he said he knew a bloke who played in a Top Rank ballroom. He'd used him on a session once, the only session Rick had ever done. So he got in touch with him, booked him, and he turned up late – got stuck on the Tube. He was very tall, blond, covered in spots, and he walked in, apologizing for being late. I told him we'd done a couple of takes and that pretty soon we'd have a master. I played him the take and I showed him a chart. He opened up this Mellotron – I was expecting to see this thing with squillions of knobs on it but it had only three knobs and an on/off switch. I guess I could have booked anyone to play it. But he knew what I wanted. We did one take and he made a mistake. Apologized. We did another one – and that was it. Pretty good really – the second session in his life and take two is the master. We also had a stylophone, which Bowie played. As for the strings, we did plan the orchestration right from the outset because I remember doing a chart – I use that term loosely, because I can't write music. I wrote all the lyrics out and did a chart that I could understand. I had different colours for different instruments – for example, brown was cello – and I wrote a sort of zig-zaggy thing under the lyrics at the point where I wanted the cello to come in. Arranger Paul Buckmaster took all the ideas I'd given him and put them together. It's possible Bowie was the first person to call Buckmaster. I can't recall, but the first sessions he did were with me and he was great, the perfect choice. 'Space oddity' was one of the very first singles to be released in stereo.

It's not true that Bowie didn't follow it up thematically. He went back in with Visconti and did 'The prettiest star', the one that Marc Bolan played guitar on, and later 'Starman' with Ken Scott. Admittedly, it wasn't exactly a speedy process; there was a gap between releases.

He didn't perform our song live in the way I produced it until much later on. The first time I saw him do it I was really cheesed off because he did it at a little gig at the Purcell Room, would you believe. It was just Bowie, solo. He looked great – he had the catsuit on and he had this projected backdrop – but it was such a disappointment because a lot of people wanted to hear 'Space oddity' as on the record, instead of which there's this bloke just banging it out on an acoustic guitar. I was really disappointed and I know the audience were, but I guess he thought it was a good idea at the time. Later, in America, I saw him do it many times in many glamorous settings, including being lowered from gantries in giant hands, singing the song into a telephone – all sorts of stuff, and all quite amusing, given that he is supposed to have dismissed the song at one point, saying, 'I'll never sing that bloody song again. It's a load of old pap.' No doubt, he couldn't really get away with not performing it.

Of course I watch his career today. At the moment I think he's musically bankrupt, which is an awful thing to say because I didn't think it would ever happen. None of us wants our heroes to slip up. I mean, I continued to buy Beach Boys records when they were making rubbish but I didn't want to admit it because I always loved The Beach Boys. It's part of the nature of the business: people just can't maintain that momentum. I just think the whole Tin Machine thing is dreadul, and the crazy thing is he spends his whole time saying he just wants to be the singer in the band. As if he *could* be just the singer in the band. He *is* David Bowie for God's sake! A major contributor to the music business and up there with the best of them. He should be allowed to make mistakes, but it doesn't alter the fact that what he's done recently – possibly since *Let's Dance* – isn't up to much. But that's just my opinion. Of course I watch his career. How could I not? It would be a challenge to work with him again. As it happens, I think it would be very successful, too. Mind you, whether he could put up with me telling him his songs were no good is another matter. Egos come with successful careers. If he wrote a great song I'd tell him; if he wrote a crap song I'd tell him. Some people don't like that, but I'd like to work with him.

As to his live appearances, if he doesn't appear on stage for three or four years and then turns up for a big charity thing with Annie Lennox – the audience are just blown away, because he's great. It's a thrill to see him and all you can do is hope it's going to be one of his *good* shows. And more often than not, it is.

TONY PALMER
Up-to-date minstrel
Observer, 7 December 1969

David Bowie first came to notice with the spectacularly good song called 'Space oddity', which surfaced in the charts a month or so ago. He then gave a sizzling concert in London's Purcell Room which was mostly ignored by the national press, presumably because they thought pop and Purcell were incompatible. Now he has released an LP of songs – including 'Space oddity' – [originally] called simply *David Bowie*.

On stage he is quite devastatingly beautiful. With his loofah hair and blue eyes, he pads around like every schoolgirl's wonder movie-star. He smiles; you melt. He winks; you disintegrate. He fumbles away on his twelve-string acoustic guitar with ferocious gusto. He apologizes that his repertoire is mostly his own songs, which he admits sound all very much the same.

It's all relaxed, chatty, informal, and you forgive him his husky voice, his strained top notes and his careless intonation. You slump back, allowing this contemporary minstrel to dazzle you with niceness. Then, suddenly, he tears into you with a violent, passionate, angry, stamping song about fear and despair – 'Our weapons were the tongues of crying rage', he shouts. Using the imagery of war and sudden death, he offers simple homilies of charity and kindliness. 'My head's full of murders/Where only killers scream', he warns.

Bowie is 22 and was born in Brixton, London, but grew up in Bromley, Kent. He now lives in Beckenham and is trying, without success, to rouse enough interest to start a local Arts Lab, modelled on Jim Haynes's now defunct Drury Lane organization. He's also moving into acting, after a miniature appearance in *The Virgin Soldiers*.

His love reveries are dreary, self-pitying and monotonous. But when he turns his eye to the absurdities of technological society, he is razor-sharp in his observations (although the sound production on his records does its best to obscure this), especially in the exquisitely scored version of his hit single, 'Space oddity'. At a time when we cling pathetically to every moonman's dribbling joke, when we admire unquestioningly the so-called achievement of our helmeted heroes without wondering why they are there at all, Bowie sings of a man called Major Tom who sets off from Cape Kennedy and just never bothers to come back. To the bewilderment of Ground Control, he just waves a sad goodbye to his wife and then shuts off the communication circuits.

TIM HUGHES

Bowie for a song

Jeremy, January 1970

It's a bitterly cold December afternoon. David is rehearsing a Save The Children charity show at the Palladium. He is going solo with acoustic guitar – wisely dispensing with the pit orchestra hastily assembled for the Royal Occasion.

Princess Margaret and Peter Sellers will be there. There's a hassle over the sound equipment. The management seem unable to produce a supplementary mike for his guitar. Justifiably, he's upset with having to make do with one.

The gigantic white safety curtain drops in. Isolated in a single spot, against mammoth projections of the Apollo space shot, David performs 'Space oddity'. It's spectacularly effective and contrasts strongly with the tatty presentation of the rest of the show.

Afterwards David sits quietly with us in the stalls. A strapping Radio 1 DJ introduces a stunningly bad parade of groups and soloists. He cracks a stream of excruciating gags and occasionally opens his dress shirt to reveal an expanse of rotating stomach flesh. Dusty [Springfield] arrives to rehearse in a trim suede trouser suit. She assumes control of the rehearsal. Out go the pit orchestra. In come her own 16 session men, sound balancers, backing girls and extra amplifiers. All of us, including David, are suitably impressed by her dazzling professionalism.

Another scene, another place. The concrete halls of the South Bank are filling up as the electronic 'A' summons the cultured to an evening's serious entertainment. Half an hour later, the serried ranks of the sober-suited may be seen on the Queen Elizabeth Hall monitor gravely grooving to the refined sonorities of a Haydn string quartet. Who would imagine that next door in the Purcell Room, Junior's Eyes are belting out the big sound, warming up a very different audience for the appearance of David Bowie?

The concert is to launch his new LP, released by Philips. The publicity says simply that it is given by 'David Bowie and Friends'. It is clear that this refers as much to the audience as to the performers. For David is not a pop star in the conventional sense. He is a very switched-on creative young man, rightly admired by the discerning for his talent and known only to the masses for his guaranteed-success single 'Space oddity'.

In the interval, the two audiences surge together for drinks and two cultures mingle strangely, the orthodox and the freaked-out. They view each other's appearance, whether bizarre or commonplace, with mixed feelings ranging from amused tolerance to confused mistrust.

But all are curiously united by the same artistic experience, whose expression alters with the vagaries of time and taste, but whose roots are constant. Oddly enough, the Bowie band looks more baroque than the Haydn mob.

After the interval, David at last appears. Perched on a stool, he begins with some quiet reflective songs, accompanying himself on acoustic guitar. Some friends join him and the sounds become more involved. Finally, Junior's Eyes plug in and suddenly there's a really hard sound and one can scarcely believe that its centre is the slight pre-Raphaelite figure who first appeared. The range is incredible. But he says of himself, 'I've been grown up for too long.'

He could never do a whole programme of unrelenting rock-and-roll, as many groups do. His creativity needs more than one outlet and he has too much to express for one medium. His background is unusually varied – art school, tenor sax with Ronnie Ross's modern jazz group, poetry, mime with Lindsay Kemp, films. And even now he feels that he hasn't really begun to tap all his resources. Mixed media fascinates him and for a time he worked with a dancer and a folk singer. He has started writing a musical based on the life story of 'someone whom everyone's mum and dad loves'.

His heroes are rather surprising – George Formby, Nat Jackley, Gracie Fields, Albert Modley – until one realizes his admiration for the artiste as an entertainer. Modern influences are Jacques Brel, Dylan, Tony Newley, John Lennon and Tiny Tim.

The car breaks down. It's raining and we arrive late to take the photos. The house is a stunning and monstrous folly of a place in deepest Beckenham. Light on. Door open. No sign of David. He's just popped down to the shops for paraffin, and meat for the night's stew.

David takes us on a conducted tour of his mansion – ramshackle yet strangely beautiful in its decay. Sweeping staircases. Huge stained-glass windows. Moulded ceilings. Carved and tiled fireplaces. Liberty print blocks. Art Deco lamps. William Morris screens. There is an almost child-like excitement about the way he pounces on each new treasure. It's infectious.

'We have only been here a month and we've hardly started yet. There is so much to do and it's the wrong time of the year.' We wonder if he doesn't get professional help. 'No. It's my first real place and I want to do it by myself. I'm just getting someone to do the ceilings. Isn't the garden wonderful? It's full of birds and animals.' Later, outside in the failing light during the photo session, squirrels leap through the branches and a fox hurries across the lawn.

David is a refreshing change from so many of the inarticulate and untalented charlatans currently littering the world of pop. He doesn't think they have anything to contribute, though the public are not taken in for long. Unlike them, he has something to say because he has bothered to think about himself, about what he wants to do and how he should do it, and about life. He hasn't come up with any startlingly original philosophy, but he differs from the herd in having a rather philosophical attitude to work and life.

Kerouac made a deep impression on him at an early age and he was genuinely affected by his recent death. He was a practising Buddhist for some time and the discipline of meditation has made him reflective. His outlook is, however, tempered by the exigencies of living in a Western capitalist society and he lacks the mindless realism of so many of his contemporaries. Money is useful. Every bloody hippie wants money to do their own non-capitalistic thing. 'Money means that I can afford to furnish my new house as I want.' He's not really materialistic – just practical.

The same attitude is seen towards relationships. 'I am a loner. I don't feel the need for conventional relationships. The few friends I have belong to the period before the success of "Space oddity". I was madly in love last year but the gigs got in the way. One needs food. I'm not really part of "the Scene". It leaves me cold. I just do what I have to. For instance, I want to write songs. At the moment the best way of having them performed is to do them myself. But being a performer gets in the way, and I look forward to the day when other people will come along and want to use my material. I have this Arts Lab at Beckenham where there's a lot going on. But I exercise a tight control over it. I have to. Free expression often means chaos, and in any case they need a leader. I don't want to be a leader – after all, who wants to be a cause? It's not cliquey like most of these joints. There's hippies and skinheads and nice young people who don't fit into any category. They just come along, and if they have something to offer they do it.'

It's the midnight hour, and the taxi drops us somewhere behind

Oxford Street. We plunge down a red stairwell. This is the Speakeasy – the club for Top Pop People. David is doing the late-night spot. Someone takes our coats and we make our way to the bar. The drinks are very expensive. The lighting is so murkily subtle that it is almost impossible to make out the features of the person standing next to us. We are dimly aware of the other inhabitants. A sprinkling of boys in bone-tight velvet pants held up by redundant broad leather belts whose heavy ornate buckles force one's eyes to midriff level. Hordes of girls with deader than deadpan faces stand in predatory clusters – these are the notorious groupies, the Scene's attendant Furies. They outnumber the boys four to one. It's just not David's scene.

The disco stops and a single spot stabs its way through layers of multicoloured light show. It's David's turn. Perched precariously on two boxes – a luminous elfin face surrounded by an aureole of blond curls – he looks very vulnerable. He works hard. Numbers from the LP . . . Jacques Brel. Some bawdy poems by Mason Williams. Buzz the Fuzz. Throughout the act there is a spattering of blasé applause. Groupies parade. People keep right on talking. No one seems involved. The reaction is disturbingly muted. It's all over, and David joins us at the bar. The elfin face looks puzzled. 'I can't believe it. The manager says I got a good reception. If that's what happens when they like you, what happens when they hate you?' A marauding groupie gropes him in the crush. 'Who was it? I ought to get a fee for that.'

Notes

1. See Kenneth Pitt, *The Pitt Report*, London, Omnibus, 1983, for details of his early career.

2. Quoted in Barry Miles (ed.), *Bowie in His Own Words*, London, Omnibus, 1980.

3. In John Mendelsohn, 'David Bowie? Pantomime rock?', *Rolling Stone*, 1 April 1971, p. 29.

4. The best coverage is in Victor Bockris' biography *Warhol*, London, Penguin, 1989.

5. In Susan Sontag, 'Notes on camp' in *Against Interpretation*, 1967, p. 279.

6. *Ibid.*, p. 280.

7. *Ibid.*

8. Johnny Rogan, *Roxy Music: style with substance – Roxy's first ten years*, London, Star, 1982, p. 42.

9. For a brief discussion of the origins of Ziggy, see Bowie's interview with Paul Du Noyer in *Q*, April 1990, pp. 66–7.

10. See Chris Brazier, 'Bowie: beauty before outrage', *Melody Maker*, 4 September 1976, pp. 17, 38.

11. From Simon Frith, 'Only dancing – David Bowie flirts with the issues', in *Zoot Suits and Second-hand Dresses*, London, Macmillan, 1989, ed. Angela McRobbie, p. 140.

12. A. C. Scott, *The Kabuki Theatre of Japan*, 1955, pp. 142–3.

13. *New Musical Express*, 9 June 1973, p. 16, cited in Susan Mensah's 'David Bowie: a construction of selves', unpublished BA dissertation, University of Exeter, 1990.

14. According to Fred and Judy Vermorel, there was something approximating an orgy going on in the audience that night. See *Fandemonium*, London, Omnibus, 1989, p. 67.

15. Jon Savage, private correspondence, 2 January 1992.

16. See Dave Laing, 'Listening', in *One Chord Wonders: Power and Meaning in Punk Rock*, Milton Keynes, Open University Press, 1985.

17. Sontag, *op. cit.*, p. 288.

18. This is mentioned also in Laing, *op. cit.*, p. 83.

19. Private interview, June 1990.

20. For readable discussions of 'call and response' performance techniques, see Richard Middleton, '"Reading" popular music', in *Form and Meaning (2)*, Milton Keynes, Open University Press, 1985, pp. 13–18; and Charles Keil, *Urban Blues*, University of Chicago Press, 1966.

21. See Dave Laing's section 'Goading and gobbing', *op. cit.*, pp. 83–6.

22. Of course, the interaction between Bowie and his fans is of crucial importance, but too big a topic to engage with here. See Simon Frith, 'Only dancing' (see above); and 'The art of posing', in *Music for Pleasure*, Cambridge, Polity Press, 1988, pp. 176–9 (see pp. 176–80 of this book). See also Dick Hebdige, *Subcultures: The Meaning of Style*, London, Methuen, 1979; Peter York, *Style Wars*, Sidgwick & Jackson, 1980.

23. Quoted in Tony Zanetta and Henry Edwards, *Stardust: The Life and Times of David Bowie*, London, Michael Joseph, 1986, p. 319.

24. *The David Bowie Story*, Radio 1, 1976 (written and produced by Stuart Grundy).

25. For a highly idiosyncratic but engaging look at Bowie displaying shamanistic qualities, see Rogan Taylor, *The Death and Resurrection Show: From shaman to superstar*, London, Anthony Blond, 1985. Taylor argues that Bowie is an 'upper-world' shaman obsessed with outer space, and his undoubted penchant for aerial, theatrical set-pieces can be linked with this.

26. The song referred to is Tin Machine's 'You belong in rock 'n' roll' from *Tin Machine II* (London/Victory Music, 1991).

27. From 'The fly', a single release from their album *Achtung Baby* (Island, 1991).

28. The desperate Horton had in fact borrowed £250 which was used to hype 'Can't help thinking about me' into the *Melody Maker* chart at number thirty-four. The disc was conspicuous by its absence from the *Record Retailer* top fifty.

29. See pp. 36–9.

30. See pp. 47–51.

TWO

Starman

JOHN MENDELSOHN

David Bowie? Pantomime rock?

Rolling Stone, 1 April 1971

Los Angeles – in his floral-patterned velvet midi-gown and cosmetically enhanced eyes, in his fine chest-length blonde hair and mod nutty engineer's cap that he bought in the ladies' hat section of the City of Paris department store in San Francisco, he is ravishing, almost disconcertingly reminiscent of Lauren Bacall, although he would prefer to be regarded as the latter-day Garbo.

In the studios of San Francisco's KSAN-FM, he assures an incredulous DJ that his last album was, very simply, a collection of reminiscences about his experiences as a shaven-headed transvestite.

In Hollywood, at a party staged in his honour, he blows the minds of arriving hot-panted honeys with Edy Williams hair, welcoming them lispily in his gorgeous gown before excusing himself so he can watch Ultra Violet give interviews from a milk bath at a party held a few blocks away in *her* honour.

Although he is the creator of one of the year's most interesting albums, *The Man Who Sold the World*, he remains mostly unfamiliar.

But perhaps not for long. The 24-year-old songwriter/singer/theatrician/magnificent outrage from London will undertake his first performing tour of this country (due to visa difficulties he was not allowed to play in public during his February visit) in April.

'I refuse to be thought of as mediocre,' Bowie asserts blithely. 'If I am mediocre, I'll get out of the business. There's enough fog around. That's why the idea of performance-as-spectacle is so important to me.'

He plans to appear on stage decked out rather like Cleopatra, in the appropriate heavy make-up and in costumes that will hopefully recall those designed in the thirties by Erté.

He says he will also interpret his own works through mime, a form in which he's been involved at several points in his career, most notably when he wrote for, acted in, and helped produce the Lindsay Kemp Mime Company of London: 'I'd like to bring mime into a traditional Western setting, to focus the attention of the audience with a very stylized, a very Japanese style of movement.'

Bowie assures us that he has already put that idea into practice with gratifying results: 'About three years ago, at the Festival Hall in London, I did a solo performance of a twenty-minute play with song that I wrote called *Yet-San and the Eagle*, which is about a boy trying to find his way in Tibet, within himself, under the pressures of the Communist Chinese oppression. I might bring it over to some of the bigger places I work in America. It was very successful – everybody seemed to understand and enjoy it.'

He is not overly concerned with American audiences' lesser experience with and consequent lesser receptivity to theatrically-enhanced musical performances: 'Should anyone think that these things are merely distractions or gimmicks intended to obscure the music's shortcomings, he mustn't come to my concerts. He must come on my terms or not at all.

'My performances have got to be theatrical experiences for me as well as for the audience. I don't want to climb out of my fantasies in order to go up on stage – I want to take them on stage with me.'

Bowie contends that rock in particular and pop in general should not be taken as seriously as is currently the fashion: 'What the music says may be serious, but as a medium it should not be questioned, analysed, or taken so seriously. I think it should be tarted up, made into a prostitute, a parody of itself. It should be the clown, the Pierrot medium. The music is the mask the message wears – music is the Pierrot and I, the performer, am the message.

'Tell your readers that they can make up their minds about me when I begin getting adverse publicity: when I'm found in bed with Raquel Welch's husband.'

MICHAEL WATTS

Oh you pretty thing

Melody Maker, 22 January 1972

Even though he wasn't wearing silken gowns right out of Liberty's, and his long blond hair no longer fell wavily past his shoulders, David Bowie was looking yummy.

He'd slipped into an elegant, patterned type of combat suit, very tight around the legs, with the shirt unbuttoned to reveal a full expanse of white torso. The trousers were turned up at the calves to allow a better glimpse of a huge pair of red plastic boots with at least three-inch rubber soles; and the hair was Vidal Sassooned into such impeccable shape that one held one's breath in case the slight breeze from the open window dared to ruffle it. I wish you could have been there to varda him; he was so super.

David uses words like 'varda' and 'super' quite a lot. He's gay, he says. Mmm. A few months back, when he played Hampstead's Country Club, a small, greasy club in North London which has seen all sorts of exciting occasions, about half the gay population of the city turned up to see him in his massive floppy velvet hat, which he twirled around at the end of each number.

According to Stuart Lyon, the club's manager, a little gay brother sat right up close to the stage throughout the whole evening, absolutely spellbound with admiration.

As it happens, David doesn't have much time for Gay Liberation, however. That's a particular movement he doesn't want to lead. He despises all these tribal qualifications. Flower power he enjoyed, but it's individuality that he's really trying to preserve. The paradox is that he still has what he describes as 'a good relationship' with his wife. And his baby son, Zowie. He supposes he's what people call bisexual.

They call David a lot of things. In the States he's been referred to as the English Bob Dylan and an avant-garde outrage, all rolled up together. The *New York Times* talks of his 'coherent and brilliant vision'. They like him a lot there. Back home, in the very stiff-upper-lip UK, where people are outraged by Alice Cooper even, there ain't too many who have picked up on him. His last but one album, *The Man Who Sold the World*, cleared 50,000 copies in the States; here it sold about five copies, and Bowie bought them.

Yes, but before this year is out all those of you who puked up on Alice are going to be focusing your passions on Mr Bowie, and those who know where it's at will be thrilling to a voice that seemingly undergoes brilliant metamorphosis from song to song, a songwriting ability that will enslave the heart, and a sense of theatrics that will make the ablest thespians gnaw on their sticks of eyeliner in envy. All this, and an amazingly accomplished band, featuring super-lead guitarist Mick Ronson, that can smack you round the skull with their heaviness and soothe the savage breast with their delicacy. Oh, to be young again.

The reason is Bowie's new album, *Hunky Dory*, which combines a gift for irresistible melody lines with lyrics that work on several levels – as straightforward narrative, philosophy or allegory, depending how deep you wish to plumb the depths. He has a knack of suffusing strong, simple pop melodies with words and arrangements full of mystery and darkling hints.

Thus 'Oh! You pretty things', the Peter Noone hit, is, on one stratum, particularly the chorus, about the feelings of a father-to-be; on a deeper level it concerns Bowie's belief in a superhuman race – *homo superior* – to which he refers obliquely: 'I think about a world to come/Where some books are found by the golden ones/It's written in pain, written in awe/By a puzzled man who questioned/What we came here for/All the strangers came today/And it looks as though they're here to stay.' The idea of Peter Noone singing such a heavy number fills me with considerable amusement. That's truly outrageous, as David says himself.

But then Bowie has an instinct for incongruities. On *The Man Who Sold the World* there's a bit at the end of 'Black country rock' where he superbly parodies his friend Marc Bolan's vibrato warblings. On *Hunky Dory*, he devotes a track called 'Queen bitch' to the Velvets, wherein he takes off to a tee the Lou Reed vocal and arrangement, as well as parodying, with a story-line about the singer's boyfriend being seduced by another queen, the whole Velvet Underground genre.

Then again, at various times on his albums he resorts to a very broad cockney accent, as on 'Saviour machine' (*The Man*) and here with 'The Bewlay Brothers'. He says he copped it off Tony Newley, because he was mad about *Stop The World I Want to Get Off*: 'He used to make his points with this broad cockney accent and I decided that I'd use that now and again to drive a point home.'

The fact that Bowie has an acute ear for parody doubtless stems from an innate sense of theatre. He says he's more an actor and entertainer than a musician: that he may, in fact, only be an actor and nothing else. 'Inside this invincible frame there might be an invisible man.' You kidding? 'Not at all. I'm not particularly taken with life. I'd probably be very good as just an astral spirit.'

Bowie is talking in an office at Gem Music, from where his management operates. A tape machine is playing his next album, *The Rise and Fall of Ziggy Stardust and The Spiders From Mars*, which is about this fictitious pop group. The music has got a very hard-edged sound, like *The Man Who Sold the World*. They're releasing it shortly, even though *Hunky Dory* has only just come out.

Everyone just knows that David is going to be a lollapalooza of a superstar throughout the entire world this year. David more than most. His songs are always ten years ahead of their time, he says, but this year he has anticipated the trends. 'I'm going to be huge, and it's quite frightening in a way,' he says, his big red boots stabbing the air in time to the music. 'Because I know that when I reach my peak and it's time for me to be brought down it will be with a bump.'

The man who's sold the world this prediction has had a winner before, of course. Remember 'Space oddity', which chronicled Major Tom's dilemma, aside from boosting the sales of the stylophone? That was a top ten hit in '69, but since then Bowie has hardly performed at all in public. He appeared for a while at an Arts Lab he co-founded in Beckenham, Kent, where he lives, but when he realized that people were going there on a Friday night to see Bowie the hit singer working out, rather than for any idea of experimental art, he seems to have become disillusioned. That project foundered, and he wasn't up to going out on one-nighters throughout the country at that particular time.

So in the past three years he has devoted his time to the production of three albums, *David Bowie* (which contains 'Space oddity') and *The Man* for Philips, and *Hunky Dory* for RCA. His first album was released in 1967, on the new Deram label, but it didn't sell outstandingly and Decca, it seems, lost interest in him.

David's present image is to come on like a swishy queen, a gorgeously effeminate boy. He's as camp as a row of tents, with his limp hand and trolling vocabulary. 'I'm gay,' he says, 'and always have been, even when I was David Jones.' But there's a sly jollity about how he says it, a secret smile at the corners of his mouth. He knows that in these times its permissible to act like a male tart, and that to shock and outrage, which pop has always striven to do throughout its history, is a balls-breaking process.

And if he's not an outrage, he is, at the least, an amusement. The expression of his sexual ambivalence establishes a fascinating game: is he, or isn't he? In a period of conflicting sexual identity he shrewdly exploits the confusion surrounding the male and female roles. 'Why aren't you wearing your girl's dress today?' I said to him (he has no monopoly on tongue-in-cheek humour). 'Oh dear,' he replied, 'you must understand that it's not a woman's. It's a man's dress.'

49

He began wearing dresses, of whatever gender, two years ago but he says he had done outrageous things before that were just not accepted by society. It's just so happened, he remarks, that in the past two years people have loosened up to the fact that there are bisexuals in the world 'and – horrible fact – homosexuals.' He smiles, enjoying his piece of addenda.

'The important fact is that I don't *have* to drag up. I want to go on like this for long after the fashion has finished. I'm just a cosmic yob, I suppose. I've always worn my own style of clothes. I design them. I designed this.' He broke off to indicate with his arm what he was wearing. 'I just don't like the clothes that you buy in shops. I don't wear dresses all the time, either. I change every day. I'm not outrageous. I'm David Bowie.'

How does dear Alice Cooper go down with him, I asked, and he shook his head disdainfully: 'Not at all. I bought his first album, but it didn't excite me or shock me. I think he's *trying* to be outrageous. You can see him, poor dear, with his red eyes sticking out and his temples straining. He tries so hard. That bit he does with the boa constrictor, a friend of mine, Rudy Valentino, was doing ages before. The next thing I see is Miss C with her boa. I find him very demeaning. It's very premeditated, but quite fitting with our era. He's probably more successful than I am at present, but I've invented a new category of artist, with my chiffon and taff. They call it pantomime rock in the States.'

Despite his flouncing, however, it would be sadly amiss to think of David merely as a kind of glorious drag act. An image, once strained and stretched unnaturally, will ultimately diminish an artist. And Bowie is just that. He foresees this potential dilemma, too, when he says he doesn't want to emphasize his external self much more. He has enough image. This year he is devoting most of his time to stage work and records. As he says, that's what counts at the death. He will stand or fall on his music.

As a songwriter he doesn't strike me as an intellectual, as he does some. Rather, his ability to express a theme from all aspects seems intuitive. His songs are less carefully structured thoughts than the outpourings of the unconscious. He says he rarely tries to communicate to himself, to think an idea out.

'If I see a star and it's red I wouldn't try to say why it's red. I would think how shall I best describe to X that that star is such a colour. I don't question much; I just relate. I see my answers in other people's writings. My own work can be compared to talking to a psychoanalyst. My act is my couch.'

It's because his music is rooted in this lack of consciousness that he admires Syd Barrett so much. He believes that Syd's freewheeling approach to lyrics opened the gates for him; both of them, he thinks, are the creation of their own songs. And if Barrett made that initial breakthrough, it's Lou Reed and Iggy Pop who have since kept him going and helped him to expand his unconsciousness. He and Lou and Iggy, he says, are going to take over the whole world. They're the songwriters he admires.

His other inspiration is mythology. He has a great need to believe in the legends of the past, particularly those of Atlantis; and for the same need he has created a myth of the future, a belief in an imminent race of supermen called *Homo superior*. It's his only glimpse of hope, he says – 'all the things that we can't do they will.'

It's a belief created out of resignation with the way society in general has moved. He's not very hopeful about the future of the world. A year ago he was saying that he gave mankind another forty years. A track on his next album, outlining his conviction, is called 'Five years'. He's a fatalist, a confirmed pessimist, as you can see.

'Pretty things', that breezy Herman song, links this fatalistic attitude with the glimmer of hope that he sees in the birth of his son, a sort of poetic equation of *Homo superior*. 'I think', he says, 'that we have created a new kind of person in a way. We have created a child who will be so exposed to the media that he will be lost to his parents by the time he is 12.'

That's exactly the sort of technological vision that Stanley Kubrick foresees for the near future in *A Clockwork Orange*. Strong stuff. And a long, long way from camp carry-ons.

Don't dismiss David Bowie as a serious musician just because he likes to put us all on a little.

WILFRID MELLERS

Still Hunky Dory, after all these years

Old people like myself, who had teenage children during the heyday of The Beatles and Dylan, cottoned on to why those pop heroes meant so much to the young. Indeed, they seemed pertinent even to me, to the degree that I wrote small books about them. David Bowie, on the other hand, was for a man of my generation a shade too way-out; I didn't try very hard to find his wavelength. It's therefore alarming to discover that Bowie's album *Hunky Dory* was made 22 years ago. Taking a belated look at and listen to it, I suspect that it has dated no more than have The Beatles and Dylan, which is hardly at all. What Bowie had to say still means something, whereas not much pop music ever meant – or was meant to mean – anything beyond its ephemeral moment. The dictionary meaning of the words 'Hunky Dory' is 'excellent'. Whether or not Bowie intended ironic undertones, one may still take the epithet straight.

Rock music was a deliberate dethronement of the 'values' of so-called Western civilization. For at least the last four centuries, European 'art' music has been preoccupied with evolution and development, with progression from A to B to Z. Most kinds of modern pop music eschew progress – not surprisingly, given the state it has landed us in. Mistrusting harmonic contradiction and resolution, rock preferred melodic 'moments' to a continuously flowing and growing line, and reinstated rhythm, or rather metre, as the dimension within which music momentarily lives. In this it was a return to the musical concepts of 'primitive' peoples and of children in most times and places. The music does not so much reflect – let alone express the feelings, much less thoughts of individual people – but rather creates a continuum within which, 'for the time being', we live, move and have our being. The anthropologist Geza Roheim spoke of the 'paradise of archetypes and repetition' within which primitive musics seek, while they last, a 'green paradise of childish loves'. Unfortunately, it may also be a black hell of infantile hates: which is why concepts of value cannot be totally extraneous to even the most wantonly vacuous entertainment. The supremacy of The Beatles in their time – and, I suspect, today also – was due in part to their creating a communal continuum as a group, while as individuals they – especially Lennon and McCartney – particularized rather than generalized. Their words and music effected a 'rebirth of wonder', most magically in their creation, in *Sgt Pepper*, of what it is not extravagant to call a new genre and medium. Drawing on many sources – English folk and pop song, music hall, American country music, Black blues and gospel – they made a polyglot demotic idiom that the young could recognize as their own. Dylan, being basically a solo artist and a poet (not merely a versifier) of distinction, worked the other way round, creating personal songs that none the less stood for an era and a generation. His sources – American pop musics, White, Black and coffee-coloured, and a fair range of literate poetry, British and American – implied more overt political and religious intentionality than did The Beatles; but his songs too simul-taneously celebrated the private and the public life.

Bowie, though not such a fine poet as Dylan, is more than a versifier; and the sequence of poem-songs that make up *Hunky Dory* creates a whole and defines a world. 'Define' is, however, too strong a word, since the heart of the Bowie experience is what has come to be called a 'crisis of identity'. Bowie is 'later' than The Beatles, or even than Dylan, in that although he doesn't dismiss notions of value, he starts from an admission that they cannot be other than elusive, and may be illusory. Dylan, though his songs are riddled with paradox and irony, worries at potential meanings like a dog with a bone. Bowie accepts bewilderment as his birthright, recognizing that the most he can hope for is to get by with a smile or guffaw. Not for nothing is the first song on *Hunky Dory* called 'Changes', with its opening lines 'I still don't know what I was waiting for/And my time was running wild'.

Bowie's ambivalence inevitably conditioned his rock idiom. On the whole, he doesn't make memorably inspired tunes, as The Beatles did in their early vernalities or in an epochal number like 'A day in the life'. Nor does he create poems that become cultural icons like Dylan's 'Mr Tambourine Man' or 'All along the watchtower' where the tunes are secondary. Bowie's strength lies rather in the authenticity of his ambiguities, as is manifest in 'Changes' which, scored for an orthodox band of piano, electric bass, drums and strings, with intermittent saxes and backing voices, creates, at a moderate 4/4 pulse, the usual unremitting continuum in which we hope to live. The difference is that it is not all that continuous and is not at all stable; the four introductory bars shift through C major with sharp seventh, to D-flat with added sixth, to D minor with added seventh, to a dominant seventh on F. Of course, The Beatles and all pop musicians also employ chord changes that, springing from oral instinct, have little to do with orthodox musical grammar. But their side-stepping shifts are recognizably part of folk traditions, compared with which the opening of Bowie's song is near-anarchic. When he starts to sing – in an airily floating high tenor that, twenty years ago, complemented his willowy, long-haired appearance – we find that anarchic freedom extends to his vocal line. For although the key now seems to be established as C major, in a basic I, III, IV, V, I progression, the tune itself is fragmented – to a more extravagant degree than the instinctively mutated, because semi-improvised, melodies of The Beatles or Dylan. Since Bowie is alluding to the transience and impermanence of the world and its values, the 'strange changes' the world inflicts on all of us, the waywardness of the vocal line and the shifts of direction in the instrumental harmonies act out the heart of the matter. When, with his voice cavorting into high register, he advises 'you rock 'n' rollers' to 'look out', his cry is naively pentatonic, like the instinctual burbles of children, and perhaps false in being in near-falsetto, while his feigned chums support him with *vocalises* on the syllables of 'changes', with ambiguous because semi-comic effect. But the coda grows suddenly grave as it admits, with a change to triple time, that although time may change him, he can't 'trace time' – cannot accommodate to it, and so doesn't know where he is. An instrumental postlude for solo sax is darkly blue, solemn as well as sultry, wavering between the major and minor third of C, while piano and strings recall the grammatically unrelated chords of the introduction.

The second number, 'Oh! You pretty things', shifts attention from the self to other (also young) people, though it carries a similar burden. For these pretty things are the young who 'can't trace time', or 'think about a world to come'. Having thrown out the books 'found by the golden ones', written 'in pain', the pretty things are 'driving your mamas and papas insane', which may be understandable, but none the less elicits from Bowie a last-minute appeal – which may or may not be ironic – to 'the *Homo superior*', in the interests, if not of the pretty things, then at least of their children, and their children's children.

Human behaviour, even in the craziest of worlds, is not necessarily arbitrary, as may be palpable in the music's nervy equilibrium between childlike wonder and distraught sophistication. The instrumental prelude for piano is notated in 2/4, in outlandishly six-sharped F-sharp major, over rocking octaves tainted with blue notes and dislocated by syncopations. The effect is zany and also childish, and when the voice enters after the piano has sidled from F-sharp to a cross between G major and E minor, it tends to pentatonic innocence, as David looks out of the morning window, glimpsing 'a crack in the sky' through which 'all the nightmares came'. The music has to be childish if it is not to drive us mad, and zaniness becomes craziness when, at the words 'don't you know you're driving your mamas and papas insane', the voice pivots from pentatonic E minor into stratospheric pentatonics in B-flat, a devilish tritone apart. The appeal to a *Homo superior* as potential guardian of the children soars even higher, to an operatic C, only to be wrenched back for the piano postlude to the original tootling-footling ditty in F-sharp major, again veering a semitone up to G, but ending back in F-sharp, and on its dominant at that! This sounds high, in more than one sense, but is too startling to be taken as optimism.

'Eight line poem' is interludial, being mainly a solo for electric guitar with piano accompaniment. For the first time the tempo is slow, and the guitar's solo line is plangently blue, with unearthly high harmonics. The piano part is in a C major that is plagally inflected, for the subdominant chord of F is almost as potent as the tonic, which is further undermined by ungrammatical lurches to triads of D and E. The brief (eight-line) poem is sung in a clearly pentatonicized C major, dialoguing with the guitar in comparably free rhythms. The words complement those of the previous song, by opposites: instead of Bowie looking through the kitchen window, a spiky cactus (a denizen of Waste Lands?) now gazes into 'the prairie of your room', picking out a spinning mobile and Clara, with her 'head between her paws'. The final line – 'But the key to the city/Is in the sun that pins the branches to the sky. Oh . . .' – is one of Bowie's occasional flashes of poetic magic, releasing from the voice a no less magical pentatonic ululation.

'Life on Mars' returns to the narrative genre, describing with Beatlesque immediacy a 'girl with the mousy hair' who is in a godawful plight because she has been thrown out by mum and dad, and her (boy?)friend is 'nowhere to be seen'. So, walking through her 'sunken dream', she's hooked to the celluloid dream of the cinema, but finds that 'the film is a saddening bore'. The adjective 'saddening' is to the point, for the film is not only a bore but a cheat: the screen's flickering images of brawling sailors, crooked lawmen and the like are nonsense, for even – or especially – in 'the best-selling show', the wrong guys always get beaten up. The cinema is also life. This song is Bowie's 'My way', harmonically complex in construction as befits its theme. The opening clauses, at a moderate rock beat and in a clear B-flat major conventionally modulating to the dominant, have something of the guilelessness of early Beatles, especially when the voice part is doubled in parallel thirds. But the illusion of the movie provokes nearlunatic shifts of triads and of key, and drives the voice into falsetto heights for the rowdy sailors. The ultimate yell, 'Is there life on Mars?' shoots to a high B-flat, clearly wanting out from a world as idiotic and as evil as ours. Of course it offers no promise of Martian bliss, and the long instrumental postlude, with a poignantly blue electric guitar solo over weirdly shifting harmonies, reveals the passion as well as pathos in the mousy girl's (and our) lost condition. The final cadence winds its way back to B-flat major, but now sounds far from guileless with its knowing reference to *Also sprach Zarathustra/2001*.

'Kooks' is again about identity in that the singer seems to be asking his son whether he wants to stay in his parents' – 'the lovers'' – story, they being kooks content to go their own sweet way, oblivious to social conventionalities. This may be fun but entails problems: David admits that he wouldn't relish fights with bullies and cads, should junior arouse their ire. The instrumental parts for solo acoustic guitar echoed by electric guitar undulate in a mesmeric 12/8 lilt, basically rooted in D major. Persistent syncopations and abrupt harmonic shifts reveal, within the music's trance, the goofiness of the Kooky state, 'hung up on romancing'. Questions of identity are latent here too, for the song is asking whether 'romance' counts for more than social reality, and offers no answer. The total effect is hilarious, but also precarious – with more than a whiff of danger in its capering piano solo and in the chromaticized, octave-leaping electric bass.

The jittery zest of this number carries us, naturally enough, into 'Quicksand' which, far from hilarious, forms the climax to the cycle. It presents the unheroic hero as living *within* the illusory distractions of media life which the other songs have evoked and commented upon. He has worn the guises of Himmler's dream, Garbo's eyes, and Churchill's lies; torn between light and dark, he can find no 'divine symmetry' and may have to herald, glumly and unportentously, 'the death of man'. It's too late to be 'tethered to the logic of *Homo sapien*' [*sic*] and to 'the great salvation/of bullshit faith'. Belief can only be deceit, and 'Knowledge comes' only 'with death's release'. The gravity of the music suggests that we're meant to take Bowie's admission that 'I ain't got the power any more' with equal gravity, and in a sense the music's forcefulness belies the words. A sustained solo line on vibes pierces through a moderately paced rocking figure in G major, with a strong, bluesy pull towards plagal subdominants. The continuity of the beat steadies us through the 'quicksand', while the vocal line, hovering pentatonically between G and C, counteracts, if it does not dispel, the sundry illusions of the poem. When the key shifts up a tone to A major, a piano solo bounces in animation, while the bass line leaps in energetic fourths and tritones. The climax comes in a paradoxical *affirmation* of negation. Only by eschewing self-deceit as well as self-conceit can one hope for any fulfilment; 'death's release' is celebrated in soaring two-part *vocalise* and the key stays up in A major – traditionally a key of youth and hope. Nor is A major, and the music's rather desperate euphoria, relaxed in the final stanzas when he admits to 'sinking' in the quicksand of his thoughts. The beat fortifies the grand asseveration until the end; solo piano burgeons, still in the dominant A major, into syncopated arabesques.

It would seem that it was necessary for Bowie to accept negation joyously before, in the next number, he can invite us to 'Fill your heart'. What we're to fill our hearts with is, of course, love, banishing fears that exist only in the mind and in the past. Lovers never lose, because love may cleanse the mind and make it free. On balance, I think we're meant to take this positive song unironically; its key, after all, is E major, which has traditionally been associated with bliss and heaven, probably because it was, in the baroque period, the sharpest, most upward key in common use. The tempo is a lilting, rather fast 12/8, with the vocal melody airily syncopated across the beats so that the singer sounds airborne, as are we with him. Solo piano, intermittently reinforced by saxophone, dialogues with the voice in a style recalling the 12/8 barrelhouse blues often favoured by John Lennon. On the word 'free' the voice cavorts in melismatic ecstasy, an abandon which is capped by jazzy chromatic riffs on piano. But the final vocal affirmations of 'yeah' are left suspended on a flat seventh, and the piano's ultimate *roulade* is microtonally echoed by wailing electric guitar.

Although the ebullience of this song doesn't seem to me to be parodistic, the rest of the album tends to deflate it, especially the next number, 'Andy Warhol'. Warhol, although a Bowie hero, is seemingly debunked. He is presented as a commercial manipulator of the media, in which dubious worlds most of the songs have operated. The words tell us that the silver screen and Andy can't be distinguished one from the other: 'He'll think about paint and he'll think about glue/What a jolly boring thing to do'. The bogus nature of the subject may be indicated by the fact that the number contains more talking than singing; even the would-be consummatory refrain in octaves is yelled rather than sung, and when the unremitting E minor *ostinato* finally veers to the subdominant major, the effect is predictably non-committal.

But the next track, 'Song for Bob Dylan', is at an opposite as well as complementary pole to the Warhol number. Bowie stresses Dylan's legendary status by addressing the song to Robert Zimmerman, as though he were separate – as in a sense he is – from the Dylan persona. He eulogizes Bob as a mythical dragon-slayer, the dragon being indentified with a painted harpy-lady, who may be a simulacrum of the various harpies that haunt Dylan's songs, but who is also in a general sense an agent of moral and social corruption. 'A couple of songs' from Bob's 'old scrap-book' can be relied upon to rout her, giving us back 'our unity, our family'. So although Bowie himself doesn't stress moral issues, he seems to acquire a vicarious conscience through Dylan; and this song pays Dylan the sincerest form of flattery in being recognizably Dylanesque, though neither passively imitative nor parodistic. Moreover, it is in E major and attains ecstasy when, in the coda, electric guitar weaves tipsy arabesques over broken chord pulses on two acoustic guitars.

Since this positive song is a gift to Dylan rather than Bowie's personal affirmation, it does not discount the apparent negation of the

Andy Warhol number, or the 'lost' state of most of the songs. And the last two numbers are more negative than positive. 'Queen bitch', some way after 'Just like a woman', is scored for acoustic and electric guitars hammering in bludgeoning euphony, at first in unsullied C major and a basic I, V, VI, I progression, with ferocious drums and prancing bass. Bowie's venom is such that he can't sing, only gabblingly declaim; at least until a sudden change of gear shifts the music from C to A to B majors. Even then, song is momentary, the voice stifled when the onslaught of diatonic triads pounds away as he phones for a cab, hopefully to bear him away from betrayal. One can't say that this number finds affirmation within negation, as did 'Quicksand', but at least aggression and assertion prove to be a way of dealing with pain or anger.

The final number, 'The Bewlay Brothers', is appropriately the most resonantly equivocal. On one level, it might be thought to refer to David and his half-brother. Bewlay Brothers was also the name given to Bowie's own publishing house. On the whole, the number comes out as happy rather than acerbic: as is promised by the introduction, in which acoustic guitars thrum a basic I, II, V, I progression in potent D major at moderate-to-fast tempo, while electric guitar inserts a serpentine, stepwise-moving solo. The vocal line, although light and airy, is not lyrically sustained, but moves in quasi-pentatonic patterns as it describes how 'the Goodmen of Tomorrow/Had their feet in the wallow' and 'bought their positions with saccharine and trust'. When the Bewlay Brothers 'swirl through the streets/Like the crust of the sun', an electric guitar soars in high *tessitura*, sweet but slightly nauseating, for the words speak of 'flashing teeth of brass/Standing tall in the dark'. The last stanza refers to 'your dwarf men' and 'your lack of conclusions', promoting a momentary shift from D major to C. The music is a shade nightmarish as the Bewlay Brothers, 'real cool traders' and 'kings of oblivion', float lyrically up to F-sharp while the original *ostinato* is reiterated at the original pitch, again subsiding on an interrupted cadence in C instead of D. Lyrical generosity is totally effaced by the coda, a metrically falling scale declining in octaves from E in the top stave to the A below middle C, bellowed in a 'low' accent and in raucous timbre. The pulsing triads now droop, not only from D to C-natural but further to F-natural, as 'he' (Bowie?) cries 'Leave my shoes, and door unlocked/I might just slip away, hey!' The subversive meanings of this song can only be difficult to decipher.

In *Hunky Dory* David Bowie encapsulated the myth of his generation in artefacts that satisfy even while being open-ended. This is an achievement, the nature of which we'll better understand if we reflect

on the words of the American poet A. R. Ammons, also written during
the early seventies:

> our young don't believe in time future and, so,
> suffer every instant's death; they don't believe
> in the thread, plot, the leading of one thing into
>
> another, consequence, developed changed: without retrospect
> or prospect, they seek the quality of experience
> a moment's dimension allows: thrill replaces
>
> goal: threat lessens and fractures times, shortening
> the distance to the abyss, immediate, a step away:
> without calm, they can't see tomorrow unfolding:
>
> . . . hell is the meaninglessness of stringing out
> events in unrelated, undirected sequence: remove danger
> (holocaust, suffocation, poisoning) from the young and
>
> their anxieties will unwind into long reaches of easeful
> seeking: . . . we now have a myth of Disaster, and that's harder
>   than
> some other kinds of myth.

Bowie, never shying away from that verity, makes music that creates
a 'self not mine but ours'.

MICHAEL WATTS

Waiting for the man

Melody Maker, 1 July 1972

It was raining the night Jim met Phil. They were total strangers to each
other, but Phil had asked Jim for a cigarette, and well . . . one thing
led to another. They've become very good friends. Phil still recalls
how Jim's hand had trembled, though.

They'd gone along to see David Bowie in Dunstable. Great fans of
Bowie they were, and Jim had almost to pinch himself when he first
heard such a grand person was actually coming to *that* place. He hated

it. Privately his mother confided that he found it difficult to make friends at work.

That Wednesday night he was there, though, clutching his copy of the new David Bowie album, *The Rise and Fall of Ziggy Stardust*, which he hoped David would autograph after the show. He was wearing his red scarf, flung nonchalantly over his shoulder, and his red platform boots.

His hair was long down the back but cropped fairly short on top so that it stuck up when he brushed his fingers through it. He hated that it was dark brown. He'd promised himself that when he eventually split to London he'd have it done bright blond. He was just turned 19.

Phil was one of the first to arrive at the Civic Hall. He'd stood in the queue for an hour and a half to get a ticket, so when he was inside he rushed quickly to the front and stood beneath the stage. He waited patiently while the Flamin' Groovies went through their set. He was to say later, in fact, that they were quite super, but after all, he'd really gone to see Dave, hadn't he?

He was so excited Phil can't remember exactly what Bowie came out wearing, but towards the end of the performance it was certain that the outfit was white satin shirt and trousers, the legs tucked into glistening thick-soled white boots. He looked like *Vogue*'s idea of what the well-dressed astronaut should be wearing. Dare it be said? A delicious space oddity.

A lesser hunk of glamour might have been upstaged by guitarist Mick Ronson with his maroon sequinned jacket, red lipstick and hair dyed peroxide as a fifties starlet, but though oohs and aaahs were directed his way, teenage hearts went fluttering out to David; for can anything dim the splendour of this ravishing creature whom all Britain is learning to love?

The newspapers were to report subsequently that this performance was one of the major turning points in David Bowie's incredible success story. The man from United Artists Records, who knows what he likes, was quite sure of that. He said afterwards that DB was definitely the biggest thing around.

To those who had seen his act before this year the format was not new. That's to say he started the set rockin' like a bitch before cooling down somewhat with 'Changes', a song of mixed tempos, and then the darkling, apocalyptic message of 'Five years', which owes something lyrically to Lou Reed ('I think I saw you in an ice-cream parlour drinking milk shakes cold and long.') And then the acoustic passages with Mick Ronson ('Space oddity' and 'Andy Warhol') culminating in a solo version of 'Amsterdam', a febrile account of rough trade, as delightfully coarse as navy blue serge.

'Now some golden oldies for you.' He announced the number as written by Jack Bruce and Pete Brown. All his fans, of course, needed no telling. 'I feel free', ripping out of the stereo PA system, choreographed by the flickering strobe lighting, it's not what you do, it's the way you do it. My, how they clapped and whistled.

The band returned for an encore. It was 'I'm waiting for the man'. But something rather strange was happening up there on stage. During the instrumental break Bowie began chasing Ronson around the stage, hustling him, trying to press his body close. The attendants at the exits looked twice to see if they could believe their eyes. The teenage chickies stared in bewilderment. The men knew but the little girls didn't understand. *Jeees – us!* It had happened.

It should be recorded that the first act of fellatio on a musical instrument in the British Isles took place at Dunstable Civic Hall. How do you top that? You don't. You get off stage.

After the show was over, scores of people were still milling around. Over the loudspeaker system *Hunky Dory* was playing. The autograph hunters were crowding round the dressing-room door, but he wasn't seen to emerge. Moist-eyed boys still hung around. After a while, Jim and Paul left the place together.

TIM KINDBERG
Muin Man

And if the homework brings you down
Then we'll throw it on the fire
And take the car downtown

Dear Da**d,
I am writing this letter uncertain that it will find you. It is not so much the address, but the question of to whom I am writing that strikes the doubt. You see, I am writing about the past: a different me, a different you. But some things, surely, remain the same? Is there not a thread that links us to our former selves, however far in the past they seem?

We have gone back to the early seventies. I have become conscious, again, that I have lost you. I think you must be lodging in some far-off place. Some pleasure must keep you bound there, so strong you must forgo the time when you will visit. There must be someone else to see, tomorrow, in another foreign place, a drive or train away. Some fresh pillow, on which you sleep and dream, and people around you, like a family, cushion your nights and keep the wolves away. I know that if you could journey home you would. I know that there are more important matters that press you now and which you cannot but master there and then, as they press.

I imagine rivers of people through which you sail, resplendent. After gigs, in Los Angeles, or Paris – wherever is the latest pit stop – their smiling faces are against the windows, they are scratching to get closer still. But you are hurrying up the man who is filling the car, or who has got out to get you cigarettes, with your screaming eyes. You are a Wanted Man, not for any crime but for shaking us out of our doldrums, our small towns and families. And I must share you with other kids, others woken along the way.

In 1971 I am 13, a vulnerable kid. And you are my main man, in my father's stead. I have had my father's absence bounced back to me, a thousand times, with silence and denial. It is a silence that looks at me with assassin's eyes and threatens: 'If you ask again, you will break the spell that holds life together.' It is only now, when I look back, that I see how you changed and animated this oppression, how you patched through the walls and came into my room with sound; yours was the music made by somebody important to me.

My brother, the one I knew about at that time, brought home *Hunky Dory*, and I knew at once who you were. You were holding your long hair like a woman would, hoping that I would not see through the disguise. Too young, too effeminate: you were not the pipe-smoking, steady type that you imagine I had dreamed up to fill the void. You couldn't have known that your guise was precisely one that would catch my eye. What did I need with a patriarch, for God's sake? Someone to start ordering me around? No thanks. I had been fed stories that varied from occasion to occasion, falsely confessional and tearful, but which gave me a picture of your worldly importance, and the glamour that secrecy confers. You were a secret agent, or the manager of a large company in Sweden. She never tried to tell me that you were a rock star.

How many other lonely little kids listened to your songs, and what voids did the music fill? They were not songs of the future then – I was barely a teenager – but songs of home. Songs of home. Settling down with small Z. The smell of new paint filled the rooms, heads lay upon the pillows. Thin with exhaustion, you got back so late after playing; your forgotten make-up smeared the pillow. You must have slept well. I know I would have slept, in my own room, like a log, with you next door. How must it have felt at last, not to be a lodger, but to be in your home, with your own family?

You were a young man telling fairy stories about the adult world, the world I had been compelled to enter too soon and which frightened me, the Bewlay Brother world of dark sibling rivalry and love. Your burning creativity, coupled with your pre-eminence at the centre of a whole family, gave you a legitimacy that transcended any scorn others could pour upon your play. You offered a bridge to the other side. It was permitted to be oneself without shame. Life would not have to be such a struggle in these conditions. I hung on to this presentiment of regaining what I had been missing.

You would wake up every morning knowing that you always had something to prove, but that you were believed in. And yet your ascent, which your father watched and nurtured, turned you loose from him. You made happen for yourself what I had had done to me. That was part of your appeal.

You were a hero. The sky was your target, whether a backdrop to sun-pinned branches or the source of a mighty hand that plucked you up. The sky represented the future. It promised explanations for those born out of joint, like the children you sang about, like me. It was as though you'd had your fingers burned when strung up in space, after being flung there in the first song; but you were ready for another try. Your fear of flying, like your other false claims, was ridiculously implausible; it was, it seemed, a mock repudiation of your goals. The trouble with the sky is that it is an object of ambivalence, like a father: from a warm blue blanket it turns into an icy absence, its reassurance against the prospect of limitless effort turns into enraging limitation.

As a blanketless youth I was warmed by the music, made to forget, made to feel I had arrived somewhere recognizable. But I was most aware of you and your self-proclaimed oddity, your communications between home and space. Mindful of the night sky's icy but compelling aspect, I felt I could look up to you.

Dear Da**d,
When my brother went to Liverpool, soon after my sister left, he took the last of the records with him. Older and free and up to that point within reach, they left without warning. I wasn't ready. But I still had you.

I purchased a record player and *Hunky Dory* was the first LP I bought. The record player was bought in a discount warehouse. It had 'quadrosound'. It seemed to me that the claps for Warhol appeared at an exact point in space, carefully rendered by my £50 machine. It was my imagination, of course, but then what couldn't I turn to to suit my fantasies where you were concerned? In my daydreams I even had you appearing at my school speech day, making an entrance covered by a blanket, and running beside me past the seated ranks of parents, to be revealed proudly at the front as I beamed from the stage.

Were you ever involved, as a parent, with something as banal as school? I imagine you would cringe at my reveries. Let's put them down to youth; I must have read too many comic features with public-school heroes. Let's put them down – and yet, remember what you said about the bullies and the cads? They were supposed to be the ones we set ourselves apart from, but it has turned out to be all too easy to bully or disown or just drop, especially when our past selves make appeals to us.

I tried to be realistic. You had your own life to lead. You were young enough to be my brother. That, too, was part of your appeal for someone scared of the schoolmasters and left at home by his real brother. And yet, by the same token, you weren't beholden to me, I had to accept that – or beholden to anyone, perhaps. That was part of the thrill. Newly grown up, you'd frighten the children away, all right. There'd be no room for me on the eleventh floor. I would only get in your way. I didn't ask; I felt that I had no rights. But it could have been me, why didn't I say?

What did you want for us kooks, anyway, Da**d? When you were trading and faking your way through the streets, what would we do? I was in over my head; but I clung on because I thought that I would turn to shameful and lonely anonymity, if it weren't for your stylish come-ons. You would describe the places, in haunting detail, but you didn't tell me what I had to do. I had to wait, wondering about how we got here, wondering at how we always went backwards, as in a film reversed, looking for the beginning that we'd missed.

After my brother left we moved, the rump family, to a new house where I had my own room for the first time, aged 13 or 14. On the first night I sat in the semi-darkness listening to the radio, and on you came. It was 'Starman'; you were letting me know you were still out there, calling out that I could meet you, if only I was ready. How could I ever be ready, with you so far away? Did you think there was anyone else around like us, someone else I could meet who'd heard you too? I denied it automatically.

I was fascinated, like you, by the picture of not knowing – or denying – where we came from, of being away from home, of never finding home – and, although I didn't know it then, of being free from home. The mystery of birth became a mystery of adolescence: waking up for what seemed like the first time, and listening to the radio; waking up with a hard-on. What a moment this promised: the moment of finding the place where I belong.

Such a moment could be earned only through imaginative living, and I looked to you as a model of this. I saw what I wanted to see, but you were no blank wall for me to write on: you were a real original, more real than I was. You were someone I could feel the loss of. I still have the record after 21 years, the oldest of my possessions. I put the outer sleeve on my wall, then lost it when I moved – but even the black record in its paper sleeve reminds me of everything I felt then.

Dear Da**d,
I saw you at the Liverpool Empire, as Ziggy. I went with my brother and his girlfriend. I never was a space cadet, a sartorial emulator of you, my model in so many other respects. I was just too shy. For the occasion I had on a green velvet jacket with teddy boy lapels, bought from a fashionable shop where my sister had taken me. My brother and his girlfriend went straight as could be.

At first I felt cheated when you started being a spaceman. You were taking your need to get away from me a little too far, weren't you? You knew I could not ascend to those reaches. From behind your mimed screen you watched us, the kids, standing on our chairs. You thought you were born out there, up in the sky or on the stage. That is the logic of your remove. What, after all, were the alternatives? To starve at home or to fight in Belfast. It was better to remain aloft and alien.

I thought at that time: I have brothers and sisters all over the world. We stay at home and feel that we are starving. We are united by a common frequency – of waves from the news guy. We listen to what the Centre says and each responds with his or her own resonance. We do not contact one another; each of us is frightened of not being special. You are not responsible for any of this, we are; we are rootless. We were born this way, trying to tune in, wandering from station to station and sometimes, catalysed, all alighting at once on the same frequency.

When my brother took me to catch the train back to Nottingham, I spotted Trevor Bolder and Mick Woodmansey at Lime Street Station. They were fresh-faced kids. I struggled to find something on which they could write their autographs. All I could come up with was a cigarette packet. They smiled and gladly signed. The glossy card wouldn't take the biro; I could think of no arresting phrase, of nothing else at hand to write on. Their scrawl was all but illegible. It was over, as quickly parted as met, like the train I took, clutching the packet of Carltons.

When I reached home I felt some relief. I wondered if the experience of being just an audience away had put an end to my romanticizing. Those boys at the train station: they were in your inner circle? The threat of ordinariness was always a mere whisker away, just as oblivion haunted the street scene in 'Five years'. I could not afford to believe in flesh-and-blood, in case it disappointed. It had become important to me not to know who my father was. I was not sure whether to be glad it wasn't you I met at Lime Street.

Dear David,

I drew a curtain over the seventies, instead of owning you or rejecting you, as I believe I would have had to do if you were really in my life instead of on the stage. Since then I have found out who my father is. He remains as much or more of an unknown as you (the real you) ever were; he lives in Canada and that seems too far to travel presently. I read that your relations with Joey are good, and that he was best man at your recent marriage. You project yourself as a family man. Perhaps you always really were.

For me, the sky is no further or nearer. I wonder what has become of your former selves who, like the stages of a rocket, brought you to stardom. You are, after all, a man with a string of selves to his credit. I once thought the need to invent yourself was endless, but it stopped after *Scary Monsters* in 1980. We have to live with them, our past selves, and with their clutter. You draw the blinds on yesterday, and it's all so much scarier. In the seventies, when self-invention seemed my only course, I felt I belonged under your wing; I have no cause for regrets.

IAIN CHAMBERS
Among the fragments
from *Urban Rhythms*

On the cover of the LP *Space Oddity* [RCA's 1972 reissue of the 1969 *David Bowie* album], the slightly dazed terrestrial David Bowie gazes out from tufts of orange hair into the middle distance. Turning the record over we find Bowie's slight frame clothed in a silverish jump suit slashed open to the waist. The singer regards us with an interrogative look, raised chin and arched eyebrows. Around his neck hangs a necklace terminating in a large glittering pendant that rests on his ivory chest. Seated, his hands pressed between his thighs, legs splayed out from the knees and tapering floorwards inside bright red boots, Bowie offers himself to the camera's eye as an image of artful disturbance. His 'feminine' pose and extravagant attire speak an indeterminate language, an androgynous code. But the narcissistic atmosphere this image invokes is in turn richly ambiguous. The object of our surprised stare, Bowie is yet simultaneously the constructor of the 'shocking image'. Such a public display in self-fascination gestures towards the possibility of loosening the sexed male subject from previous, more predictable, moorings.

Glam or glitter rock's inroads into the public perception of male sexuality, in which the chameleon figure of David Bowie was seminal, seemed to crack an image brittle with repression. Yet various commentators insisted that all that was really involved was a commercial manipulation of sexual ambiguities, a shallow contortion. Understood in that key, glam rock becomes simply a conspicuous part of a general retreat by pop music from more committed concerns: from the wider aspirations of the counterculture, or the instinctive assertions of working-class habits and tastes. What this view overlooks is that *within* the cultural economy of pop, playing with sex and the erotic imagination – with its imagery and possible senses – can hardly be considered a retreat: more a return with a vengeance to the music's central social referents. Like several other tendencies coming out of the tail end of the counterculture, it highlighted that 'development which has made sexual characteristics a major organizing element in our culture.'[1]

But this is a description of glam rock which is usually accepted only with some reluctance. It was elsewhere that it was considered to be more innovatory. In its sophisticated reaches (Bowie, Roxy Music, Lou Reed), glam rock offered an aesthetic prospective that was markedly different from that of progressive music. Its 'artistry' went beyond traditional European aesthetic canons, and, like pop art, looked to the shiny ones of modern industrial life and its continual reproducibility. The rhetorical gesture of progressive rock, which had sought to separate commerce from conscious, artistic poise, was brusquely abandoned. The two were now indiscriminately mixed together on the same palette. In this fashion, the objects of everyday life – the sense of music, of sex, of art, of pleasure – were disturbingly rearranged, and unexpected suggestions were able to emerge. Inside that process, 'good' and 'bad' taste were superseded by the disturbance of 'kitsch' and journeys towards the frontiers of excess: out there where 'a-lad-insane' (David Bowie, *Aladdin Sane*, 1973), could continue a perverse research for new extremes. The reception of this music was not organized through the appeal of an abstract aesthetic. Its futuroid imagery – an exaggeration of the present in anticipation of the future – celebrated a tangible technology, stardom and commerce. The invasion of psychic and social spaces by these realities was not refused, as had been the case with the counterculture and progressive rock, but accepted, absorbed, investigated.

However, the 1970s opened preoccupied with other prospects. It was 'art' and 'musicianship', rather than explicit tamperings with sexuality, the pleasures of 'kitsch' and disruptive avant-gardist theories, that set the tone. It was the abstract chimera of 'art' surrounding the music of such groups as Yes, Jethro Tull, Genesis, Emerson, Lake and Palmer, and The Moody Blues that continued to exert a disproportionate influence on the direction and sense of much pop music, distributing judgment and dividing the musical field into frequently quite rigid divisions. And, up until the autumnal triumph of the progressive music ideal with Mike Oldfield's *Tubular Bells*, it remained the most privileged sector of critical attention.

Between the distinctive intentions of progressive rock and sophisticated glam, pop's more predictable elements reproduced themselves. Variations on the electric blues format even enjoyed something of a mini-revival in the early 1970s. The Rolling Stones were joined by other blues-tinged sounds, as diverse as Rod Stewart and The Faces or Free. But it was the loud pummelling beat and flamboyant guitar antics of heavy metal that most decidedly occupied the centre of blues-riffing. Alongside heavy metal and electric blues there was a recall to pop styles that pre-dated the geological shifts of the late 1960s: the Saturday night rock-and-roll euphoria of Creedence Clearwater Revival, and the wistful pop lyricism of Elton John.

What appears most clear about this moment is the new arrangement within pop. Under the umbrella of progressive music, all the above-mentioned styles constituted a rock 'mainstream', set apart from the rest of pop. Although the boundary was often decidedly hazy, rock in general considered itself separate from the pop-show business world of television variety shows, Radio One and Engelbert Humperdinck. This meant that while glam rock star Marc Bolan, or even Bowie, might remain uncertain cases, Deep Purple were 'in' and Tom Jones definitively 'out'.

Rock music was increasingly occupied with its own internal affairs. The more open, experimental atmosphere of the late 1960s had evaporated. Rock was now taking itself 'seriously'. This self-conscious reality was fittingly caught in the rise of the professional rock critic: the writer, working not only in the musical press, but also on 'alternative' (*Time Out*, *Rolling Stone*) and 'quality' papers, who is paid to expound views and theories on rock as a particular body of musical work. While this was going on, pop's long-standing affair with modes of sexuality and the extravagance of male style experienced a compensatory inflation. Glam rock, certain parts of heavy metal, and teeny-bopper pop, with their diverse economies of the corporeal image and its possible sexualities, suggested a very different set of concerns from those embroiled in the rock/pop demarcation dispute.

. . . It is largely against the precise artistic and musical proposals of progressive rock, rapidly turning into a new orthodoxy in the early 1970s, that developments elsewhere in British pop can be fruitfully defined. Some of these continue to enjoy an ambiguous relation to the status and artistic command of the progressive rock world, others fall decidedly outside it. But all, whether involving the pubescent stirrings of teenybopper pop, the burlesque camp of a Gary Glitter or an Alvin Stardust, the crude insistency of heavy metal, or the sophisticated claims of David Bowie and Roxy Music, can be viewed as part of a firm objection to progressive music's more ethereal claims. Still, progressive music continued to cast influential shadows over many of these tendencies. It indirectly taught Bowie and Roxy Music, for instance, to combine commercial success with a well-publicized 'artistry', encouraged pop to incorporate the 'authentic' sounds and sentiments of country music, and provided the initial formulae for the rough populism of heavy metal. More than this, it had shifted the whole of pop, including the sense of a 'mainstream', out beyond earlier bearings. In the subsequent readjustment and fall-out, pop music as a whole emerged substantially transformed: notably wider in its musical heterogeneity, but tending for the moment to be more exclusive in its internal divisions.

Around 1970–1, while the main body of progressive rock continued to inflate, glitter or glam rock appeared to propose a flight towards a sensationalist aesthetic of the 'strange'. Behind its disturbing theatrics, the masks, make-up, hair dye, platform heels and changing costumes, glam rock betrayed a wildly contradictory range of cultural motifs. Unashamedly caught up in the commercial meshes of the music industry, it also proved to be a sharp, mocking reply to the illusions of progressive rock. Further, it raised disturbing questions about male sexuality and styles from within a masculine universe. Apparently seduced by its own narcissism, sophisticated glam rock knowingly advertised the artifice and construction of the 'star'. It was quite clearly not lacking in some intellectual pretensions of its own. With all these intentions, glam rock became pop's most self-conscious expression. It tended to fragment older modes of reception, whether these were simply associated with 'fun' or the recently gained, but traditionally exercised, reign of 'art'. At the same time, much glam rock was itself simultaneously popular and yet, in its sophistication, often painfully 'artistic'. In this fashion, it held together a diversity of influences and heterogeneous publics. Perhaps its final significance lay in its rich and suggestive 'confusion of levels' (Ben Gerson).

For many, glam rock simply represented a novel twist in pop's public style and commercial stratagems: the latest fashion fad, encouraging an escape from immediate concerns and obvious commitment. Whether it was the glittering spectacle of Rod Stewart or the allusive communion of Bowie's show, it was considered simply to involve rhetorical stage costumes and commercial acumen. Behind this façade, older musical and cultural rhythms apparently continued unperturbed. Examined in this manner, glitter rock signalled a return to a presumed 'golden age' of pop, when the mood was joyous, the beat insistent, and the music basically implied 'fun'. Here glitter frequently crosses tracks with the more precise focus of teenybopper pop. It is true that many performers insisted on the basics of pop music, on its beat (Slade), its R & B and soul heritage (Rod Stewart) and its lyricism (Elton John). Sometimes, there was a barely disguised revivalism, a glittering parody of rock-and-roll and beat music (Gary Glitter, Alvin Stardust); elsewhere, the synthesis was more subtle. When ex-mod, ex-underground singer Marc Bolan took up an electric style in 1970 and launched T Rex, his guitar echoed the immediate inheritance of Jimi Hendrix, but his riffs came straight from the US pop of the 1950s: Chuck Berry, Eddie Cochran and Ricky Nelson. Backstage, among the props and show business machinery, however, there was also another story; one that connected glam rock's 'camp' appearance to a more significant script.

Already in 1966, New York – increasingly the symbol of the modern city in crisis and breakdown – offered, with the music of The Velvet Underground, a bleak alternative to the open optimism of California's budding counterculture. As a dark, isolated voice, oblivious of utopian release, the music of the New York group seemed destined to be aware only of the fragile prospects of defiance and snatched comforts in the 'mean streets' of the eastern metropolis. If LSD and its promise of widening vistas was the West Coast cult drug, then New York was the habitat of the terminal prospects of heroin. It was as early as 1965 that the 'plastic' values and disposable aesthetics of metropolitan collapse issued their manifesto. *Andy Warhol's Plastic Exploding Inevitable* opened in New York in November of that year. A multimedia event, it deployed The Velvet Underground, stroboscopes, the singer Nico, and such Warhol films as *Eat, Sleep, Banana* and *Blow Job*. There was no 'public'. Anyone who walked in off the street instantly stepped into the spectacle, everyone was temporarily a 'star'.

Warhol, and behind him pop art, became quite a momentous connection with a small but significant area of pop. At that time, Warhol's influence, apart from a short-lived and rather obscure co-operation with The Velvet Underground on their first LP (complete with Warhol banana cover), was minimal. But the exploration by the American and British pop art movement of the ironic expressive possibilities of the mass media and popular culture in figurative and iconic art was to be influential. Reproducing reproductions – Warhol's silk screen series of Campbell soup cans or Marilyn Monroe – was a celebration of the artist as 'thief', stealing and borrowing techniques, suggestions and images from wherever in contemporary culture. But it was productive 'robbery', and deeply instructive. It took and transformed the existing sign systems of popular culture (advertising, cinema, comics, photography) into fresh meanings, oblique messages about themselves and their place in the modern world: a soup can reproduced in a certain field becomes an art work. This, together with the deeply connected idea of the individual who *constructs* himself (or herself) as the 'self-referential object of his art',[2] became an important prosaic tendency in British pop after its introduction by sophisticated glam rock,[3] the lesson being that it is the gesture, the momentary perspective, that might be original, not the object.

The music of The Velvet Underground was part of this 'realistic', urban appraisal. It was a music stripped down to metallic guitar rhythms, electric 'noise' and inhuman vocals. The perpetual threat of cacophony was counterbalanced by the harsh monotones and arresting associations of many of the songs: 'I'm waiting for the man', 'Heroin', 'Sister Ray'. These dark comments were later complemented by the theatrical violence of Iggy Pop and The Stooges from Detroit ('No fun'), and the transvestite New York Dolls ('Personality crisis', 'Trash', 'Pills'). The overall effect was that of a sleazy East Coast, urban sound.

A subversive musical sneer that irreverently cast doubts on the 'authenticity' of the singer-songwriter confessionals or the 'sincerity' of progressive rock's 'art'.

In a twilight, urban imagination of fragmentation and moral crack-up, the trash aesthetics of the American metropolis turned out to have an important appointment with European 'decadence'; in particular, with the latter's morbid fascination with the stylized gestures of the extreme. To the vivid scenes of American 'street life' songs, Bowie brought the cold dramaticity of a dehumanized future, while Roxy Music proposed shiny projections and alluring icons – see the music and record sleeve of *For Your Pleasure* (1973) – that ironically reflected nothing . . . but themselves. The 'flatness' of the artifice was paradoxically its profoundest statement: the construction was revealed, the borrowings exposed and mocked, the style shared.

It was above all Bowie who was the (self-admitted) master-thief. His songs were miniature films, where the 'camera is the eye of a cruising vulture' (William Burroughs). The resulting song strips were full of startling images that apparently mated Marvel comics with Burroughs's eschatalogical vision. In the early 1970s, Bowie's songs and personae were organized through a changing series of sexually ambiguous protagonists (Ziggy Stardust, Aladdin Sane, the diamond dogs) who move through flashes of time and disparate, colliding images, just like the adolescent homosexual warrior bands of the future that rove through Burroughs's novel *The Wild Boys* (1971). These songs emerge as a disturbing montage that spans Bowie's music from *David Bowie* (1969, reissued in 1972 as *Space Oddity*) to the moment in which he closes this part of his mannequined career with *Diamond Dogs* (1974) and swaps a sci-fi future for the uniform of white soul boy, neurotic funkster and a doomed dandyism.

With both Bowie and his protégé Lou Reed (Bowie produced *Transformer*, 1972), a musical mixture of the commonplace (orthodox pop song structures, frequent hard rock timbres and instrumentation) and the unusual (suggestive images drawn from the darker corners of the urban night) provocatively focused on the ambiguities of male sexuality. Bowie, Reed and the android image of Brian Eno of Roxy Music, represented lives and habits beyond the pale of the common imagination, they were 'extra-terrestrial' in more senses than one. Embracing the ambiguities of the hermaphrodite, the transvestite, the bisexual and the homosexual, they appeared as 'forbidden heroes' whose 'walk on the wild side' (Reed) confronted pop's normal gallery with the subversive suggestions of an unstable male sexuality. Although already hinted at in Jagger's stage performance and the more relaxed, softer male style of the hippies, it was Bowie and Reed who refined and concentrated this possibility to a sharp and shocking degree. The condemned melancholy of Weimar Berlin, or the harsh splendours of a decadent, futuroid New York, provided the dislocating backdrops that encouraged the emergence of something previously unspoken. It confronted male youth cultures with what was most disturbing to it: the shifting, sliding, but material signs (it was there in the music, the clothes, the body) of an uncertain 'maleness' – the androgynous humanoids who 'fell to earth'.[4] A previously mute urban male romanticism began to speak in confusing and contradictory voices. The stability of a time-honoured sexual security was threatened by an ambiguous future.

Such 'ambiguity' appears to beckon us on to speculative ground, away from the firmer footholds of explanation so far employed. Glam rock was, after all, a self-advertised refusal of 'reality', a glittering façade that perpetually slipped away from explicit contexts. Yet, on its inside, buried in its researched solipsism, fleeting personae and studied vacuity, we can discover the tangible condensation of wider forces. In particular, Bowie and Roxy Music inadvertently exposed a certain cultural proximity to the counterculture. Of course, the connections were tangential, disguised, subconsciously recognized if at all; they remain lost in a bohemian fog. That is not important; conscious intentions are hardly the point here. What was significant was that the radical sexual and 'camp' styles found in metropolitan counterculture and glam rock shared common ground when an apparently 'private' narcissism transformed itself into public theatrics and took to a wider stage.

Public displays of sexuality – from advertising to cinema – had moved ahead by leaps and bounds in the 'swinging sixties'. These had been accompanied, encouraged according to malicious comment, by a series of liberal reforms relaxing controls on personal sexual and public moral conduct. This development was now encountering mounting resistance. Encouraged by the more rigorous climate of the Heath administration (1970–4), and the tightening of moral belts that invariably accompanies the observation of crisis clouds on the horizon, public celebrations of sexual hedonism were decisively challenged. 'Permissiveness' was declared to have gone too far. The 'cost' to British society of permitting the liberal movement of the citizen not only among consumer, but also moral goods, was proving too high. With a world economic crisis rearing its head and an all too obviously unprepared Britain, the spaces for social experiment began closing down; earlier boundaries were pulled back and prospects retracted as the solid values of 'tradition' closed ranks.

Against these mounting prospects, the 'frivolous' proposals of

Bowie, Reed and Roxy Music are not merely light relief, but promise a 'dangerous affirmation' (David Bowie). The extraordinary attention paid by these glam rock performers to 'the outward appearances of role implies that roles and, in particular, sex roles are superficial – a matter of style'.[5] It was this seemingly hidden script that points to the possibility of a profounder sense in glam rock. To propose sexual ambiguities, and hence draw public attention to the details of sexuality, justifies some comment when precisely at that time a new, authoritarian morality was spreading over Britain's cultural landscapes, prosecuting for obscenity, 'cleaning up' television, campaigning against abortion, reasserting traditional views on sexuality, and swelling into a high wave of moral rearmament. In a tangential and distractive fashion, glam rock revelled in a display that was intent on demonstrating that the assumed 'privacy' of sexual matters, then being so fervently insisted upon by Mrs Whitehouse, was an illusion. Sexuality was as much part of the public domain as politics, class and subcultures. This often proved to be as uncomfortable for many radicals as it was for the moral crusaders.

It was Bowie, above all, who pioneered the shift of rebelliousness and images of resistance into the parade of male sexual ambiguities: in rock music (i.e. *Ziggy Stardust and The Spiders From Mars*, 1972), and then with disco (*Young Americans*, 1975), before moving off into funk experimentation. Among Bowie's and glam rock's fiercest critics, it was reluctantly accepted that the music's primary audience was made up of white, working-class teenagers. Glam rock was a '"focal cult" in working-class youth culture'.[6] The same commentators also admitted that the imaginative 'night life' that Bowie and his kind projected 'provided working-class youth in general, and working-class girls in particular, with a way of participating in leisure consumption that has not been built into the traditional institutions of class'.[7] Actually this part of the spectrum of glam rock – Bowie, Reed, Roxy Music – also had a significant student and art school following. But what was important here were the new possibilities, particularly involving the public construction of sexual roles in youth culture, that glam rock held out. Strange as it may initially seem, the commodity on sale here – and glam rock blatantly represented a 'commercial sound' – frequently offered greater expressive and imaginative potential than the means found within the narrow cultural pathways and pinched perspectives of its varied publics.[8]

In everyday life, the cultural map of glam rock was destined to remain largely restricted to pop music's internal geography. Attempts to translate its imaginative gestures into the more rigid performances of daily cultures often encountered vindictive male outrage:

One evening on the Wall by Monmouth Estate, Tommy arrived looking
like David Bowie, complete with make-up and streaked hair. Chorus of
hoots, wolf whistles and jeers from the Wall gang. Then, Mick, who used
to be a close friend of Tommy's but is now more involved with his motor
bike, starts to have a go at him. 'Where's your handbag, dearie? Going
out with your fella then?'[9]

Such a turning to 'face the strange' on the part of male youth,
particularly amongst working-class boys, had to settle accounts with
some very entrenched patterns and attitudes. To play with 'masculinity' was still condemned to remain more an imaginary than a practical
option for the majority of boys – involved with their motor bikes –
participating in popular culture.[10] It had, however, widened the reach
of the public imagination and become a permanent interlocutor in
pop's future.

Contributing to such a sense of instability were Bowie's frequent
public metamorphoses: Ziggy Stardust, Aladdin Sane, White soul boy,
Berlin émigré. Such characters underlined the continual sign production of the mass media, that possibility foreseen by Warhol in which
everyone would be a 'star' for fifteen minutes, a hero 'just for one
day'. If all is 'falsehood', a media-induced 'illusion' of constructed
images, then this, conversely, becomes the basis of a new 'reality'. At
times the imagery seemed to take alarming directions: Roxy Music in
Nazi uniforms, or 'Hitler was the first superstar. He really did it right'
(David Bowie). But the disguises kept changing, their wider, historical
associations perversely ignored. They were not so much statements
about the world, as passing gestures of provocation. They did not
'represent' anything apart from themselves. For all was concentrated
in the possibilities of the image; a careful construction revealed in the
self-conscious deftness of the David Bowie or Bryan Ferry persona.
Bowie, with his dyed hair, make-up and leotard spider costume; Ferry
in rakish evening wear and a late-1940s Dry Martini pose; Reed the
trash poet, ashen-faced behind dark glasses, topped off with peroxide
hair: these were the 'artists' constructing their public 'selves'. The
ultimate profanity of the star was ironically exposed through the sheer
exaggeration of the image constructed.

In its music, this part of glam rock eschewed the simple continuities
and revivalist spirit of more mainstream glitter rock for a brittle,
shifting collage of researched musical effects. Both Bowie and Roxy
Music scoured the post-progressive musical terrain with an impressive
series of constructs, posing themselves as ironic commentators as they
knowingly produced their own musical itineraries. Bowie proposed an
aesthetic of musical and cultural fragmentation that moved from the
hard rock sounds of *The Man Who Sold the World* (1971) through the

'plastic soul' (his definition) of *Young Americans* (1975) and on to the tortured funk experiments of *Station to Station* (1976). In a less intense, more whimsical fashion, Roxy Music explored the inheritance of the 1960s. They produced a free-wheeling musical *bricolage* of sounds, timbres and styles drawn from diverse sources. Synthesized together, the novelty, well exposed on their early records, lay precisely in the unusual juxtaposition and attenuation of already existing elements. Glam rock's fascination with the image and potential metamorphosis of the performer was a fitting fetish to accompany such labours.

Irony and image: these are highly familiar themes. Their undeniable centrality to the sophisticated play of glam rock's White aesthetic ultimately hinted at other cultural spaces and sonorities. Although it had been banished from critical concern by progressive music, modern soul had continued to pursue its own intentions confidently and coolly within pop throughout the late 1960s and early 1970s. By 1974–5, the young, White record-buying readership of *Record Mirror* was reading about and dancing to disco music. Meanwhile, the urban stylists at clubs such as Crackers, The Global Village and other London spots were moving to the hottest soul sounds imported from the States. Up North, this music was *the* sound of Saturday night (and Sunday morning in the case of the 'all niters'), and everywhere, in one variant or another – Tamla, Stax, the 'Philly Sound', 'Northern Soul', disco – the music for dancing.

Set alongside the meticulous moves of Bowie through the icy reaches of stylized extreme, the sequined frenzy of contemporary American soul and disco seemed a world apart. But the release of Bowie's own 'avant-garde disco' (Peter York) record, *Young Americans*, in 1975, dramatically revealed an unsuspected connection. The LP, recorded at the Sigma Studios, Philadelphia – the headquarters of the Philly Sound – was influential in bringing disco music to Bowie's predominantly White audience. Occupying a position between a researched artistic pose and a mythologized Black urban 'cool', David Bowie was one of the first White performers to open up an important passage between sonorial experiments in White music and the timbres of contemporary Black musics. It marked the recognition of the return of the excluded and buried 'exotica' of the latter into the 'legitimate' considerations of White pop.

PETER HOLMES

Gay rock

Gay News, July 1972

The event: Saturday 8 July, Bowie played at London's Royal Festival Hall in a benefit for the Friends of the Earth's Save the Whale campaign fund. Two weeks before the concert you couldn't get a seat in the RFH for deviant practices or money. Your reporter got in early with a couple of quid and there he was, just a few yards out from the stage and enough amplification equipment to set up a small to medium-sized radio station.

Cuddly Ken Everett is compere. Introduces Marmalade and the JSD Band, who replace Mott. It seems podgy Scots boys with glasses are in this week. They get a reasonable reception. But we're waiting for the star. The crowd isn't noticeably campy, even though the aftershave lies slightly heavier on the air than at most concerts at the RFH. Then Ken Ev ('I even went a bit gay'! *Nova*) in a fetching jumpsuit of blue denim with massive white buttons, showing how he got in and how he meant to get out, says he fought his way through the feather boas to the star's dressing room. 'He insists on introducing himself in about four minutes' time, so here is the second greatest thing, next to God . . . David Bowie,' says Ken. The speakers boom out the Moog martial version of the 'Ode to Joy' from *A Clockwork Orange*.

The capacity-plus crowd claps in time and in the dark as people sneak across the stage in the murk. It ends. A single spot picks out a thin, almost drawn jester. Red hair, white make-up and a skintight, red and green, Persian-carpet-print space suit. All this on top of red lace-up space boots. 'Hello, I'm Ziggy Stardust and these are The Spiders From Mars.' More lights and we have Mick Ronson, Trevor Bolder, Mick Woodmansey. A few seconds and we have the mind-blowing electric music of Bowie from the amps matched by the words that make Burroughs look like a slouch. And on stage, Bowie rampant.

Until now, Bowie's never been a star, but he's studied some of the best, like Garbo and Presley, and now he's on top and he knows what to do. Sometimes he plays guitar, sometimes just sings with his eerie thin voice, but sometimes that voice grows. Bowie is the understudy who's been waiting in the wings for years. Finally his big day comes, and he's got every step, every note, every voice-warble right. A star is born.

He's a showman all right. Even the pubescent girls who'd spent their Saturday-mornings-at-Woollies wages on a seat, or crowded into the gangways, screamed. He says, 'Tonight we have a surprise for you.' And everyone knows what it is. Lou Reed. The *New Musical Express* and other pop papers carried that secret during the week in inch-and-a-half caps. 'Tonight we're going to do a number by Cream – "Free".' Anticlimax swamps the hall. But the Bowie voice is haunting in the few lines of the words at the beginning of the number. Then he leaves it to The Spiders to get on with it.

. . . Then our David's back. Now he's in a white satin space suit that leaves only how he got into it to the imagination. Garbo on Mars. And, offhand, he says, 'If you've seen us before, you'll know we do some numbers by The Velvet Underground. And tonight we have, for the first time on any stage in England, Lou Reed.'

And the Velvets' former leading light bounds on in black to match Bowie's white. We get a set of Velvet numbers. David plays to Lou. Lou plays to Mick. Mick plays to David. While they're having fun on stage there's enough electricity generated in the RFH to keep the national grid pulsing high-voltage goodies all over the land.

They end, and the front several hundred of the 3000-plus crowd mobs the stage. Time for the expected encore. Ziggy and The Spiders reappear and do 'Suffragette city'. Orange handouts with their pictures on explode from the stage.

In this hour-and-a-bit, Bowie has passed from wild electric rock to simple ballads, such as 'Space oddity', and a Jaques Brel poem, 'Amsterdam', and back to wild electric rock. His words span concepts from science fiction and the coming of a super-race to sexual liberation. And we all had a bloody good time.

David Bowie is probably the best rock musician in Britain now. One day he'll become as popular as he deserves to be. And that'll give gay rock a potent spokesman.

RAY COLEMAN

A star is born

Melody Maker, 15 July 1972

When a shooting star is heading for the peak, there is usually one concert at which it's possible to declare, 'That's it – he's made it.' For David Bowie, opportunity knocked loud and clear last Saturday at London's Royal Festival Hall – and he left the stage a true 1972-style pop giant, clutching flowers from a girl who ran up and hugged and kissed him while a throng of fans milled around the stage. It was an exhilarating sight.

Bowie is going to be an old-fashioned, charismatic idol, for his show is full of glitter, panache and pace. Dressed outrageously in the tightest multicoloured gear imaginable, Bowie is a flashback in many ways to the pop star theatrics of about ten years ago, carrying on a detached love affair with his audience, wooing them, yet never surrendering that vital aloofness that makes him slightly untouchable.

On Saturday, the magic was boosted by an unadvertised appearance by Lou Reed. The American jammed with David and his group, and although mutual admiration societies like this are often disappointing ego trips, an electrifying heat came across that stage as David and Lou roared into 'White light', 'I'm waiting for the man' and 'Sweet Jane'. Their obvious admiration for each other's style was great to watch. Bowie did the back-up vocal work to Lou's haunting singing, and though his words were hard to pick up, Reed's presence was terrific. In black-sequinned jump-suit and gold shoes, he stood with feet tripping into a neat criss-cross movement at the breaks in his songs – rather like The Shadows used to do in that much-mocked leg-crossing stage movement.

There was something beautifully earthy, cool and all-knowing about Lou Reed, and the crowd who had come mainly to see Bowie were obviously in love with the memory of Lou's Velvet Underground history. Reed now needs to strengthen his simmering popularity here with a full-scale tour of his own. The time is now.

But this concert still belonged to Bowie, legs astride as wide as possible, his face painted incongruously to project a Danny La Rue profile and his diction quite splendid. His music naturally comes mainly from the *Ziggy Stardust* hit album, but little on this record equals the canny 'Changes' from the *Hunky Dory* set, or the classic 'Space oddity'. At the start, the sound was imperfect, but once this settled Bowie came over powerfully, oozing with histrionic confidence, with Mick Ronson turning in a potent lead guitar.

'Star man', 'Five years', 'Andy Warhol', a straight solo on 'Amsterdam' and a superb encore, 'Suffragette city', were the high-spots of a show which saw Bowie dressed in two outfits, obviously revelling in stardom, strutting from mike to mike, slaying us all with a deadly mixture of fragility and desperate intensity, the undisputed king of camp rock.

The concert, presented by Friends of the Earth to save the doomed whale, also featured Marmalade and the JSD Band . . . a superb night's music, because all of them have roots. Like Marc, Bowie has been a long time coming, but a more certain Bolan-chaser I never saw. At the end, two 'Ziggy' banners were extended by fans over the balcony. Bowie has arrived – a worthy pin-up with such style.

Notes

1. J. Weeks, *Sex, Politics and Society*, London, Longman, 1981, p. 287.

2. D. Graham, 'The end of liberalism', *ZG* 2, London, Macmillan Press, 1981.

3. Such self-referring constructs were the shifting personae of David Bowie and Lou Reed, the ironic, glossy packaging of Roxy Music and, more indirectly, the subsequent facial masks and sartorial kaleidoscope of punk and such post-punk manifestations as the new romantics: 'three times removed from fiction' (Steve Strange).

4. Directed by Nic Roeg, the film *The Man Who Fell to Earth* appropriately featured Bowie as an extraterrestrial humanoid moving blankly through a science fiction script.

5. R. Dyer, *Stars*, London, British Film Institute Publishing, 1979, p. 67.

6. Ian Taylor and Dave Wall, 'Beyond the skinheads – Comments on the emergence and significance of the glam rock cult', in *Working Class Youth Culture*, ed. Geoff Mungham and Geoff Pearson, London, Routledge & Kegan Paul, 1976, p. 106.

7. *Ibid.*, p. 109.

8. It is no accident that much of the most illuminating research into how consumer goods are *actively* transformed into meaningful cultural signs and expression has been that examining the particular situations and experiences of those generally assumed to be the most 'passive' in their consumption – women. Arguments about the contradictory potentialities of consumption and its active appropriation/transformation run com-

pletely counter to Taylor and Wall's wholly negative view of glam rock. For them, Bowie was a 'plastic' disguise, an offensive commercial and cultural 'emasculation' of the once 'authentic' values of the 'underground'. So, while they acknowledge glam rock's importance in permitting working-class girls to enter directly into new leisure institutions, they conclude that 'this process has been accelerated, if not actually precipitated by, the new marketing of leisure' (p. 110). All the *contradictory* evidence of glam rock's and Bowie's success is reduced to being merely the latest move by capitalism to organize proletarian leisure. But the real question, given that the commercialization of popular culture has been going on for at least a century or more in Britain, is not whether this tendency exists, but *how* it exists. To adopt an epochal explanation of the details of British popular culture – the contradiction between capital and working-class culture – does not carry us very far towards understanding the active and imaginative changes made in the cultural textures and social experiences of popular culture by subordinate groups as they transform cultural commodities into their own (determined) culture.

9. D. Robins and P. Cohen, *Knuckle Sandwich*, Harmondsworth, Penguin, 1978, p. 81.

10. For a revealing account of the construction of 'masculinity' in the male working-class experience of school, see P. Willis, *Learning to Labour*, Farnborough, Saxon House, 1977. It should be read alongside Angela McRobbie's criticism of male-oriented subcultural studies in 'Settling accounts with subcultures', *Screen Education* 34, London.

THREE

Changes

ELLEN WILLIS

Bowie's limitations

New Yorker, 14 October 1972

In England, David Bowie may become – may already be – a real star, but in the American context he looks more like an aesthete using stardom as a metaphor. I'm not entirely happy with this conclusion; it seems almost ungrateful. A week ago, I went to see Bowie's New York début at Carnegie Hall and ended up standing on my seat; at that, he was subdued by a virus and was much less exciting than when I saw him perform at a British rock club three months ago. Bowie is personally appealing, his act is entertaining theatre, his band rocks, and Mick Ronson, the guitarist, is so sexy he crackles. Yet after both concerts I felt unsatisfied; more than that, I felt just the slightest bit conned. Something was being promised that wasn't being delivered.

Part of the problem is Bowie's material. *Hunky Dory*, the first of his albums to get much critical attention, has become one of my favourite records, but his more recent stuff bores me. When *Hunky Dory* came out, I took one look at the album cover – a soft, vague picture of the artist looking soft and vague – and anticipated a soft, vague sensibility. Instead, Bowie turned out to be an intelligent, disciplined, wry Lou Reed freak. To say that his current opus, *The Rise and Fall of Ziggy Stardust and The Spiders From Mars* (suggested alternate title: 'Jefferson Starship vs. Powerman & Moneyground'), fulfils the threat of the *Hunky Dory* cover would be unfair, but not very. Some of the songs are OK – 'Hang on to yourself', 'Starman', even 'Five years' when it manages to transcend the self-pity inherent in its theme (the end of the world). But the idea of a pop star from outer space (read pop star as explorer, prophet, poet of technology, exotic on the outside but merely human on the inside, and so on) just doesn't make it, except maybe as a spoof, and Bowie – or should I say Ziggy? – takes it seriously. 'We got five years, my brain hurts a lot/Five years, that's all we've got'? Ouch! On stage, 'Ziggy's' deficiencies are obscured by

Bowie's flash and Mick's crackle. Still, Bowie is at his best doing other people's songs – 'Waiting for the man', 'White heat/white light', 'I feel free'. On the other hand, the worst song in his repertoire isn't anything from *Ziggy*.' It's 'Amsterdam', by Jacques Brel.

A lot of nonsense has been written about Bowie. The ubiquitous comparisons to Alice Cooper, in particular, can only be put down to wilful incomprehension. There is nothing provocative, perverse or revolting about Bowie. He is all glitter, no grease, and his act is neither overtly nor implicitly violent. As for his self-proclaimed bisexuality, it really isn't that big a deal. British rock musicians have always been less uptight than Americans about displaying, and even flaunting, their 'feminine' side. Androgyny is an important part of what The Beatles and The Stones represent; once upon a time Mick Jagger's bisexual mannerisms and innuendos were considered far out. Bowie's dyed red hair, make-up, legendary dresses, and on-stage flirtations with his guitarist just take this tradition one theatrical step further. In any case, Bowie's aura is not especially sexual; Ronson is the turn-on of the group, and his attractiveness – platinum hair, high heels, and all – is very straight, if refreshingly non-macho. What Bowie offers is not 'decadence' (sorry, Middle America) but a highly professional pop surface with a soft core: under that multicolored Day-Glo frogman's outfit lurks the soul of a folkie who digs Brel, plays an (amplified) acoustic guitar, and sings with a catch in his voice about the downfall of the planet.

I've been thinking about all this ever since July, when RCA Records, with unusual promotional zeal, flew a bunch of American journalists to London to see Bowie on his home ground. As it happened, Lou Reed was also in town to see Bowie, who is producing Reed's second solo album. The night of our arrival, Lou was scheduled to perform at the King's Cross Cinema, a proletarian Fillmore that features weekend shows lasting from midnight till six in the morning, and a number of us dedicated fans, undeterred by the fact that we hadn't slept in some thirty hours, decided to go. The performance could have been better; Reed's new band not only wasn't The Velvet Underground but wasn't even barely competent. Lou wore black eye make-up, black lipstick, and a black velvet suit with rhinestone trimming. (The Reed–Bowie influence, it seems, has gone both ways.) His voice had an unaccustomed deadpan quality, but it still conveyed that distinctive cosmic sadness. It occurred to me that one reason I loved Reed was that he didn't invite us to share his pain – he simply shared ours. I went to bed at 4 am feeling sombre and drained. The next night, our party was bused to the Bowie concert which was held at a club called Friars, at Aylesbury, thirty miles away. Friars was considerably more middle-class than the King's Cross, and it was mobbed by pink-cheeked teenagers. They were crazy about Bowie. I was susceptible but confused. Afterward, a group of us went back to the King's Cross Cinema to see some American expatriates – Iggy Pop and The Stooges, one of the original Detroit high-energy bands. Iggy's thing is hostility: he leaps into the audience and grabs people by the hair. His best song is called 'Hungry'. He is also a great rock-and-roll dancer. Unlike David Bowie, he sweats.

On Sunday afternoon, I went for a walk in Hyde Park with Iggy and Dave Marsh, the editor of *Creem*. We spent a long time trying unsuccessfully to hunt down a vendor who would sell Iggy a cold Coke. 'This country is weird, man,' said Iggy. 'It's *unreal*.' Later, Dave and I talked about Bowie. What was is that was missing? 'Innocence,' Dave suggested. But maybe it's just that unlike Lou Reed (who will never be a star here, either) or Iggy (who just might), Bowie doesn't seem quite real. Real to me, that is – which in rock-and-roll is the only fantasy that counts.

TIMOTHY FERRIS

David Bowie in America

Rolling Stone, 9 November 1972

Tony Frost came across the lobby of the Memphis Downtowner Motor Inn in a hurry. You could pick him out because he was the only one in the lobby wearing a judo robe and black belt over his slacks.

Waiters in white coats were carting liquor and mix into an adjoining meeting room where David Bowie's post-concert party was to be held. A dozen travellers and their kids were clustered at the desk, bleating quietly over delays in getting their rooms. Frost ignored all of them and with strides remarkable in so small a man, zoomed up to Al DeMarino, the booking agent for Bowie's tour.

'Has the lobby been booked?' he asked eagerly.

The *lobby*? Frost was one of Bowie's three bodyguards and his steely grip had been felt upon the biceps of just about everybody on the tour. He had fingered, gripped and questioned everyone who stumbled anywhere within waving distance of the star, and many who had not. Now he was worried about all these loose people in the lobby of the Downtowner Motor Inn. Strange middle-aged men in sports shirts, gooey children with no visible means of support, rock writers lacking proper respect . . . All these strangers were lurking in the lobby, which after all was only a door away from the room in which Bowie himself would appear in little more than an hour.

Had the lobby been booked? Well, what difference does it make? Are you one to shrink back when action is demanded? Hustle that gang of two-pants suiters out quick, drive those gasheads down Elvis Presley Boulevard, show them a taste of the old judo if they give you any lip, teach them to get smart with rock-and-roll.

'No, the lobby hasn't been booked,' said DeMarino.

Frost shot away like a billiard ball off a cushion.

David Bowie's manager is Tony De Fries (pronounced as in 'deep freeze,' not as in 'French fries'). His background as a London solicitor left him with the mental hardware to handle the legalities of Bowie's business affairs and with a lawyer-like paunch which he now enshrouds not in pinstripes but in tanktops and the like. His long, pointed nose is out of Dickens. His complexion is an uneven white. He favours fat black cigars. When he smokes one, he resembles a ball of oatmeal on a stick.

When I interviewed De Fries at the Plaza Hotel in New York, he turned on his own cassette tape recorder when I started mine. This was to enable him to double-check any quotes I might attribute to him in print.

. . . 'I want to make it clear right at the start that Bowie is a star and we don't need any of you,' he began, 'especially you writers. You are a worthless band of eels, sucking the blood of artists. *You* particularly I don't need. If you should ever show up in London, I'll have one of the big boys loosen you up so good you'll be able to store your elbows in your ears . . .'

. . . No, he didn't. He didn't say that. I can't pretend he did because he made *his own* tape of the whole interview, which he could produce and prove me a liar. What he actually said was this:

'If you're taking a performer who's going to be . . . the most important artist in his area within a very short space of time, which already happened to Bowie in England, then you find yourself dealing with an audience who want to get *to* your artist *by whatever means possible* . . .

'If you don't have security, the artist suffers, because you get break-ins, riots, people hurt and all that sort of thing . . . That is not going to happen to Bowie if I can help it.'

De Fries spoke with the measured tones of a lawyer talking as much for the transcript on appeal as for immediate effect. He kept an eye on the TV screen, awaiting an expected news spot on his boy.

'Bowie is setting a standard in rock-and-roll which other people are going to have to get to if they want to stay around in the seventies. I think he's very much a seventies artist. I think most of the artists who are with us at the moment are sixties artists, and Bowie, certainly to me, is going to be the major artist of the seventies. In 1975, he will be at his peak in music. What he does after that is going to depend on what his talents are in other fields.'

Other fields?

'I want to see him on film. I want to see him making feature films . . .'

'. . . And doing the soundtracks for them for RCA', inserted Stu Ginsberg, the red-haired RCA publicity man, from across the room.

'. . . films in which he is developing another aspect of his personality. As well as being a mime he is also an actor . . . Bowie himself often says he is not a musician, and he really isn't. To me, he has the potential to be a major force in films in the way he has been in music.'

Then De Fries became more philosophical.

'He is one person of many facets and many talents who can be and will be an industry on his own,' he said.

'You see, I've always seen David as a building. I visualize him as a building. Something rather like the Pan Am building on Park Avenue.'

The Bowie report came on TV.

'It's all part of the current trendy decadence of rock', said newsman Scott Osborne over a film showing Bowie and his Spiders From Mars in a blaze of strobe lights and feedback. A backstage interview with Bowie followed.

What do you want your audience to think when they see you?

I don't want them to think anything. They're probably just as confused about my writing as I am. I mean, I'm the last one to understand most of the material I write.

How would you describe yourself?

Partly enigmatic, partly fossile . . .

Fossile?

Yes.

One eye is green, the other alternately green and orange. The boots are bright red with two-and-a-half-inch risers. The blouse is orange see-through. The hair, dyed bright carrot, sticks straight up above the brow. Bowie was thin before he arrived in America and he has lost weight since; his smooth white skin is stretched from bone to bone in his face like telegraph wire along poles. He changes expression constantly as wind blowing across a lake, instantly as static electricity. Everything about his appearance is extreme.

He is sitting primly in an armchair in a Cleveland hotel room. Through the windows are the multiple new buildings of downtown Cleveland, each on its lot; it looks like the showroom of an office building manufacturer. Two reporters – one from a Cleveland newspaper, one from *Creem* magazine – question Bowie. He answers in a soft voice, often mumbles. He looks his interrogator in the eye, then drops his gaze to the floor. Everything about his manner is moderate.

'Do you think the whole bisexual scene in England owes a lot to Ray Davies?' asks Mr Creem.

'I think there's always been a bisexual scene in England,' says Bowie.

'I know, but I mean, bringing it to the fore.'

Mr Cleveland interrupts: 'Davies doesn't come out and talk about it, though. He seems to have evaded the issue. In two specific interviews I read he beat around the bush talking about it.'

'It's not for me to interpret,' says Bowie.

'The great story line behind "Five years", how did that come about?' says Mr Cleveland.

'It . . .'

'It's obviously a science fiction, future-type thing, but how did it come about exactly, deciding the world was going to end in five years?'

'It was a bad afternoon.'

'Oh. Do you write most of your stuff on piano?'

'On bad afternoons.'

'What's the story about "I wanted TV but I got T Rex"? Where did that song come from?'

'It was written specifically for Marc Bolan. It was the first song I've written for somebody else. They were at the point of breaking up as a band and I told them not to, because I thought they were a very good band. I told them I'd write them a hit single. And I did. It was easy.'

Today, people involved with Bowie will tell you that he represents the new rock of the seventies and that his American tour is an example of the business style of this new rock.

The substance of his business arrangement is a deal between De Fries and RCA whereby the record company agreed to underwrite the tour by means of a low-interest loan. Record promotion would help stir up concert audiences, and the shows in turn would sell records. RCA figured that even if it lost money on the tour (which, as it turned out, it probably didn't), it would still be worth it.

Otherwise, the trick was to treat Bowie as a star even if nobody knew he was yet. De Fries, who like many managers refers to both an artist and his music as the 'product', but who unlike American managers pronounces it 'pro-duct', put it this way:

'I think making America listen to Bowie in terms of listening to the product, and making them aware of the product before he came here, is one way of doing it. The other way is to bring him here without anyone knowing anything about him, and putting him on a second bill, and letting them learn about him firsthand in sleazy, dingy little places for two or three years. I don't think that necessarily is the right way . . .'

The product and his wife arrived on the *Queen Elizabeth II* in September and took a bus to Cleveland. Bowie doesn't like to fly but found he liked the chartered Greyhound; he often sat alone in the back, writing songs or gazing out at the countryside.

The early shows met with mixed critical reaction. Some reviewers seemed disappointed that Bowie didn't turn out to be a super-Alice Cooper, a queen of fag rock and an all-purpose high-voltage degenerate. A few moments on stage may have elated these souls – such as when Bowie kneels and performs a kind of fellatio on Mick Ronson's guitar strings – but overall they had to face it: there was not a limp wrist in the set.

So assessments varied widely. My own was that Bowie is the strongest figure to appear in rock in years.

He is one of those performers who easily commands the eyes of the audience every moment he is on stage. In his controlled theatrics, his ability to put across highly compressed lyrics and in the sustained anxiety he arouses in an audience, he reminds me of Dylan. He has borrowed from Dylan, as from The Beatles, Elvis and a half-dozen others, but what emerges is substantially his own.

The songs hold up. Solid, interesting material like 'Life on Mars', 'Space oddity' and 'Changes' turn out in concert to be still more powerful. And Bowie's voice, no more than adequate on the records, is startling on stage; it takes him about a half hour to get it cranked up, after which it becomes not only the most important but the most compelling instrument on stage.

The show – worked out in two weeks of rehearsal in the Stratford East theatre in London – has a lot of flash. The Spiders From Mars favour luminescent snakeskin suits, dyed hair and tight riffs. Bowie keeps moving, strikes poses reminiscent of a dozen earlier rockers and behaves much of the time like a puppet. He looks the way he says he feels – like an actor playing the role of a rock star. The thesis of that role is that freedom on stage is an illusion paid for by freedom.

For all this preparation, the show retains a lot of spontaneity in a period when most big-name concerts seem to come out of cans. It compares to the last Rolling Stones tour the way watching a fight from ringside compares to viewing a tape of it a year later from the bar of a 747.

New York in September and October harboured a wretched strain of flu which eventually extended its unwelcome tendrils across the nation. Victims could look forward to a two-week variety show, featuring a new symptom each day. It might be an eye-crossing cough one day, kidneys full of steel wool the next, then fever enough to make the patient glow in the dark. The hideous last stages, not fully describable in a family magazine, brought with them galley-slave joints and chronic reductions in IQ.

Bowie managed to do shows in Cleveland and Memphis before the flu caught up with him. When he reached Carnegie Hall it was showing off its way with a fever.

Waiting in the audience were the New York critics, less friendly than the flu. In fact, many were not exactly in the audience, but in the bar; these consider it an act of philanthropy just to come to a concert, and will emerge from the bar and actually enter the hall itself only upon receiving word of an assassination, a virgin birth or an appearance by Dylan.

Al Aronowitz, pop critic for the *New York Post*, was not there. He will not enter Carnegie Hall at all because, he says, the manager once insulted him. To the Bowie concert he sent a 'scout' who reported that there sure were some strange-looking people in the audience, like Andy Warhol, but the music seemed OK.

On his dressing-room door Bowie discovered a scrawled message: 'New York ain't jiving, is it?' He did a pallid imitation of his usual show and returned to his hotel without ceremony.

The flu had progressed to its stupefaction stage when I visited Bowie in his room at the Plaza a few days later. He responded to questions in the flu sufferer's manner, with a blank stare into space for about the time it takes to ride a bicycle up a long hill, followed by a fretful harvest of words.

'I'm not an intellectual by any stretch of the imagination,' he said, with a sniffle. 'I was very worried when I saw some of the pre-tour publicity about me in America, which cited me as being part of some kind of new-wave intelligentsia. I'm not a primitive either. I would describe me as a tactile thinker. I pick up on things . . .

'I'm a pretty cold person. A *very* cold person, I find. I have a strong lyrical, emotional drive and I'm not sure where it comes from. I'm not sure if that's really me coming through in the songs. They come out and I hear them afterward and I think, well, whoever wrote that really

Davie Jones and the King Bees, 1964 (*David Wedgbury*)

David Bowie plays
Stylophone on 'Space oddity'

George Underwood's painting for
Walter Tevis's novel *The Man Who
Fell to Earth*. Underwood, now a
freelance artist, went to school
with Bowie and played with him
in the Konrads and the King Bees

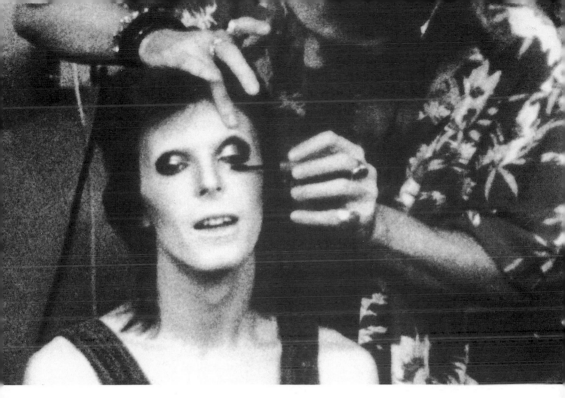

Preparing for Ziggy's
'farewell', London, July 1973.
The concert was filmed by
D. A. Pennebaker
(*BFI/Movie Acquisitions*)

Bowie lookalikes
(*Rex Features*)

London billboard, 1976

The Man Who Fell to Earth, 1976 (BFI/Movie Acquisitions)

'Spiritual Pilgrim'
by David Oxtoby
(photo: Miki Slingsby)

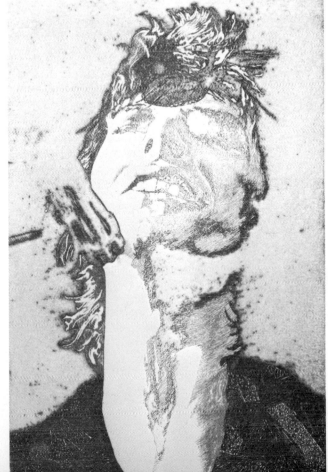

'Ziggy' by David Oxtoby
(photo: Miki Slingsby)

David Bowie in *The Hunger*, 1983 *(BFI/UPI)*

On the set of *The Hunger*, 1983 *(BFI/UPI)*

In *Merry Christmas, Mr Lawrence*, 1983 *(BFI/Mayfair Entertainment)*

With director Nagisa Oshima, 1983 *(BFI/Mayfair Entertainment)*

Serious Moonlight tour, 1983 *(Nancy Scariati/LGI/Rex Features)*

Seeking anonymity in Tin Machine? *(Rex Features)*

felt strongly about it. I *can't* feel strongly. I get so numb. I find that I'm walking around numb. I'm a bit of an iceman.'

Psychology aside, Bowie talked about the difficulties of charting out his career as The Star of the Seventies.

'It's so difficult to determine which way this new era is going in rock. There's definitely *some* kind of new era coming in . . . There's definitely a resurgence of spirit in entertaining. But there is also a cross-mesh of social significance, and it's quite hard to determine whether the next artists are going to exist as large artists on their entertainment merit, as Doris Days or Engelbert Humperdincks, or whether they're going to be large because they have some kind of redeeming social value.

'Now, me, I don't know which of those I fit into. As much as I enjoy just going out and making sure that a show goes on, I also like to feel that some of the things I'm writing about mean something to some people. So I'm pretty unstable about my stability as an artist. I won't be able to say much about it until maybe a year or so from now. I'll see where I've been pushed by the public.'

Such are the calculations of a seventies artist. Dylan doubtless thought about the same things, but he sure as hell didn't say them out loud. That is one difference between the two decades, I suppose.

There are others. The image of the new rocker that emerges is that of a clear-headed rider of a well-oiled carriage. With record company money under him and sound counsel at his side, he is skilfully to steer his career to the top. No dope, no hassles, no surprises. Every star will be Elvis, with no Col. Parkers.

'What I am doing with RCA,' says De Fries, 'is involving them in a business venture of which David Bowie is the pro-duct.'

Cool (he describes himself as 'a robot' off stage), professional, multi-talented, Bowie seems perfect for the new Apollonian order. Audiences should like it too, if it turns out any more rock of the same high quality as Bowie's. In fact it seems to be fun for everyone except those who go along on tour.

They get to watch the bodyguards throw out everybody backstage while Bowie performs, manhandling anyone who gets out of step – including members of Bowie's band. They get to attend the parties, dreary affairs which end early; the one in Cleveland was guarded by a doorman told simply to let nobody in, a dictate which limited attendance to the aggressive, the crude, the impolite and journalists.

The atmosphere of the tour was a little like that of a Roman division camped behind trenches in Germania, if you can imagine the Romans setting up stage and performing for the barbarians. Perhaps the barbarians, being Americans who already have signed over much of their lives to corporations, won't mind if even their funkiest, most outrageous and best music springs from corporate mentalities, as we have been told for years it inevitably must. Perhaps, for the performers, it will be a relief.

Bowie doesn't mind. He is well past thinking about rock as having any of the cultural or evangelic trappings once attributed to it. 'I feel like an actor when I'm on stage, rather than a rock artist,' he said. 'I very rarely have felt like a rock artist. I don't think that's much of a vocation, being a rock-and-roller.'

Bowie's wife Angela – cheerful, intelligent, her hair dyed white with streaks of sherbet red and anemone purple – appeared as Bowie was saying he doesn't think rock has much universality either.

'In just about every country except England and America there are strangely strong family ties,' he said. 'Very few countries need rock-and-roll. Very few. It's America and England that need it, and probably Germany. But France and Italy, no way. They don't need it. Rock provides a family life that is missing in America and England. It provides a sense of community.'

Angela: 'I think Mick Jagger would be astounded and amazed if he realized to how many people he is not a sex symbol . . .'

David: 'But a mother image!'

ROBERT CHRISTGAU

Growing up grim with Mott The Hoople

Newsday, December 1972

. . . For the English, rock-and-roll has never involved doing what comes naturally. No matter how well off the prospective American rock musician may be, it seems that he is closer to down-home funk than his (often working-class) English counterpart, and (due largely to the inspiration of The Beatles, of course) he is no longer embarrassed about showing it. Occasionally, England will produce some mad blues avatar like Eric Burdon or Joe Cocker, but for the most part the English work out their built-in detachment aesthetically. Invariably, their music redefines that old catch-all: art rock . . .

What is most striking about all art rock is that it isn't very sexy.

Bands like Jethro Tull make head music, using the physical compulsion of beat and volume to involve the mind. Bands like Led Zeppelin, on the other hand, make body music of an oddly cerebral cast, arousing aggression rather than sexuality. This means that the second kind of English hard rock – Led Zeppelin and Mott The Hoople's – has a strange potential double audience. It can attract intellectuals, and it can attract working-class kids.

Only two American bands of any consequence have made such music, and they split this audience down the middle. The Velvet Underground, nurtured by Andy Warhol before nestling down in Boston's academic ghetto, was America's first and greatest critics' band. And Alice Cooper, after an early flirtation with the Zappaphiles, has become the focus of the entire downer generation. It's curious that the only American 'English hard rock' bands are also the only American bands with an explicit connection to homosexuality – Alice Cooper through Alice's since-abandoned transvestism, not to mention his assumed name, and The Velvets through the Warhol superstars.

In England such connections are commonplace, from Mick Jagger's androgyny and Ray Davies' camping all the way to David Bowie, who in case you haven't heard is a singer-composer-producer who is also a transvestite and a bisexual and a trained mime and who is currently trying to ride a massive hype into superstardom. Bowie's manager is Tony De Fries. De Fries also manages Mott The Hoople, Lou Reed of The Velvets, and Iggy, whose band, The Stooges, doesn't rank with The Velvets or Alice Cooper because it never developed a real following. For the record, The Stooges weren't into homosexuality. Iggy liked to make himself bleed on stage though.

Like everyone else, De Fries and his stable want to reach a new rock audience that barely remembers The Beatles. In England this audience has far-out tastes, going for the fey fantasies of T Rex and the crude generational hostility of Slade, where the Americans go for The Osmonds and Grand Funk. But the fact that English tastes once took over America doesn't mean they will again – in a sense, The Beatles were a one-shot. Artistically, the English groups are superior, but as phenomena they are no more real. By the time of *Brain Capers*, Mott The Hoople had a substantial English following. In America, however, they had a Velvet Underground reputation when they would have preferred an Alice Cooper market. When their US record company dropped them, they were so disheartened they were ready to disband. But De Fries and Bowie persuaded them to give it one more try.

The reason was 'All the young dudes', a song Bowie wrote and produced for Mott The Hoople. A big hit in England, it made only top fifty here, which, since Mott's new label was pushing hard, doesn't mean a thing. No matter. 'All the young dudes' is the most exciting piece of White rock-and-roll released all year. It recalls The Stones at their peak, when all that ironic density still pertained to us as well as them. Like 'I'm eighteen', the hit single that transformed Alice Cooper from the group that slaughtered chickens to the group that destroyed stadiums, 'All the young dudes' is an attempt by an over-25 to get under the skins of the new rock audience. But where the American produced a defiant cry of joyful alienation, the English art rocker tried to suggest paradoxes of power and frustration, solidarity and isolation.

Because Mott The Hoople are produced by David Bowie and open the *All the Young Dudes* album with 'Sweet Jane', a Velvet Underground song, it is generally assumed that the band is flirting with the trendy gayness now threatening the red-blooded American boogie. Hmph, just listen to the very first stanza of 'Sweet Jane': 'Now Jack he's in his corset, and Jane she's in her vest.' Only thing is, the crucial line in that song is the next one: 'Me, I'm in a rock-and-roll band.' In 'One of the boys', which opens side two, the same identification is reconfirmed: 'I borrowed a gypsy Gibson just to show them/And now I'm a rock-and-roll star I don't want to know them/If they want a straight they better go out and grow one.'

Lately, the old figure of the self-conscious rock-and-roll star has been turning into the even more traditional world-weary art hero, with all the effeteness that implies – Mick Jagger's coat is worn and frayed, and he wants to shout, but he can't hardly speak, while Bowie's own persona, Ziggy Stardust, is an androgynous alien trying to conjure some love out of a dying planet. But whereas Jagger really is a fagged-out ten-year music veteran, and Bowie really is an art scene outsider trying to reach the masses through music, Ian Hunter is the lead singer of a genuine second-level touring band. He is familiar enough with the kinks of the pop world, but fame has not separated him – not totally, anyway – from his own class and generational origins. If he is part of a subculture in which love's sweet sentiment seems a thing of the past, as it does in 'Sweet Jane', he can also remember how he grew his hair to scare the teacher as one of the boys: 'I don't say much but I make a big noise.'

In 'All the young dudes', the rock-and-roller who knows Jack and Jane and the rock-and-roller who is one of the boys combine to undermine the notion that Jack and Jane are merely weird or the boys merely ordinary. For this is a dying planet in the sense that economic pressures break down traditional roles faster than anyone can find comfortable new ones – Dad wears a secret tummy-flattener to the PTA, and Mom affects a suede jerkin around the office. Meanwhile, the kids cope. A generation because they are a market, they band together, fortified by details of style against their own fate: 'Don't want to stay alive when you're twenty-five.'

Singing against an unforgettable chorus, an inspiriting, somewhat brutal-sounding hymn to subgenerational solidarity – one line, 'All the young dudes carry the news', repeated over and over – Hunter reveals the cruel limits of such solidarity. Whether the dudes are homosexuals, droogs, mods, rockers or mockers – or just the boys – doesn't matter. Whoever they are, they are united by a style ('He dressed like a queen . . .') against time, and they're out on the street determined to face it down together ('. . . but he can kick like a mule'). They're not 'juvenile delinquent wrecks', they tell us: 'We can love, we can really love.' But in the end the love and the face-down are inextricable, for the only accessible adversaries are those contemporaries who don't conform to their style. As the chorus repeats to a fade, Hunter calls out: 'Hey, you there. You with the glasses. I want you. I want you in the front. Now.' Soon, he loves and faces down his victim, who I imagine as some hapless Emerson, Lake and Palmer fan. 'How did it feel?' someone asks. Hunter's reply is barely audible, the last word of the song: 'Sick.'

Obviously, this is not exactly trendy gayness. The dudes love only in their apparently sexless camaraderie, and on the rest of side one Hunter plays an unusually vindictive rock misogynist. As the harsh rhythms of English hard rock imply, both homosexual and heterosexual contact is likely to be understood in terms of the patterns of dominance and submission that accompany any struggle, including the struggle for identity. Side two is a little more hopeful. Organist Verden Allen sings of a woman who is his sexual equal, and guitarist Mick Ralphs declares that he is 'ready for love' before Hunter closes with 'Sea diver', a somewhat ambiguous lament for the wasted chances of youth. 'Oh Lord, I wish I could escape this iron veil', he moans, and then answers himself, apparently in another voice: 'Write on, my son, write on, my son/Write until you fail.'

Especially in comparison to the raucous aggression of *Brain Capers* and the earlier albums, this is mature, reflective stuff. Its mood is reinforced by Bowie's well-pruned production and Hunter's almost tender reading of the final song. Under Bowie's direction Hunter has become a Dylan imitator on a new level – he wants his music to enlighten as well as entertain. In 'All the young dudes' he comments: 'We need TV but we got T Rex.' Even though he can't make it with The Beatles or The Stones – they're for his older brother, sitting at home – he knows there is something better than Slade's hostility and T Rex's fantasy. And so Mott The Hoople enter the battle for the soul of English working-class adolescents, capturing their angry confusion but trying to point beyond it too. That sort of transcendence is what art rock really ought to be about.

DAVE LAING AND SIMON FRITH

Bowie Zowie: Two views of the glitter prince of rock

Let It Rock, June 1973

What you think of Bowie depends on your idea of rock-and-roll. It's no good criticizing him for falling short in what he's trying to do, because he's right there. The point is – is Ziggy Stardust Like A Rolling Stone, does he belong in Heartbreak Hotel or in Strawberry Fields, does he Let It Rock?

One thing all great rock music has in common is that it stands outside the dominant ethos of traditional pop: the ethos of showbiz. Now showbiz isn't just a matter of where you play, what kind of outfit you wear and the length of your hair. It involves a whole philosophy of what music (or films, plays, novels) is for, how it relates to the rest of our lives. It's not simply that showbiz is part of *leisure*, something completely separate from our living and loving time and something to take us away from who and where we are. It also reinforces the stereotyped (conservative) images of ourselves and others that come at us from all of the media most of the time. The Engelbert ballad of impossible romantic love ends up by making it easier for the housewife to bear the drudgery of her existence.

OK, Bowie isn't Humperdinck. At times he has the poetic power of Dylan, the demonic presence of Jagger. But he has compromised with showbiz, with the whole manipulative process of image and stardom. Of course, any rock musician who achieves any kind of success can't help but get involved to some extent in that process. The way music is organized – as an industry – it's the only way he or she can reach large numbers of people. But with the best of them, there's always something there behind the image and the stardom. Often, it's nothing as simple as a *message*, it comes through in a tone of voice, a turn of phrase. And, however imperceptibly, it makes a difference to how we go about our daily lives.

But take away Bowie's image, and there's nothing left. The image itself is dense with weird and wonderful things – myths of inner and outer space, intimations of bizarre sexuality – but somehow they never lead anywhere except down the hole in the centre of the record. It's partly because he's too knowing. He knows everything that has been said and every lick that made a top ten hit, but ends up communicating nothing. His weakness for puns is crucial here: he uses them like Danny La Rue not John Lennon or John Donne. Clever, not witty.

And this is the sense in which Bowie is truly decadent, not his make-up or hip camping. His stuff reminds me increasingly of The Beatles just before they split – the aimless doodlings of *Abbey Road*, when they had nothing to say and everything to say it with. One alternative to Bowie is the subsequent work of two of The Beatles: Lennon and Harrison. For the last few years they've been trying to reconcile and unite their lives and beliefs with their music. Maybe they haven't succeeded, maybe they each have a long way to go. But David Bowie, he hasn't anywhere to go. Still, if he falters, there's always Gary Glitter.

* * *

Arguing about pop stars is mostly a loony thing to do. So many of the judgments involved are subjective that the inarticulacy of a Juke Box Jury is entirely right – I like the backing and so what? David Bowie is pretty and witty but *he'll* have to convince you, not me. The only words worth flinging about have a much more general concern – not with Bowie's aesthetic appeal but with his purpose and effect. So, Bowie bashing (roll up! roll up!) isn't much different from Bolan bashing and other past delights. It's the back page of *Melody Maker* and the selling-out argument. Bowie has sold his talent for fame, fortune and a white fur rug; a once creative artist is now slipping on Woolworth's glitter; shameless, Bowie has become a showbiz star.

I know who Bowie's sold out to; I don't understand what he's sold out from. Where is this authentic rock tradition, pose-less and glamour-free? Elvis? The Beatles? No way. Dylan wasn't a bootlace maker, pulling himself up. They're all pop stars, big business livery-chauffeured. Rock is not some pure order, under constant threat of worldly corruption; it operates from the heart of the beast itself and its achievement is the result of its context. Rock is entertainment that suggests – by its energy, self-consciousness, cultural references – something more. The Bowie question is not whether he's sold out, but whether the music he makes from his pop star stance is more than good fun, whether it illuminates its situation.

Bowie constructs his music around an image rather than a sound or a style and it's this that disturbs rock purists. I mean, what a cheek, deciding to be a star before he'd even got a fan. But it isn't a con trick. Ziggy Stardust is the loving creation of a genuine rock addict and the purpose of the Bowie show isn't to give pop a falsely glamorous glow but to point up the reality of the continuing star–audience relationship. Since 1967 and peace and love, rock has been faking a community, as if Jimmy Page, by being scruffy, became a man of the people. But smoking dope together in a field doesn't turn an audience into a society, and it's this pretence that Bowie rips apart.

I'd welcome Bowie to rock if only because his live act (down to the flaunted bisexuality) makes explicit aspects of pop usually ignored. But it's equally fascinating to follow his attempts to create a musical style to support the theatrics. His aim is to combine a tone of voice (world-weary, narcissistic), an instrumental urgency (Mick Ronson's aggressive and melodic riffs) and a lyrical mythology (science fiction plus New York depravity). It doesn't always work, but when it does the result is a gripping rock statement. Cold and calculated, maybe, but a scarily complete vision of life in the rock culture – sensual, selfish, endless. Heartbreak Hotel has become a Drive-in Saturday (Seattle–Phoenix) and Dave Laing's regret is a waste of emotion.

BEN GERSON

Aladdin Sane

Rolling Stone, 19 July 1973

A lightning bolt streaks across David's face; on the inside cover the lad is air-brushed into androgyny, a no less imposing figure for it. Though he has been annointed to go out among us and spread the word, we find stuffed into the sleeve, like dirty underwear, a form requesting our name, address, 'favourite film and TV stars', etc., plus $3.50 for membership of the David Bowie Fan Club (materials by return mail unspecified).

Such discrepancies have made David Bowie the most recently controversial of all significant pop artists – all of it owing to the confusion of levels on which he operates. His flamboyant drive for pop star status has stamped him in many people's eyes a naked opportunist and poseur. But once it is recognized that stardom represents a metaphysical quest for Bowie, one has to grant at least that the question of self-inflation is in his case unconventional.

The twin impulses are to be a star (ie Jagger) and to be a star (ie Betelgeuse). *The Rise and Fall of Ziggy Stardust and The Spiders From Mars* depicted an impending doomsday, an extraterrestrial visitation and its consequences for rock and society. Although never so billed, *Ziggy* was a rock opera, with plot, characters, and musical and dramatic momentum. *Aladdin Sane*, in far less systematic fashion, works over the same themes – issuances from the Bowie schema which date back to *The Man Who Sold the World*. Bowie is cognizant that religion's geography – the heavens – has been usurped, either by science or by actual beings.

If by conventional lights Bowie is a lad insane, then as an Aladdin, a conjurer of supernatural forces, he is quite sane. The titles may change from album to album – from the superman, the *Homo superior*, Ziggy, to Aladdin – but the vision, and Bowie's rightful place in it, remain constant. The pun of the title, alternately vaunted and dismissive, plays on his own sense of discrepancy. Which way you read it depends upon whether you are viewing the present from the eyes of the past or the future.

Bowie's programme is not complete, but it involves the elimination of gender differences, the inevitability of Armageddon, and the conquering of death and time as we know them. Stardom is the means towards attaining a vantage point from which to foresee, and an elevation from which to lead. The awesome powers and transformations civilization associates with heaven and hell will be unleashed on earth.

The title song is this album's 'Five years'. Ominously, within parentheses after the title, are the dates '1913–1938–197?' The first two are the years before the outbreak of the First and Second World Wars, respectively, and we have no reason to think that 197? represents anything but a year prior to the date of the third. The music is hothouse orientalism, jagged, dissonant and daring, yet also wistful and backward-looking. Phrases like 'battle cries and champagne' evoke images of earlier, more romantic wars. The impatient chug of the machine (the electric guitar) gently clashes with the wilder, more extreme flailings of a dying culture (the piano). We have been deposited in the realm of Ives and Stravinsky.

Mike Garson's long piano solo is fabulously imaginative and suggestive, incorporating snatches of *Rhapsody in Blue* and 'Tequila'. The reference to sake, the Japanese drink, in the first verse, and the last verse's 'Millions weep a fountain/Just in case of sunrise' suggest the land of the rising sun as a potentially significant future locale. While writing this album, Bowie decided to tour Japan (where he has recently been performing), and Ziggy was described on the last album as 'like some cat from Japan'. The relationship of Aladdin's visitations to the outbreak of war is not clear. Is it his appearance, or our failure to embrace him, which plunges us into strife?

Although a good portion of the songs on *Aladdin Sane* are hard rock-and-roll, a closer inspection reveals them to be advertisements for their own obsolescence – vignettes in which the baton is being passed on to a newer sensibility. 'Watch that man', the album's opening number, is inimitable Stones, *Exile* vintage. Mick Ronson plays Chuck Berry licks via Keith Richard, Garson plays at being Nicky Hopkins, Bowie slurs his lines, and the female back-up singers and horns make the appropriate noises. Like *Ziggy*, one of the subjects of *Aladdin Sane* is rock-and-roll (and its linchpin, sex), only here it is extended to include its ultimate exponents, The Stones.

Taking up the warning he gave in 'Changes' – 'Look out you rock-and-rollers/Pretty soon you're gonna get a little older' – David presents 'an old-fashioned band of married men/Looking up to me for encouragement.' To emphasize the archaism of these fellows, there are references to Benny Goodman and 'Tiger rag'. Jagger himself has become so dainty 'that he could eat you with a fork and spoon'.

'Let's spend the night together' continues The Stones preoccupation. Here, one of the most ostensibly heterosexual calls in rock is made into a bi-anthem: The cover version is a means to an ultimate revisionism. The rendition here is campy, butch, brittle and unsatisfying. Bowie is asking us to re-perceive 'Let's spend the night together' as a gay song, possibly from its inception. Sexual ambiguity in rock has existed long before any audience was attuned to it. However, though Bowie's point is well taken, his methods are not.

'Drive-in Saturday' was conceived during Bowie's passage through the Arizona desert. It is a fantasy in which the populace, after some terrible holocaust, has forgotten how to make love. To learn again they take courses at the local drive-in, where they view films in which 'like once before . . . people stared in Jagger's eyes and scored'.

'Panic in Detroit' places us right in the middle of a battered urban scape. Ronson deals out a compelling Bo Diddley beat which quickly leads into a helter-skelter descending scale. The song is a paranoid descendant of the Motor City's earlier masterpiece, Martha and The Vandellas' 'Nowhere to run'. The hero is 'the only survivor of the National People's Gang', the revolutionary as star (shades of Sinclair), Che as wall poster. By the end of the song, all that is left to claim his revolutionary immortality is a suicide note, an 'autograph' poignantly inscribed 'Let me collect dust'.

Rock and revolutionary stardom are not the only varieties which are doomed. In his work Bowie is often contemptuous of actors, yet he is, above all, an actor. His intent on 'Cracked actor', a portrait of an ageing screen idol, vicious, conceited, mercenary, the object of the ministrations of a male gigolo, is to strip the subject of his validity, as he has done with the rocker, as a step towards a redefinition of these roles and his own inhabiting of them. The homosexuality of 'Cracked actor' is not, as elsewhere, ground-breaking and affirmative, but rather decadent and sick. 'The prettiest star', the album's other slice of cinematic life, again asserts the connection between secular and celestial stardom: 'You and I will rise up all the way/All because of what you are/The prettiest star'. But the song itself is too self-consciously vaudeville.

'Time' is a bit of Brecht/Weill, a bit of Brel. All the world's not a stage, but a dressing-room, in which Time holds sway, exacts payment. Once we're on, as in all theatres, time is suspended and will no longer be 'Demanding Billy Dolls' – a reference to the death of New York Dolls drummer Billy Murcia in London last summer.

The appeal to an afterlife, or its equivalent, which is implied in this song, using the theatre as its metaphor, is further clarified in 'Lady grinning soul'. The song is beautifully arranged; Ronson's guitar, both six-string and twelve, elsewhere so muscular, is here, except for some faulty intonation on the acoustic solo, very poetic. Bowie, a ballad singer at heart, which lends his rock singing its special edge, gives 'Lady grinning soul' the album's most expansive and sincere vocal.

The seeming contradictions intrinsic to this album and the body of the last four albums are exasperating, yet the outlines are sufficiently legible to establish the records from *The Man Who Sold the World* to *Aladdin* as reworkings of the same obsessions – only the word 'obsession' smacks too much of psychological enslavement. Partly, the difficulty derives from the very private language Bowie employs; partly, I suspect, it is the function of a very canny withholding of information. Each album seems to advance the myth, but perhaps it is only a matter of finding new metaphors for the same message, packing more and more reality (in *Aladdin's* case, the America Bowie discovered on tour) into his scheme, universalizing it.

Aladdin is less manic than *The Man Who Sold the World*, and less intimate than *Hunky Dory*, with none of its attacks of self-doubt. *Ziggy*, in turn, was less autobiographically revealing, more threatening than its predecessors, but still compact. Like David's Radio City Music Hall show, *Aladdin* is grander, more produced: David is, more than ever, more mastermind than participant. *Aladdin's* very eclecticism makes it even less exposed, conceptually, than *Ziggy*. Three of the tracks 'The prettiest star', 'Let's spend the night together' and the related 'The Jean genie', are inferior; they lack the obdurate strength of the remaining songs, not to mention the perfection of *Hunky Dory* and *Ziggy*. The calmness of the former, the inexorability of the latter (which manages to subsume the question of each individual song's merit) are not *Aladdin Sane's*.

You needn't buy the mumbo-jumbo to accept Bowie's provocative melodies, audacious lyrics, masterful arrangements (with Mick Ronson) and production (with Ken Scott). As a strictly *musical* figure Bowie is of major importance. His remoteness, his stubbornness, do not describe a man at the mercy of the media or his audience, ready to alter his course at their behest, but one who wills them to do his bidding – the arrogance of the true believer. David has organized his career according to a schedule to which he steadfastly adheres. With Time waiting in the wings, an apocalypse near at hand, he lacks the freedom to tamper with it.

Certainly there is a general sense of oncoming catastrophe afoot in the land; many of his other concerns enjoy equal currency. But Bowie, uniquely among the pop musicians of today, sees them as the province of popular music (and popular music, by extension, as a world-shaking force). He is attempting to seize hold of these questions with the energy and commitment The Beatles and Dylan evinced towards their areas of concern in the sixties. With the benefit of hindsight, he seeks the kind of power The Beatles and Dylan had to *discover* they could have. However, it is not his goal just to return music to its stature as more than music. With the benefit of hindsight, it is to take it one step further.

CRAIG COPETAS
Beat godfather meets glitter Mainman
Rolling Stone, 28 February 1974

William Seward Burroughs is not a talkative man. Once at a dinner he gazed down into a pair of stereo microphones trained to pick up his every munch and said, 'I don't like talk and I don't like talkers. Like Ma Barker. You remember Ma Barker? Well, that's what she always said. "Ma Barker doesn't like talk and she doesn't like talkers." She just sat there with her gun.'

This was on my mind as much as the mysterious personality of David Bowie when an Irish cabbie drove Burroughs and me to Bowie's London home on 17 November ('Strange blokes down this part of London, mate'). I had spent the last several weeks arranging this two-way interview. I had brought Bowie all of Burroughs' novels: *Naked Lunch, Nova Express, The Ticket That Exploded* and the rest. He'd only had time to read *Nova Express*. Burroughs for his part had heard only two Bowie songs, 'Five years' and 'Starman', though he had read all of Bowie's lyrics. Still they had expressed interest in meeting each other.

Bowie's house is decorated in a science fiction mode: a gigantic painting, by an artist whose style fell midway between Salvador Dali and Norman Rockwell, hung over a plastic sofa. Quite a contrast to Burroughs' humble two-room Piccadilly flat, decorated with photos of Bryan Gysin – modest quarters for such a successful writer, more like the Beat Hotel in Paris than anything else.

Soon Bowie entered, wearing three-tone NASA jodhpurs. He jumped right into a detailed description of the painting and its surrealistic qualities. Burroughs nodded, and the interview/conversation began. The three of us sat in the room for two hours, talking and taking lunch: a Jamaican fish dish, prepared by a Jamaican in the Bowie entourage, with avocados stuffed with shrimp and a beaujolais nouveau, served by two interstellar Bowieites.

There was immediate liking and respect between the two. In fact, a few days after the conversation Bowie asked Burroughs for a favour: a production of *The Maids* staged by Lindsay Kemp, Bowie's old mime teacher, had been closed down in London by playwright Jean Genet's London publisher. Bowie wanted to bring the matter to Genet's attention personally. Burroughs was impressed by Bowie's description of the production and promised to help. A few weeks later Bowie went to Paris in search of Genet following leads from Burroughs.

Who knows? Perhaps a collaboration has begun; perhaps, as Bowie says, they may be the Rodgers and Hammerstein of the seventies.

Burroughs: Do you do all your designs yourself?

Bowie: Yes, I have to take total control myself. I can't let anybody else do anything, for I find that I can do things better for me. I don't want to get other people playing with what they think that I'm trying to do. I don't like to read things that people write about me. I'd rather read what kids have to say about me, because it's not their profession to do that.

People look to me to see what the spirit of the seventies is, at least fifty per cent of them do. Critics I don't understand. They get too intellectual. They're not very well versed in street talk; it takes them longer to say it. So they have to do it in dictionaries and they take longer to say it.

I went to a middle-class school, but my background is working-class. I got the best of both worlds, I saw both classes, so I have a pretty fair idea of how people live and why they do it. I can't articulate it too well, but I have a feeling about it. But not the upper class. I want to meet the Queen and then I'll know. How do you take the picture that people paint of you?

Burroughs: They try to categorize you. They want to see their picture of you and if they don't see their picture of you they're very upset. Writing is seeing how close you can come to make it happen, that's the object of all art. What else do they think man really wants, a whiskey priest on a mission he doesn't believe in? I think the most important thing in the world is that the artists should take over this planet because they're the only ones who can make anything happen. Why should we let these fucking newspaper politicians take over from us?

Bowie: I change my mind a lot. I usually don't agree with what I say very much. I'm an awful liar.

Burroughs: I am too.

Bowie: I'm not sure whether it is me changing my mind, or whether I lie a lot. It's somewhere between the two. I don't exactly lie, I change my mind all the time. People are always throwing things at me that I've said and I say that I didn't mean anything. You can't stand still on one point for your entire life.

Burroughs: Only politicians lay down what they think and that is it. Take a man like Hitler, he never changed his mind.

Bowie: *Nova Express* really reminded me of *Ziggy Stardust*, which I am going to be putting into a theatrical performance. Forty scenes are in it and it would be nice if the characters and actors learned the scenes and we all shuffled them around in a hat the afternoon of the performance and just performed it as the scenes come out. I got this all from you, Bill . . . so it would change every night.

Burroughs: That's a very good idea, visual cut-up in a different sequence.

Bowie: I get bored very quickly and that would give it some new energy. I'm rather kind of old school, thinking that when an artist does his work it's no longer his . . . I just see what people make of it. That is why the TV production of *Ziggy* will have to exceed people's expectations of what they thought *Ziggy* was.

Burroughs: Could you explain this Ziggy Stardust image of yours? From what I can see it has to do with the world being on the eve of destruction within five years.

Bowie: The time is five years to go before the end of the earth. It has been announced that the world will end because of lack of natural resources. Ziggy is in a position where all the kids have access to things that they thought they wanted. The older people have lost all touch with reality and the kids are left on their own to plunder anything. Ziggy was in a rock-and-roll band and the kids no longer want rock-and-roll. There's no electricity to play it. Ziggy's adviser tells him to collect news and sing it, 'cause there is no news. So Ziggy does this and there is terrible news. 'All the young dudes' is a song about this news. It is no hymn to the youth as people thought. It is completely the opposite.

Burroughs: Where did this Ziggy idea come from, and this five-year idea? Of course, exhaustion of natural resources will not develop the end of the world. It will result in the collapse of civilization. And it will cut down the population by about three-quarters.

Bowie: Exactly. This does not cause the end of the world for Ziggy. The end comes when the infinites arrive. They really are a black hole, but I've made them people because it would be very hard to explain a black hole on stage.

Burroughs: Yes, a black hole on stage would be an incredible expense. And it would be a continuing performance, first eating up Shaftesbury Avenue.

Bowie: Ziggy is advised in a dream by the infinites to write the coming of a starman, so he writes 'Starman', which is the first news of hope that the people have heard. So they latch on to it immediately. The starmen that he is talking about are called the infinites, and they are black-hole jumpers. Ziggy has been talking about this amazing spaceman who will be coming down to save the earth. They arrive somewhere in Greenwich Village. They don't have a care in the world and are of no possible use to us. They just happened to stumble into our universe by black-hole jumping. Their whole life is travelling from universe to universe. In the stage show, one of them resembles Brando, another one is a Black New Yorker. I even have one called Queenie the Infinite Fox.

Now Ziggy starts to believe in all this himself and thinks himself a prophet of the future starman. He takes himself up to incredible spiritual heights and is kept alive by his disciples. When the infinites arrive, they take bits of Ziggy to make themselves real because in their original state they are anti-matter and cannot exist in our world. And they tear him to pieces on stage during the song 'Rock 'n' roll suicide'. As soon as Ziggy dies on stage the infinites take his elements and make themselves visible. It is a science fiction fantasy of today and this is what literally blew my head off when I read *Nova Express*, which was written in 1961. Maybe we are the Rodgers and Hammerstein of the seventies, Bill!

Burroughs: Yes, I can believe that. The parallels are definitely there, and it sounds good.

Bowie: I must have the total image of a stage show. It has to be total with me. I'm just not content writing songs, I want to make it three-dimensional. Songwriting as an art is a bit archaic now. Just writing a song is not good enough.

Burroughs: It's the whole performance. It's not like somebody sitting down at the piano and just playing a piece.

Bowie: A song has to take on character, shape, body and influence people to an extent that they use it for their own devices. It must affect them not just as a song, but as a lifestyle. The rock stars have assimilated all kinds of philosophies, styles, histories, writings, and they throw out what they have gleaned from that.

Burroughs: The revolution will come from ignoring the others out of existence.

Bowie: Really. Now we have people who are making it happen on a level faster than ever. People who are into groups like Alice Cooper, The New York Dolls and Iggy Pop, who are denying totally and irrevocably the existence of people who are into The Stones and The Beatles. The gap has decreased from twenty years to ten years.

Burroughs: The escalating rate of change. The media are really responsible for most of this. Which produces an incalculable effect.

Bowie: Once upon a time, even when I was 13 or 14, for me it was between 14 and 40 that you were old. Basically. But now it is 18-year-olds and 26-year-olds – there can be incredible discrepancies, which is really quite alarming. We are not trying to bring people together, but to wonder how much longer we've got. It would be positively boring if minds were in tune. I'm more interested in whether the planet is going to survive.

Burroughs: Actually, the contrary is happening; people are getting further and further apart.

Bowie: The idea of getting minds together smacks of the flower power period to me. The coming together of people I find obscene as a principle. It is not human. It is not a natural thing as some people would have us believe.

Copetas: What about love?

Burroughs: Ugh.

Bowie: I'm not at ease with the word 'love'.

Burroughs: I'm not either.

Bowie: I was told that it was cool to fall in love, and that period was nothing like that to me. I gave too much of my time and energy to another person and they did the same to me and we started burning out against each other. And that is what is termed love . . . that we decide to put all our values on another person. It's like two pedestals, each wanting to be the other pedestal.

Burroughs: I don't think that 'love' is a useful word. It is predicated on a separation of a thing called sex and a thing called love and that they are separate. Like the primitive expressions in the old South when the woman is on a pedestal, and the man worshipped his wife and then went out and fucked a whore. It is primarily a Western concept and then it extended to the whole flower power thing of loving everybody. Well, you can't do that because the interests are not the same.

Bowie: The word is wrong, I'm sure. It is the way you understand love. The love that you see, among people who say, 'we're in love', it's nice to look at . . . but wanting not to be alone, wanting to have a person there that they relate to for a few years is not often the love that carries on throughout the lives of those people. There is another word. I'm not sure whether it is a word. Love is every type of relationship that you think of . . . I'm sure it means relationship, every type of relationship that you can think of.

Copetas: What of sexuality, where is it going?

Bowie: Sexuality and where it is going is an extraordinary question, for I don't see it going anywhere. It is with me, and that's it. It's not coming out as a new advertising campaign next year. It's just there. Everything you can think about sexuality is just there. Maybe there are different kinds of sexuality, maybe they'll be brought into play more. Like one time it was impossible to be homosexual as far as the public were concerned. Now it is accepted. Sexuality will never change, for people have been fucking their own particular ways since time began and will continue to do it. Just more of those ways will be coming to light. It might even reach a puritan state.

Burroughs: There are certain indications that it might be going that way in the future, real backlash.

Bowie: Oh yes, look at the rock business. Poor old Clive Davis. He was found to be absconding with money and there were also drug things tied up with it. And that has started a whole clean-up campaign among record companies; they're starting to ditch some of their artists.

I'm regarded quite asexually by a lot of people. And the people that understand me the best are nearer to what I understand about me. Which is not very much, for I'm still searching. I don't know, the people who are coming anywhere close to where I think I'm at regard me more as an erogenous kind of thing. But the people who don't know so much about me regard me more sexually.

But there again, maybe it's the disinterest with sex after a certain age, because the people who do kind of get nearer to me are generally older. And the ones who regard me as more of a sexual thing are generally younger. The younger people get into the lyrics in a different way, there's much more of a tactile understanding, which is the way I prefer it. 'Cause that's the way I get off on writing, especially William's. I can't say that I analyse it all and that's exactly what you're saying, but from a feeling way I got what you meant. It's there, a whole wonder-house of strange shapes and colours, tastes, feelings.

I must confess that up until now I haven't been an avid reader of William's work. I really did not get past Kerouac to be honest. But when I started looking at your work I really couldn't believe it. Especially after reading *Nova Express*, I really related to that. My ego obviously put me on to the 'Pay colour' chapter, then I started dragging out lines from the rest of the book.

Burroughs: Your lyrics are quite perceptive.

Bowie: They're a bit middle-class, but that's all right, 'cause I'm middle-class.

Burroughs: It is rather surprising that such complicated lyrics can go down with a mass audience. The content of most pop lyrics is practically zero, like 'Power to the people'.

Bowie: I'm quite certain that the audience that I've got for my stuff listen to the lyrics.

Burroughs: That's what I'm interested in hearing about . . . do they understand them?

Bowie: Well, it comes over more as a media thing and it's only after they sit down and bother to look. On the level they are reading them, they do understand them, because they will send me back their own kind of write-ups of what I'm talking about, which is great for me because sometimes I don't know. There have been times when I've written something and it goes out and it comes back in a letter from some kid as to what they think about it and I've taken their analysis to heart so much that I have taken up his thing. Writing what my audience is telling me to write.

Lou Reed is the most important writer in modern rock. Not because of the stuff that he does, but the direction that he will take it. Half the new bands would not be around if it were not for Lou. The movement that Lou's stuff has created is amazing. New York City is Lou Reed. Lou writes in the street-gut level and the English tend to intellectualize more.

Burroughs: What is your inspiration for writing, is it literary?

Bowie: I don't think so.

Burroughs: Well, I read this 'Eight line poem' of yours and it is very reminiscent of T.S. Eliot.

Bowie: Never read him.

Burroughs: [Laughs] It is very reminiscent of 'The Waste Land'. Do you get any of your ideas from dreams?

Bowie: Frequently.

Burroughs: I get seventy per cent of mine from dreams.

Bowie: There's a thing that, just as you go to sleep, if you keep your elbows elevated you will never go below the dream stage. And I've used that quite a lot and it keeps me dreaming much longer than if I just relaxed.

Burroughs: I dream a great deal, and then because I am a light sleeper, I will wake up and jot down just a few words and they will always bring the whole idea back to me.

Bowie: I keep a tape recorder by the bed and then if anything comes I just say it into the tape recorder. As for my inspiration, I haven't changed my views much since I was about 12 really, I've just got a 12-year-old mentality. When I was in school I had a brother who was into Kerouac and he gave me *On The Road* to read when I was 12 years old. That's still a big influence.

Copetas: The images that transpire are very graphic, almost comic-booky in nature.

Bowie: Well, yes, I find it easier to write in these little vignettes; if I try to get any more heavy, I find myself out of my league. I couldn't contain myself in what I say. Besides, if you are really heavier there isn't much more time to read that much, or listen to that much. There's not much point in getting any heavier . . . there's too many things to read and look at. If people read three hours of what you've done, then they'll analyse it for seven hours and come out with seven hours of their own thinking . . . whereas if you give them 30 seconds of your own stuff they usually still come out with seven hours of their own thinking. They take hook images of what you do. And they pontificate on the hooks. The sense of the immediacy of the image. Things have to hit for the moment. That's one of the reasons I'm into video; the image has to hit immediately. I adore video and the whole cutting up of it.

What are your projects at the moment?

Burroughs: At the moment I'm trying to set up an institute of advanced studies somewhere in Scotland. Its aim will be to extend awareness and alter consciousness in the direction of greater range, flexibility and effectiveness at a time when traditional disciplines have failed to come up with viable solutions. You see, the advent of the space age and the possibility of exploring galaxies and contacting alien life forms poses an urgent necessity for radically new solutions. We will be considering only non-chemical methods, with the emphasis placed on combination, synthesis, interaction and rotation of methods now being used in the East and West, together with methods that are not at present being used to extend awareness or increase human potentials.

We know exactly what we intend to do and how to go about doing it. As I said, no drug experiments are planned and no drugs other than alcohol, tobacco and personal medications obtained on prescription will be permitted in the centre. Basically, the experiments we propose are inexpensive and easy to carry out. Things such as yoga-style meditation and exercises, communication, sound, light and film experiments, experiments with sensory deprivation chambers, pyramids, psychotronic generators and Reich's orgone accumulators, experiments with infrasound, experiments with dream and sleep.

Bowie: That sounds fascinating. Are you basically interested in energy forces?

Burroughs: Expansion of awareness, eventually leading to mutations. Did you read *Journey Out of the Body*? Not the usual book on astral projection. This American businessman found he was having these experiences of getting out of the body – never used any hallucinogenic drugs. He's now setting up this astral air force. This psychic thing is really a rave in the States now. Did you experience it much when you were there?

Bowie: No, I really hid from it purposely. I was studying Tibetan Buddhism when I was quite young, again influenced by Kerouac. The Tibetan Buddhist Institute was accessible so I trotted down there to have a look. Lo and behold, there's a guy down in the basement who's the head man in setting up a place in Scotland for the refugees, and I got involved purely on a sociological level – because I wanted to help get the refugees out of India, for they were really having a shitty time

112

of it down there, dropping like flies due to the change of atmosphere from the Himalayas.

Scotland was a pretty good place to put them, and then more and more I was drawn to their way of thinking, or non-thinking, and for a while got quite heavily involved in it. I got to the point where I wanted to become a novice monk, and about two weeks before I was actually going to take those steps, I broke up and went out on the streets and got drunk and never looked back.

Burroughs: Just like Kerouac.

Bowie: Go to the States much?

Burroughs: Not since '71.

Bowie: It has changed, I can tell you, since then.

Burroughs: When were you last back?

Bowie: About a year ago.

Burroughs: Did you see any of the porn films in New York?

Bowie: Yes, quite a few.

Burroughs: When I was last back, I saw about thirty of them. I was going to be a judge at the erotic film festival.

Bowie: The best ones were the German ones; they were really incredible.

Burroughs: I thought that the American ones were still the best. I really like film . . . I understand that you may play Valentine Michael Smith in the film version of *Stranger in a Strange Land*.

Bowie: No, I don't like the book much. In fact, I think it is terrible. It was suggested to me that I make it into a movie, then I got around to reading it. It seemed a bit too flower-powery and that made me a bit wary.

Burroughs: I'm not that happy with the book either. You know, science fiction has not been very successful. It was supposed to start a whole new trend and nothing happened. For the special effects in some of the movies, like *2001*, it was great. But it all ended there.

Bowie: I feel the same way. Now I'm doing Orwell's *1984* on television;[1] that's a political thesis and an impression of the way in another country. Something of that nature will have more impact on television. People having to go out to the cinema is really archaic. I'd much rather sit at home.

Burroughs: Do you mean the whole concept of the audience?

Bowie: Yes, it is ancient. No sense of immediacy.

Burroughs: Exactly, it all relates back to image and the way in which it is used.

Bowie: Right. I'd like to start a TV station.

Burroughs: There are hardly any programmes worth anything any more. The British TV is a little better than American. The best thing the British do is natural history. There was one last week with sea-lions eating penguins, incredible. There is no reason for dull programmes, people get very bored with housing projects and coal strikes.

Bowie: They all have an interest level of about three seconds. Enough time to get into the commentator's next sentence. And that is the premise it works on. I'm going to put together all the bands that I think are of great value in the States and England, then make an hour-long programme about them. Probably a majority of people have never heard of these bands. They are doing and saying things in a way other bands aren't. Things like the Puerto Rican music at the Cheetah Club in New York. I want people to hear musicians like Joe Cuba. He has done things to whole masses of Puerto Rican people. The music is fantastic and important. I also want to start getting Andy Warhol films on TV.

Burroughs: Have you ever met Warhol?

Bowie: Yes, about two years ago I was invited up to The Factory. We got in the lift and went up and when it opened there was a brick wall in front of us. We rapped on the wall and they didn't believe who we were. So we went back down and back up again till finally they opened the wall and everybody was peering around at each other. That was shortly after the gun incident. I met this man who was the living dead. Yellow in complexion, a wig on that was the wrong colour, little glasses. I extended my hand and the guy retired, so I thought, 'The guy doesn't like flesh, obviously he's reptilian.' He produced a camera and took a picture of me. And I tried to make small talk with him, and it wasn't getting anywhere.

But then he saw my shoes. I was wearing a pair of gold-and-yellow shoes, and he says, 'I adore those shoes, tell me where you got those shoes.' He then started a whole rap about shoe design and that broke the ice. My yellow shoes broke the ice with Andy Warhol.

I adore what he *was* doing. I think his importance was very heavy, it's become a big thing to like him now. But Warhol wanted to be cliché, he wanted to be available in Woolworth's, and be talked about in that glib type of manner. I hear he wants to make real films now, which is very sad because the films he was making were the things that should be happening. I left knowing as little about him as a person as when I went in.

Burroughs: I don't think that there is any person there. It's a very alien thing, completely and totally unemotional. He's really a science fiction character. He's got a strange green colour.

Bowie: That's what struck me. He's the wrong colour, this man is the wrong colour to be a human being. Especially under the stark neon lighting in The Factory. Apparently it is a real experience to behold him in the daylight.

Burroughs: I've seen him in all light and still have no idea as to what is going on, except that it is something quite purposeful. It's not energetic, but quite insidious, completely asexual. His films will be the late-night movies of the future.

Bowie: Exactly. Remember *Pork*? I want to get that on to TV. TV has eaten up everything else, and Warhol films are all that is left, which is fabulous. *Pork* could become the next *I Love Lucy*, the great American domestic comedy. It's about how people really live, not like Lucy, who never touched dishwater. It's about people living and hustling to survive.

That's what *Pork* is all about. A smashing of the spectacle. Although I'd like to do my own version of *Sinbad The Sailor*. I think that is an all-time classic. But it would have to be done on an extraordinary level. It would be incredibly indulgent and expensive. It would have to utilize lasers and all the things that are going to happen in a true fantasy.

Even the use of holograms. Holograms are important. Videotape is next, then it will be holograms. Holograms will come into use in about seven years. Libraries of video cassettes should be developed to their fullest during the interim. You can't video enough good material from your own TV. I want to have my own choice of programmes. There has to be the necessary software available.

Burroughs: I audio-record everything I can.

Bowie: The media is either our salvation or our death. I'd like to think it's our salvation. My particular thing is discovering what can be done with media and how it can be used. You can't draw people together like one big huge family, people don't want that. They want isolation or a tribal thing. A group of 18 kids would much rather stick together and hate the next 18 kids down the block. You are not going to get two or three blocks joining up and loving each other. There are just too many people.

Burroughs: Too many people. We're in an over-populated situation, but even with fewer people that would not make them any less heterogeneous. They are just not the same. All this talk about a world family is a lot of bunk. It worked with the Chinese because they are very similar.

Bowie: And now one man in four in China has a bicycle, and that is pretty heavy considering what they didn't have before. And that's the miracle as far as they're concerned. It's like all of us having a jet plane over here.

Burroughs: It's because they are the personification of one character that they can live together without any friction. We quite evidently are not.

Bowie: It is why they don't need rock-and-roll. British rock-and-roll stars played in China, played a dirty great field, and they were treated like a sideshow. Old women, young children, some teenagers, you name it, everybody came along, walked past them and looked at them on the stand. It didn't mean a thing. Certain countries don't need rock-and-roll because they were so drawn together as a family unit. China has its mother-father figure – I've never made my mind up which – it fluctuates between the two. For the West, Jagger is most certainly a mother figure and he's a mother hen to the whole thing. He's not a cockadoodledoo; he's much more like a brothel-keeper or a madame.

Burroughs: Oh, very much so.

Bowie: He's incredibly sexy and very virile. I also find him incredibly motherly and maternal clutched into his bosom of ethnic blues. He's a White boy from Dagenham trying his damnedest to be ethnic. You see, trying to tart the rock business up a bit is getting nearer to what the kids themselves are like, because what I find, if you want to talk in the terms of rock, a lot depends on sensationalism and the kids are a lot more sensational than the stars themselves. The rock business is a pale shadow of what the kids' lives are usually like. The admiration comes from the other side. It's all a reversal, especially in recent years. Walk down Christopher Street and then you wonder exactly what went wrong. People are not like James Taylor; they may be moulded on the outside, but inside their heads is something completely different.

Burroughs: Politics of sound.

Bowie: Yes. We have kind of got that now. It has very loosely shaped itself into the politics of sound. The fact that you can now subdivide rock into different categories was something that you couldn't do ten years ago. But now I can reel off at least ten sounds that represent a kind of person rather than a type of music. The critics like being critics, and most of them wish they were rock-and-roll stars. But when they classify they are talking about people *not* music. It's a whole political thing.

Burroughs: Like infrasound, the sound below the level of hearing. Below 16 MHz. Turned up full blast it can knock down walls for 30 miles. You can walk into the French patent office and buy the patent for 40p. The machine itself can be made very cheaply from things you could find in a junk yard.

Bowie: Like black noise. I wonder if there is a sound that can put things back together? There was a band experimenting with stuff like that; they reckon they could make a whole audience shake.

Burroughs: They have riot-control noise based on these soundwaves now. But you could have music with infrasound, you wouldn't necessarily have to kill the audience.

Bowie: Just maim them.

Burroughs: The weapon of the Wild Boys is a bowie knife, an 18-inch bowie knife, did you know that?

Bowie: An 18-inch bowie knife . . . you don't do things by halves, do you? No, I didn't know that was their weapon. The name Bowie just appealed to me when I was younger. I was into a kind of heavy philosophy thing when I was 16 years old, and I wanted a truism about cutting through the lies and all that.

Burroughs: Well, it cuts both ways, you know, double-edged on the end.

Bowie: I didn't see it cutting both ways till now.

LESTER BANGS
Swan dive into the mung

Creem, August 1974

D-d-d-*decadence*, that's what this album's all about, thematically and conceptually. You've all heard of that stuff, and now you can buy it red hot and regurgitated from the poor stiffs who actually have to live it and your local platter vendor. Only trouble is, we gotta question whether Bowie of all people actually *does* live it. Aw hell, he's a goddam family man, he doesn't hardly take drugs, and perhaps the most perverted thing about Bowie's music is that in trowelling on the most studious sort of retching emotionalism he always comes out precisely as cold as we know him to be. Lou Reed's always talking about atrophied sensations, but Lou really can feel (that's his problem); I don't think Bowie can feel, and the irony is that in making albums about future brats' hysterical detachment from feeling he really does them feelinglessly. All the hysteria is contrived.

But that's OK, because the same thing applies to the great Sonny

Bono's vintage work, and *Diamond Dogs* reaffirms what an incredible producer Bowie is even if most of the songs are downright mediocre. The decadence angle comes in mostly because Bowie knows how cool it was in 1972 to be wasted, so even though he's not wasted himself he's put up a big front in the form of a wasted-sounding album. He was always weary, and pretentiously likes to think of himself as the prescient chronicler of a planet falling to pieces, so this again is a quasi-Orwellian concept album about a future world where the clock-work orangutans skulk like dogs in the streets while the politicians etc. and blah blah blah. Also this is the sloppiest Bowie album yet, so if the theory goes that it's better the more decadent it is, and decadence is not caring at all, then this must be Bowie's masterpiece, since he really doesn't seem to care as much as he used to. Or maybe that's all part of the total set-up: what's certain is that for the first time his production has a dense, smoky, eccentrically rough and claustrophobic touch, and it can't be an accident because he doesn't have any which is one of the things that's wrong with him.

'Future legend' opens the beast with a snarl of noise reminiscent of the intro to *Berlin*, from which Bowie emerges with his thickest-tongued quasi-poetics yet: 'And in the death, as the last few corpses lay rotting on the slimy thoroughfare . . .'. Sounds like Tom Wilson's 'Let them rot in the stifling air of their flowerspun graves' rap at the beginning of the first Beacon Street Union album. A brief off-key snatch of 'Bewitched, bothered and bewildered', and Bowie screams 'This ain't rock-and-roll, this is genocide.'

Which isn't the dumbest line on the album. All production phantas-magorias aside, I'm getting a bit tired of his broken-larynxed vocals; they're so queasily sincere they reek of some horrible burlesque, some sterilely distasteful artifice. It's the same old theatrical delivery of pretentious lyrics: 'You're dancing where the dogs decay/Defecating ecstasy'; 'Oh, I love you in your fuck-me pumps'. 'Choking on you lightly'. *Really*. There are moments when his words are less embarrass-ing: at one point you can't tell if he's saying 'my friend Celine' (great line if so) or 'I keep the vaseline' (bad one but good comedy maybe). I'm glad he didn't enclose a lyric sheet with this sludgesluice.

Musically the album is uneven. 'Rock 'n' roll with me' and 'We are the dead' are mediocre ballads unredeemed by vocal melodramatics, 'Sweet thing/Candidate' is two jumbled songs saved only by brilliant production, and the title track is a sloppier, slushier 'Watch that man' out of 'Brown sugar' and New Orleans R & B complete with saxes. It's supposed to be some spew of get-it-on desperation, but really sounds pretty tired in spite of some earnest garage Keith Richard guitar work by Bowie. You miss Mick Ronson consistently, but Bowie's playing is somehow oddly satisfactory because it's so like a kid – proud, a bit off, show-offy.

Meanwhile, he's singing more like Jagger than ever, which falls flat in 'Diamond dogs' but makes 'Rebel rebel' one of his best ever: solid guitar hook, and the whole thing remixed from the single to give it the same density as the rest of the album. Great lyrics for once: 'You've torn your dress . . ./Your face is a mess . . . *Hot tramp*, I love you so.' If only Bowie could settle for that kind of simplicity all the time.

I think that Bowie was attempting a sort of futurist *Exile on Main Street* here, trying to put across a similarly hazy, messy brilliance, an equally riveting vibe. I think he failed, and the reason he failed is that *Exile* contained real commitment, a certain authentic last-ditch desperation which Bowie has not really captured since *The Man Who Sold the World*. That doesn't mean, of course, that Bowie fans aren't going to find a way to like this, or that other listeners won't find a certain amount of entertainment in the murk.

Notes

1. The project came to nothing, but Bowie's Orwellian obsession surfaced on *Diamond Dogs*.

FOUR

Let's Dance

LESTER BANGS

Jonny Ray's better whirlpool: The new living Bowie

Creem, January 1975

It wasn't exactly the première of *Le Sacre du Printemps*. Nor was it as opulent as Sly's wedding. More like the opening of a moderately high-energy new discotheque.

What it was was David Bowie's return to the boards in Afro-Anglican drag. Now, as we all know, White hippies and beatniks before them would never have existed had there not been a whole generational subculture with a gnawing yearning to be nothing less than the downest, baddest *niggers* they could possibly be. And of course it was only exploding plastic inevitable that the profound and undeniably seductive ramalama of negritude should ultimately penetrate the kingdom of glitter. Everybody knows that faggots don't like music like David Bowie and The Dolls – that's for teenagers and pathophiles. Faggots like musical comedies and soul music. No gay bars have 'Rebel rebel' on the jukebox; it's all Barry White and the big discotheque beat booming out while everybody dances his or her ass off. I'm not saying that Black and gay cultures have any special mysterious affinity for each other – I'll leave that for profounder explicators, Dr David Reuben, say – what I'm saying is that everybody has been walking around for the last year or so acting like faggots ruled the world, when in actuality it's the *niggers* who control and direct everything, just as it always has been and properly should be. If you don't believe it, just go ask respected social commentator Lou Reed, who wrote and recorded a song for *Sally Can't Dance* called 'I wanna be Black' which unfortunately eventually became an out-take (probably realized he'd revealed too much).

So it was only natural that Bowie would catch on sooner or later. After all, he's no dummy. But he is pretty weird. That's what the kid standing behind us in line was saying as the rioters who got a fin apiece from manager Tony De Fries came storming across the street at the door for the third time: 'I like Bowie's music, but I don't like his personality. He's too weird.' He went on to say that he wanted to buy a copy of The New York Dolls album but didn't because he was afraid somebody would see the cover lying around the house and get the wrong idea. He, like most of this audience, leaned much farther to denims than glitter. In fact, they were downright shabby. In the traditional sense.

Which is something you certainly couldn't say about Bowie. What would *you* think of a guy who came on stage in blackface with white gloves, top hat and tails over Isaac Hayes chains and a dildo with Josephine Baker's face on the head, singing 'Old folks at home' and 'Darktown strutters' ball' in a trilling limey warble masquerading as a down-home bullfrog belch as he waved his hands in the air and twirled his cane while sixty or seventy Michael Jackson lookalike pickaninnies chanted 'Hi-de-ho! Hi-de-ho!' behind him, all massed afront a backdrop of magnolias and sharecropper shacks?

You would think the man had some imagination in his tack, but you can't because he doesn't. At least when it comes to spadedelia. Because he did none of the above. What he did instead was hire himself a tightly professional backup for a weird and utterly incongruous melange of glitter sentiment, negritudinal trappings, cocaine ecstasy and Vegas schmaltz.

We walked in to a scene right out of *God's Trombones* as rendered by The Ohio Players. The stage was covered with Black people – two percussionists (Emir Ksasan, Pablo Rosario), bass (Dennis Davis), the florid Mike Garson on piano, two guitarists (Carlos Alomar and Earl Slick), the ubiquitous Dave Sanborn on sax, and a clutch of 'dancer/ singers', as my informant at MainMan put it: Guy Andressano, Geoffrey MacCormack, Luther Vandross, Anthony Hinton, Ava Cherry, Robin Clark and Diana Sumler. In fairness, not all of these people are Black, but they all of course are artists, and they sho' is funky. Opening with 'Love train', they funkifized the sweet bejesus out of that audience, who talked all the way through their set.

After the opening ensemble whoop-up, Garson plunged into a typically grandiose piano solo, which as always reminded me of the progeny of an unholy shtup between Liberace and Cecil Taylor. There was a loud drum solo which mildly roused the crowd, whose mean age was 17, although the girl in front of me just kept giggling breathily: 'Daaaaaay-vid! Daaaaaayvid! Ooh, when he comes out I'm just gonna . . . *touch* him!' Ava Cherry, a curvaceous Black girl with butch blonde hair, sang soul torch, followed by Luther Vandross (who is fat and much given to Stepin Fetchit rolling and popping of eyes) and one of the other Black girls crooning and making eyes at each other like April Stevens and Nino Tempo playing the Apollo in blackface. Ava and Geoffrey MacCormack, a slender White with black curly hair and black silk shirt who gives off the kind of gay showbiz vibes which insist on shouting from the housetops that he is just *rhapsodically* thrilled over this whole affair (I later thought he was going to stoop to kiss Bowie's toe as part of handing him an acoustic guitar), ran through a sort of Lambert, Hendricks and Ross/Pointer Sisters scat-jazz quicktalk routine. There were two solo vocals: Vandross sang something which I believe was entitled 'Funky music', and MacCormack actually sat on the piano with one knee raised and sang 'Stormy Monday' to the band. Strange change that a lounge act should open for such a self-made anomaly as Bowie? Depends on your perspective, kid.

At this point in my concert scrawlings there is the notation 'fat ass in face', referring to the concert patron who happened to be moving past me at that moment. It seemed as germane as the rest of the action.

Bowie's entrance was hardly as fraught with magisterial pomp as Elvis's *2001* routine: Garson played something that sounded like the theme from *The Edge of Night*, Sanborn cut loose with a fine King Curtis-style sax solo, and the singer/dancers, now mutated into gospel choir, began booming something to the effect that the 'star machine is coming down/We're gonna have a party.'

And here he came, spindling, crackling out: white gleaming face, brilliantined hair cut short and combed back for definite early-fifties effect, grey jacket cut at the waist, blue shirt, tie slightly loosened. It was not quite stunning, although he did manage to radiate tides of nervous energy, accent the nervous, along with enough sweat to float a fleet of gondolas. I peered and peered, trying to catch the ultimate vibe . . . *Johnny Ray*. Johnny Ray on cocaine singing about 1984. Except that his opener was 'John, I'm only dancing', transformed into a driving new arrangement in the most surging PAAAAAARTY style. It worked, which was more than you could say for David's attempts at dancing, which were stiff, jerky – at times he actually began to resemble Jobriath. A parody of a parody, except that Bowie could never really sink to self-parody because he was a parody at his inception.

Still, he worked the crowd in the finest tradition, slapping hands all night, accepting first a glass and then a whole bottle of wine from somebody ('Hope it's got LSD in it,' said a seatmate), running back and forth from one end of the stage to the other, falling to his knees, kneeling down and rocking back and forth in 'Rock 'n' roll with me', indulging varying brands of mikestand English, including at one point a definite parody of a biker stance.

Mugging, grimacing, moving his hands in arcs that might have been sensual if you couldn't *see* him thinking how sensual they were, he had definite flash but there was something brittle about it, as there was something hollow when I saw him two years ago on his first post-Ziggy tour, padding around lightly while Ronson served up all the moves, just as without all the gauche props and stage business the recent live album is a dismal flatulence. Bowie has always made a point of being distant on every level, from the way he treated his audience to the strong-arm tactics used by his goons on photographers. Now he is posing as a get-down dude, as if he had just decided that we won't get fooled again, that there is a we after all, which may or may not be true but is irrelevant to him in any case.

This was particularly apparent in the segment of the show where he sang his new songs, from the upcoming album which he has claimed is the 'most personal' thing he's ever done, blah, blah, and you can see where he's coming from with this one just like you could read those 'I've travelled, I've seen who rules the world, and I'm frightened' pronunciamentos. Bowie's new material seems to be comprised mainly of 'love songs', melodramatic ballads about apparently wholesome teenage boys and girls and David's search for sincerity on this pathetic bitch of an earth. The most memorable, because most characteristic, was 'Young Americans', and of course you couldn't miss the line 'Ain't there one damn song that can make me break down and cry?' Touching, touching, like Johnny Ray coming on as Frankie Laine, except when he would stick one hand in front of his crotch and touch the mike delicately, mutating for himself at least into Tina Turner. He also utilized that stool that Perry Como used to fall off of on the Steve Allen show for one particularly poignant vignette. I prefer Charles Aznavour myself.

Mike Garson kept looking around as if in wonderment, bluefaced with delicate five o'clock shadow and carrying definite Richard Carpenter vibes, gazing reverently at Bowie and rolling his eyes at the band while playing piano so turgid it was downright bouncy. And the singer/dancers all massed like The Mormon Tabernacle Choir in the background, snapping their fingers, jutting their arms and shaking their butts around in perfervid Stoneground/Mad Dogs and Englishmen pep rally.

This show is going to wow them in Vegas, and it certainly didn't do badly in Detroit. But don't be fooled: Bowie is as cold as ever, and if you get off on his particular brand of lunar antibody you may well be disappointed in his latest incarnation, because he's doubling back on himself and it fits about as well as those boxing gloves he had last time out. You don't set yourself up as Mr Sleaze and then come on like Jerry Lewis at the palsy telethon, unless you realize that you are just about as full of ersatz sincerity as Jerry Lewis and might as well ooze it from every pore because your audience doesn't care, they just want you to hit them hard and fast and then come back and hit them again, slightly altered, a little to the right this time. As far as the PAAAAAARTY goes, Bowie has just changed his props: last tour it was boxing gloves, skulls and giant hands, this tour it's Black folk. As far as I'm concerned, if that pastyfaced snaggletoothed little jitterbug doesn't give me an interview pretty soon, I'm going to stop doing him all these favours.

BRUNO STEIN

UFOs, Hitler and David Bowie

Creem, February 1975

'Have you got any metal in your body?' asked the flying saucer man.

'Yeah, I've got one pin,' said David Bowie.

Well, it turned out David was in luck then. If he went to a little town in Missouri at a certain time, he would be able to see in a seemingly empty field a fully equipped flying saucer repair shop at work.

It was one of those fascinating things you learn at a Bowie soirée. This evening the gathering was rather intimate. There was Corinne, David's charming personal secretary, who ducked out early due to exhaustion (although another participant gossiped that she had someone interesting waiting for her in her hotel room).

There was a tired newspaper reporter trying to get a question in edgewise now and then. There was Ava Cherry, the effervescent, razor-thin, husky-voiced Black singer and dancer with white bleached hair who was part of David's backup vocal group on his 'soul' tour. There were three more young Black ladies, members of Ava's 'gang' when she was growing up, whom she invited over now that she was back in her home town for a night.

There was a nice young roadie who had just resigned from David's crew for some mysterious reason, which David wanted to find out

127

about. The roadie had brought along two local friends, a guy and girl, and the guy was the flying saucer man, who had actually seen UFOs, both in flight and on the ground.

And, of course, there was Mr Bowie himself, somewhat tired from the energetic performance he had given to a packed audience less than an hour before. He looked relaxed in a loose-fitting, uncolourful overall outfit, and although his eyes seemed weary and his voice was a bit hoarse, as the conversation twisted and turned among the subjects of music, extraterrestrials and political conspiracies, he gradually grew animated and energetic, jumping up to make a point, stalking around the hotel suite while listening to someone else, dancing while seated on a chair and singing along as he played tapes of his forthcoming soul album.

'I used to work for two guys who put out a UFO magazine in England,' he told the flying saucer man. 'About six years ago. And I made sightings six, seven times a night for about a year, when I was in the observatory.

'We had regular cruises that came over. We knew the 6.15 was coming in and would meet up with another one. And they would be stationary for about half an hour, and then after verifying what they'd been doing that day, they'd shoot off.

'But, I mean, it's what you do with the information. We never used to tell anybody. It was beautifully dissipated when it got to the media. Media control is still based in the main on cultural manipulation. It's just so easy to do. When you set up one set of objectives toward the public and you've given them a certain definition for each code word, you hit them with the various code words and they're not going to believe anything if you don't want them to.

'That's how the Mayans were ruling South America thousands of years ago. That's what the media is. That's how it works. The Mayan calendar: they could get the crowds to go out and crucify somebody merely by giving them a certain definition, two or three words, primed in terms such that they could tell what day the people would react and how they would react . . . I sound like a subversive.'

The reporter protested that he knew the media all too well and they weren't organized enough to carry off any kind of conspiracy or manipulation.

'It's seemingly disorganized,' replied David. 'It's not disorganized, because I've been in the media as well. I used to be a visualizer for an advertising agency, and I know exactly what – I mean the advertising agencies that sell us, they are killers, man. Those guys, they can sell anybody anything. And not just products. If you think agencies are just out to sell products, you're naive. They're powerful for other reasons. A lot of those agencies are responsible for a lot of things they shouldn't be responsible for. They're dealing with lives, those ad agencies.'

Somehow, to make a point about how humans are all manipulated, David brought up Hitler's Germany and said that Hitler, too, was controlled. He wasn't really the man in charge. The reporter asked how was that possible when Hitler's personal military mismanagement probably cost the Germans the war.

'Oh he was a terrible military strategist,' said David, 'the world's worst, but his overall objective was very good, and he was a marvellous morale booster. I mean, he was a perfect figurehead. And I'm sure that he was just part of it, that he was used . . . He was a nut and everybody knew he was a nut. They're not gonna let him run the country.'

But what about losing the war, asked the reporter. Was that part of the plan too?

'No, that's not what I said,' said David, exasperated. 'I said I don't believe that he was the dictatorial, omnipotent leader that he's been taken for.'

At this point, the flying saucer man broke in to try and help put things in perspective. 'I think that you have to look at it as the same thing as your band,' he said to David. 'You'll sing, out of a zillion notes, you'll sing X amount. But you are the figurehead of the band. You're the main man. Hitler was the main man of his entourage.'

David seemed somewhat taken aback at being put in the same category as Hitler. 'Yes . . . well. I'm the leader, the apparent organizer and whatnot, but the product which takes place is a contributed product, and responsibility lies with the whole lot, and the direction is on many shoulders.'

'The responsibility lies with you,' maintained the flying saucer man, sounding like a Nuremberg prosecutor.

'No it doesn't,' David protested. 'Once you get out there and start working actively, the responsibility's on everybody's shoulders.'

'Yes, but with the public—' began the saucer man.

'Exactly!' interrupted David. 'That's what I'm saying, man. It looks like Hitler but the actual effect was produced by a number of people, all working their own strategies of where it was going to go.'

At this point the tension suddenly broke. David and everyone in the room broke into laughter at the seriousness with which a rock-and-roll star and some acquaintances of one evening were presuming to figure out the way the world ran. Everyone lightened up, and David put on tapes of the new album on an elaborate studio tape deck that RCA had delivered to his suite. Ava Cherry sang her parts, and David sang his, along with the tape, which was full of exciting soul-type music, taking David a step farther in the direction he started on the *David Live* album.

After listening to four numbers, Ava and her girlfriends persuaded David to leave with them. Ava knew a millionaire who lived not far away in a modernistic mansion full of strange delights. David gulped down another cup of coffee, with cream and sugar, put on a striking green coat – it looked like mohair – and followed them out of the suite.

It was 2.30 am, and the sluggish night crew of the small but elegant hotel barely looked up as the red-haired rock star and four giggling Black girls made their way through the lobby to the waiting limousine.

LESTER BANGS

Chicken head comes home to roost

Creem, April 1976

It's tough having heroes. It's the hardest thing in the world. It's harder than being a hero. Heroes are generally expected to produce something or other to reconfirm their mandarin-fingered clinch on the hot buns of the bitch muse, which sometimes comes closer to resembling a set of clawmarks running down and off the edge of a shale precipice. At sunset, even. And that's no office party, kiddo.

But hero-worshippers (fans) must live with the continually confirmed dread of hero-slippage and humiliating personal compromises in your standards and plain good sense about, oh, two to three weeks after the new LP masterwork first hits our turntables.

A very great man (I think it was The Isley Brothers) once said that the real bottom line truism re life on this planet is that it is merely a process of sequential disappointments. So there's no reason even to romanticize your betrayals. Just paying dues, kid. I get burned, therefore I exist. No words in the history of the rock poetic genre, from Dylan to Bernie Taupin, ever said it better than Sandy Posey's pithy catalogue in 'Born a woman': 'Born to be stepped on, lied to, cheated and treated like dirt.' And are we not all in some sense women, the niggers of the world according to contemporary social commentators (I tried to get a call through to Toynbee to confirm this like a good journalist but the bastard had the nerve to fucking *die* in the same week, *my* week!)?

Yes, we are. A great many David Bowie fans felt burned, turned into veritable women (de-virilized, as Pope Paul would have it) when David released *Young Americans*. Why? Because, interestingly enough, they thought David was trying to turn *himself* into a nigger. I was not, however, one of these people.

Now, as any faithful reader of *Creem* magazine is probably aware, David Bowie has never been my hero. I always thought all that Ziggy Stardust homo-from-Aldebaran business was a crock of shit, especially coming from a guy who wouldn't even get in a goddam airplane. I thought he wrote the absolute worst lyrics I had ever heard from a major pop figure with the exception of Bernie Taupin; lines like 'Time takes a cigarette and puts it in your mouth' delivered with a face so straight it seemed like it would crack at a spontaneous word or gesture, seemed to me merely gauche. As for his music, he was as accomplished an eclectician (aka thief) as Elton John, which means that though occasionally deposited on stage after seemingly being dipped in vats of green slime and pursued by Venusian crab boys, he had Showbiz Pro written all over him. A façade as brittle as it was icy, which I guess means that it was bound to crack or thaw, and whatever real artistic potency lay beneath would have to stand or evaporate.

Crack Bowie did, in the last year or so, and the result was *Young Americans*. It was not an album beloved of trad Bowiephiles, but for somebody like your reviewer, who never put any chips on the old chickenhead anyway, it was a perfectly acceptable piece of highly listenable product. More than that, in fact – it was a highly personal musical statement disguised as a shameless fling at the disco market, the drag perhaps utilized as an emotional red herring: *Young Americans* wasn't Bowie dilettanting around with soul music, it was the bridge between melancholy and outright depression, an honest statement from a deeply troubled, mentally shattered individual who even managed, for the most part, to skirt self-pity. Like many of his peers, Bowie has cracked – and for him it was good, because it made him cut the bullshit. *Young Americans* was his first human album since *Hunky Dory*, and in my opinion the best record he ever put out.

Till now. The first things to be said about *Station to Station* are that it sounds like he's got a real live band again (even if star guitarist Earl Slick reportedly split between the sessions and the new tour), and that this is not a disco album either (though that's what the trades, and doubtless a lot of other people, are going to write it off as) but an honest attempt by a talented artist to take elements of rock, soul music

131

and his own idiosyncratic and occasionally pompous showtune/camp predilections and rework this seemingly contradictory melange of styles into something new and powerful that doesn't have to cop either futuristic attitudes or licks from Anthony Newley and The Velvet Underground because he's found his own voice at last.

This is the first Bowie album without a lyric sheet, and I'm glad, because aside from reservations voiced above I've always agreed with Fats Domino that it's more fun to figure them out for yourself. The first line on the album is the worst: 'The return of the thin white duke/ Throwing darts in lovers' eyes.' Somehow, back in Rock Critics' Training School, when they told me about 'pop poetry', I didn't and still don't think that they were talking about this, which is not only pretentious and mildly unpleasant, but I am currently wrestling with a terrible paranoia that this is Bowie talking about himself. I have a nightmare vision in my mind of him opening the set on his new tour by striding out on stage slowly, with a pained look in his eyes and one spotlight following him, mouthing these words. And, quite frankly, the idea terrifies me. Because if it's true, it means he's still as big an idiot as he used to be and needs a little more cocaine to straighten him out.

But I'm really not worried. Because you can always ignore the lyrics if you want, since this is one of the best *guitar* albums since *Rock 'n' Roll Animal*, it has a wail and throb that won't let up and rolls roughshod over the words. So who gives a shit what 'TVC 15' means, it's a great piece of rock-and-roll. And when words do appear out of the instrumental propulsion like swimmers caught in a rip tide not sure whether they wanna call for the lifeguard or just enjoy it, well, at those moments, dear reader, I know you're not gonna believe this but *those words usually make sense*! In fact, in (for Bowie) relatively simple, unconvoluted language, they bespeak a transition from the deep depression of the best of *Young Americans* (and here's a case of scientific proof that depression should never be knocked or avoided, it's a means to an end of division from self, aka remission) to a beautiful, swelling, intensely romantic melancholy in which the divided consciousness may not only have kissed and made up with itself but even managed to begin the leap towards *recognizing that other human beings actually exist*! And can be loved for something besides the extent to which they feed themselves to the artist's narcissism.

Specific examples of this remission are not hard to come by: lines like 'Don't have to question everything in heaven or hell', along with the melodic mood that is their context, can be intensely moving according to *your* mood, and it doesn't even matter that 'Wild is the wind' is an old Dmitri Tiomkin movie theme – even if Bowie did it for camp reasons and to indulge a personal idiosyncrasy, it doesn't sound like he did, it sounds right with the rest of the album.

Which is so impressive, such a great rocker and so promising of durability even exceeding *Young Americans*, that I'm going to go out on a limb and say that I think that Bowie has finally produced his (first) masterpiece. To hell with *Ziggy Stardust*, which amounted to starring Judy Garland in *The Reluctant Astronaut*, fuck trying to be George Orwell and William Burroughs when you've only read half of *Nova Express* – this and *Young Americans* are the first albums he's made which don't sound like scams. Bowie has dropped his pretensions, or most of them at any rate, and in doing that I believe he's finally become an artist instead of a poseur, style collector and (admittedly always great, excepting *Raw Power*) producer. He'll still never have a shot at becoming my hero, because he's neither funny nor Black enough, but I can hardly wait to hear what he's going to have to say next.

JEAN ROOK

Waiting for Bowie – and finding a genius who insists he's really a clown

Daily Express, 5 May 1976

Interviewing David Bowie is a scarring experience. To showbiz, he is a super-planet. To rock, a messiah. To his fans, a god. To his pensioned Beckenham mother, an ungrateful little rotter who doesn't even send her postcards from California.

To the nervous, Bowie is sinister. A leader of troops of youths who wear his thirties suits and slicked-back hair like uniforms. The nearest the world could come to a Fourth Reich. Waiting for him is the worst. It makes you sweat, like Godot. And his bodyguard of what look like storm-troopers in black leather pants doesn't help.

Physically, Bowie is not disappointing. He looks terribly ill. Thin as a stick insect. And corpse pale as if his life blood had all run up into his flaming hair. Did Bowie say that Britain needs a fascist Prime Minister and that, at 28, he is the man to fit the goose-stepping boots? Bowie would blush if he could spare the blood.

'If I said it – and I've a terrible feeling I did say something like it to a Stockholm journalist who kept asking me political questions – I'm astounded anyone could believe it. I have to keep reading it to believe it myself. I'm not sinister. I'm not a great force – Well, not that sort of force. I don't stand up in cars waving to people because I think I'm Hitler. I stand up in my car waving to fans – I don't write the captions under the picture.'

So long as it's publicity, does it matter?

'Yes, it does. It upsets me. Strong I may be. Arrogant I may be. Sinister I'm not.'

Then why look it?

'How do I look?'

Like Dracula, Berenice, a zombie or an emaciated Marlon Brando playing a Hitler youth.

'No, no, no' – his still faintly Brixtonian voice snaps, and when he slaps a thigh, as thin as your wrist, you're scared it will be the next to go. 'I'm Pierrot. I'm Everyman. What I'm doing is theatre, and only theatre. All this business about me being able to raise 7000 of my troops at the Empire Pool by raising one hand is a load of rubbish. In the first place the audience is British, and since when will the Brits stand for that? What you see on stage isn't sinister. It's pure clown. I'm using myself as a canvas and trying to paint the truth of our time on it. The white face, the baggy pants – they're Pierrot, the eternal clown putting over the great sadness of 1976.' He asks if I remember him as Ziggy Stardust. Who could forget him in high heels, a scarlet bottle-brush hair-do, one chandelier ear-ring, and more Max Factor than Marilyn Monroe?

'Ziggy was putting over the bizarre in our time. Now Bowie's putting over the sadness.'

If you hadn't seen – and heard – Bowie perform, you'd accuse him of swotting up the lyrical phrases for the interview.

In fact Bowie is a poet, possibly a modern-day genius.

What W. B. Yeats – referring to an Irish dustman – called 'living poetry' flows from his death-pale lips (pancake make-up, and not, thank God, leukaemia).

He describes his one ear-ring, Ziggy Stardust period as 'looking like a cross between Nijinsky and Woolworth's' without self-consciousness of his own cleverness. The words his mother wouldn't understand pour naturally out of him. Like Dylan Thomasian chat.

This would bring us to the rumoured feud with his mother, if I can get up the guts to ask the question that nearly stopped *The Russell Harty Show* when Harty had the nerve to ask it.

'What would you like to say about your mother?' I asked of the millionaire whom his mother claims leaves her to languish on an £11.50 a week pension. The ice blue-green-grey eyes that froze Russell Harty to his chair, swivelling with terror, meet mine. The bones in the aesthetic face are cold.

'Nothing,' Bowie said.

By comparison, asking about his off-beat sex life would seem safe. Bowie has, at various times, declared himself all things to all women. Or men, without embarrassment. His wife Angie has spoken freely of free love as and when it comes. The fact remains that the Bowies' seven-year itchless marriage has lasted. Yesterday, they were together at his secret London hide-out – Angie glamorous, thinner even than he is, with ginger eye make-up to match his hair, and looking incestuously like his twin sister. Asked if she expects to be married to the man she seldom sees in ten years' time, she unhesitatingly says yes. When Bowie says, of her, 'How could I ever let go of this divine being?', he means it.

All this, added to their surrealistic sex views, if not sex life, should be confusing to their 5-year-old son Zowie, but somehow isn't. What do you tell a kindergarten child about his red-haired, white-faced, mascara'd father? 'That that's the way Daddy makes his money,' said Bowie. When Bowie becomes David Jones, proud father and talks of his son's pony riding and French lessons, his image cracks up. Even the bones in the incredibly beautiful and terrifyingly unisex face soften.

'Are you telling me Bowie is just another doting parent at heart?' I said.

'Yes, yes, it's all there – of course it is,' Bowie smiles, and the Brixton-born Jones boy comes through. Looking back on 'shy, quiet' David Jones, how does David Bowie see him?

'I liked him. I still like him if I could only get in touch with him,' said Bowie, who has an unnerving habit of talking about himself as if he were in the past. 'We've been apart for a long time, and I've so many more changes to make. Jones is real. Bowie isn't real. There's nothing real about standing up in front of 7000 people. I suppose that doing that is a bit sinister when you think about it but, if it is, the only person I brainwash and scare stiff is myself.'

The bodyguard is looking nervous. I click my notebook and shake the leader's skeletal hand. I'm surprised – and even game to tell his mother – that I've found David Bowie one of the most mystical, exquisite, thoroughly odd and totally nice people I've ever met.

'Don't be surprised,' said Bowie the god, standing up and looking like David Jones in need of a good feed. 'After all, it *is* only rock-and-roll.'

DEREK JEWELL
Bowie and Bassey
Sunday Times, 9 May 1976

Shirley Bassey and David Bowie on successive nights. So contrasting, yet so similar. She a peach in maturity; he fragile as a stick insect, and just as elusive to discern, define, deny. Similar? Certainly. Both are children of our time, climbing out of Tiger Bay and Brixton, and so, enabling audiences to identify with them, are archetypal popular music idols.

She feeds middle-aged fantasy, epitomized in beautiful songs like 'Yesterday when we were young'. He encourages a younger army, bored with their external characters, to seek within themselves alternative egos; as artist-hero, he kills off his past roles – Ziggy Stardust, spaceman, bisexualist, rebel – like clockwork, with only the orange coxcomb of his hair for continuity. His disciples dutifully ape him.

Both, too, are beyond normal criticism, defying purely musical assessment. Bassey over-sings (but thrillingly) and cannot perform except with total commitment. Bowie over-plays (but rivetingly) and demands attention by his extravagant idiosyncrasy, which is as professionally adamantine as hers. She devours the audience; he incites it. Each earthquakingly demonstrates the power of personality.

Shirley Bassey sang, in all, to 25,000 at the Albert Hall last week. Tuesday, second house, was an outstanding triumph. Standing ovation after standing ovation, the emotion aroused by her beauty and her passionate singing flooding the arena. She is at her peak. She still goes over the top sometimes, which is Bassey magically being herself, but she knows more about light and shade than ever. She whispers the final note of 'The way we were'; within 'Something', the orchestration leaves momentary sounds of silence. Her world conquests are richly earned.

David Bowie entertained 50,000 at Wembley. On Monday, after a boring surrealistic movie, greeted with cynical derision, his casual entry was spellbinding. He has murdered Ziggy, appearing glitterless in plain black trousers, waistcoat and white shirt, looking like a refugee from Isherwood's Berlin cabarets. The lighting, with Bowie trapped in harsh white cross-beams, was rock's most brilliantly theatrical effect. He sang 14 songs, and when the hundreds of mini-Bowies leapt on seats, miming every gesture, he played with them, smiling. He's rejected soft orchestrations (as on 'Space oddity') for a thunderous R & B backing, which is tiresomely flairless. It ruined 'Stay', the best of his *Station to Station* album. But Bowie's personal performance was monstrously successful, more of a charged-up crooner than an Alice Cooper rival.

Is he sinister? There are, undeniably, visual Nuremberg overtones. Bowie-obsessiveness is sterile. But mostly, I suspect, he's the prisoner of his own publicity, his need to keep changing his image. Musically, he's limited as yet. It's where he ends up that matters. Meantime his own lyric, 'Fame, bully for you, chilly for me, gotta get a raincheck on pain', may yet be his epitaph.

PAULINE KAEL

Notes on evolving heroes, morals, audiences*

New Yorker, 8 November 1976

Nicolas Roeg's *The Man Who Fell to Earth*, which stars David Bowie, is *The Little Prince* for young adults; the hero, a stranger on earth, is purity made erotic. He doesn't have a human sex drive; he isn't even equipped for it – naked, he's as devoid of sex differentiation as a child in sleepers. (He seems to be the first movie hero to have had his crotch airbrushed.) Yet there's true insolence in Bowie's lesbian-Christ leering, and his forlorn, limp manner and chalky pallor are alluringly tainted. Lighted like the woman of mystery in thirties movies, he's the most romantic figure in recent pictures – the modern version of the James Dean lost-boy myth. Nicolas Roeg has a talent for eerily easy, soft, ambiguous sex – for the sexiness of passivity. In his *Don't Look Now*, Donald Sutherland practically oozed passivity – which was the only interesting quality he had. And at the beginning of *The Man Who Fell to Earth* (which was shot in this country with an American cast except for Bowie), when the stranger splashes down in a lake in the Southwest and drinks water like a vampire gulping down his lifeblood, one is drawn in, fascinated by the obliqueness and by the promise of an erotic sci-fi story. It is and it isn't. The stranger, though non-human, has visions of the wife and kiddies he has left – an old-

* Excerpted from a longer article.

fashioned nuclear family on the planet Anthea. He has come to earth to obtain the water that will save his people, who are dying from drought, but he is corrupted, is distracted from his mission, and then is so damaged that he cannot return. Although Roeg and his screenwriter, Paul Mayersberg, pack layers of tragic political allegory into *The Man Who Fell to Earth*, none of the layers is very strong, or even very clear. The plot, about big-business machinations, is so uninvolving that one watches Bowie traipsing around – looking like Katharine Hepburn in her transvestite role in *Sylvia Scarlett* – and either tunes out or allows the film, with its perverse pathos, to become a sci-fi framework for a sex-role confusion fantasy. The wilted solitary stranger who is better than we are and yet falls prey to our corrupt human estate can be said to represent everyone who feels misunderstood, everyone who feels sexually immature or 'different', everyone who has lost his way, everyone who has failed his holy family, and so the film is a gigantic launching-pad for anything that viewers want to drift to.

A former cinematographer, Roeg has more visual strategies than almost any director one can think of. He can charge a desolate landscape so that it seems ominously alive, familiar yet only half recognizable, and he photographs skyscrapers with such lyric glitter that the United States seems to be showing off for him (the better to be despoiled). The people pass through, floating, using the country without seeing its beauty. Roeg's cutting can create a magical feeling of waste and evil, but at other times his Marienbadish jumpiness is just trickery he can't resist. In *The Man Who Fell to Earth*, the unease and sense of disconnectedness between characters also disconnect us. Roeg teases us with a malaise that he then moralizes about. His effects stay on the surface; they become off-puttingly abstract, and his lyricism goes sentimental – as most other Christ movies do. In *Blow-Up* and *The Passenger*, Antonioni showed a talent (and a propensity) for mystification; it would be a present to audiences if just once he would use his talent frivolously – if, instead of his usual opaque metaphysical mystery, he'd make a simple trashy mystery, preferably in those *Réalités* travel spots he's drawn to. And it would be a blessing if Nicolas Roeg – perhaps the most visually seductive of directors, a man who can make impotence sexy – turned himself loose on the romance of waste.

Bowie's self-mocking androgyny is not a quality that one associates with the heroes of imperial nations. Imperial movie heroes are just about gone, and even much of what comes out on the American screen as sexism isn't necessarily the result of conviction; it may be the sexist result of simple convenience. In the movies or on television, the two cops in the police car don't have to think about each other. When a cop-hero's partner is shot, it's supposed to be worse than anything, but the reason it's worse then anything is always explained *after* he's been shot. Then the survivor – let's call him Frank – explains that Jim took the bullet for him, that Jim was the one Frank spent more time with than anyone else. And Frank's wife can say, 'Frank and Jim were more married than we are' – and she says it sympathetically. She understands. The theme of mateship is such a clean, visible bond. It doesn't have the hidden traps of the relationship between men and women, or between lovers of the same sex. In a number of movies, the actors playing the two cops seem palpably embarrassed by the notion that women are those creatures who come into the story for a minute and you jump them. Some are embarrassed that that's all you do with them; others are relieved that that's all you have to do – because if there's anything more it may involve the problem of what men are supposed to be in relation to women.

FIVE

Hang On To Yourself

ERIC TAMM

Soul robots: Eno and Fripp with Bowie

Every note obscures another.   Brian Eno

In 1979, former King Crimson guitarist Robert Fripp expounded on what he perceived as the similarities between himself, David Bowie and Brian Eno. This trio of rock renegades, according to Fripp, were of similar age and 'more or less working-class backgrounds'. They were all keen self-promoters. But at the same time, 'Each of us finds it difficult to accept the responsibility of having feelings. So we tend toward cerebration and bodily involvement rather than the exposure of one's feelings.'

On rare occasions, the music that's innovative is the same music that sells. Haydn and Stravinsky were successful in projecting their ideas to the acclaim of wide international audiences; Bach and Bartók had more difficulty gaining the acceptance of their contemporaries outside an inner circle of devotees. The late 1970s were one of those special eras, when – however briefly, and limited to specific local geographical regions in the Western world – the entrenched border-lines between low art and high art, between the demands of the market-place and those of aesthetic conscience, seemed to shimmer and vanish. Bowie, Fripp and Eno were at the forefront of this ferment, pushing back boundaries, goading each other – and their audiences – into taking musical and conceptual chances, carrying the flag for rock as a serious art form. Not *too* serious, though: they all despised the pretension, bombast and pathetic *Weltschmerz* of the classic/gothic rock of the early 1970s – even though Fripp, through King Crimson, had been among the leaders of that ill-fated charge of the heavy

143

brigade, and Bowie and Eno, as devoted, though by nature ephemeral glitter rockers, had cheered heartily from the sidelines.

Those days gone by, in the late seventies, Brian Eno was pioneering a new, soft-edged style he called 'ambient'. He was using synthesizers to make music that was luscious, beautiful, slow, tantalizing and mesmerizingly repetitive, unfolding elusively like mist – music you could listen to at the level of pure listening, but which nevertheless didn't shout for attention. Ambient music was designed to tint the atmosphere with sharp intelligence and classical repose.

At that time, Fripp's mind had been blown by years of gruelling touring and studio work with a kaleidoscopically changing King Crimson. Having put out albums containing both soaring visions and noodling inanities, having established new standards for both thinking persons' rock and endlessly tedious one-chord jams, he had gone on a three-year retreat from the music industry, undertaking a deep inner journey and making an intensive study of the living philosophy of Gurdjieff as transmitted through the British teacher John Bennett. In 1977 he was ready for something new, but didn't yet know quite what it would be.

Fripp and Eno had already collaborated extensively: they'd recorded the epochal minimalist/raga/rock manifesto *No Pussyfooting* in Eno's home studio in 1972, worked on Eno's solo rock albums and done a mini-tour of Europe. Throughout their amicable work together, Eno played the idiot savant to Fripp's intellectual virtuoso.

In gross commercial terms, Bowie was by far the biggest star of the three, but by 1977, following a string of successes, he had hit a wall. According to Eno, Bowie was interested in working with him because he had found that his own creative ideas were running out. Bowie had heard Eno's *Another Green World* (1975), and 'saw in that an approach he liked'. *Another Green World* was Eno's progressive rock masterpiece and a turning point in his own career and compositional output. On side one of the album, he had carried the timbral and textural manipulations of his previous solo work to new heights, taking the raw forms of rock music and forging out of them something uncannily strange, distant and compelling, like robots playing soul music. On side two he had crafted a set of insinuating, sometimes virtually pulseless pieces that hinted strongly at the ambient style yet to be born, but were not without their roots in the erotic pulsations of rock.

Eno had admired Bowie's *Station to Station* (1976) and accepted Bowie's invitation to work together. In their collaborations on three studio albums between 1977 and 1979 – *Low*, *"Heroes"* and *Lodger* – Eno was able to nudge Bowie beyond the limits of rock. Fripp, who attended some of the sessions and added a few lacerating guitar lines, played a less than central role in the proceedings, but for his part found the musical chemistry a powerful tonic: soon after the *"Heroes"* sessions, Fripp stormed back into the battleground of musical commerce with a rejuvenated attitude and a reformulated creative agenda.

Bowie and Eno got together at Conny Plank's studio in Cologne and set about making *Low*, which was released in 1977. *Low* contains 11 tracks; Eno is listed as co-composer with Bowie on only one of them, 'Warszawa', but he was an active contributor throughout the sessions.

Given the immediate background, and the content of the album, it makes sense to view *Low* as Bowie's *Another Green World*. Like Eno, he opted for a double-fisted, two-sided approach to the organization of the album as a whole, with the more outwardly conventional rock songs on the first side and the more experimental instrumentals on the second. If anything, Bowie outdid Eno with the segregational approach: the pieces are all either strictly rock or non-rock, with little Enoesque exploration of the no-man's-land between.

Throughout side two of *Low* – the non-rock, experimental, mostly instrumental side – Eno's musical personality is distinctly evident in an array of metallic and grating sounds, primitive drum machine backings, guitar 'treatments' and sweeping, string-like synthesizer lines. Bowie was paying heed to Eno's input but, all things considered, the music still seems much more Bowie than Eno. Bowie has always had a penchant for strange harmonic twists of a kind Eno, benignly relentless in his diatonicism, tends to avoid. Moreover, Bowie's compositions are considerably more 'active' in traditional terms, if not a great deal more linear in a teleological sense, than Eno's: they contain more simultaneous, active melodic lines, more counterpoint, more harmonic activity and a greater density of events, resulting in a fatter, busier sound texture. *Low* also features such typical Bowieisms as saxophone and octave-doubled melodies.

Eno made the instrumental tracks for 'Warszawa' by himself in the studio while Bowie was away for two days. Upon returning, Bowie added the vocals. 'Warszawa' is a slow, severe, frightening piece based on piano drones, organ-like synthesizer and flute-mellotron tones that set up successions of harmonies quite uncharacteristic of Eno's solo work. After several minutes, Bowie's voice enters, singing indecipherable words or vocalizations to simple melodies. The whole piece is carefully *composed* – that is, non-improvised – with a great deal of harmonic and structural pre-planning, and represents a case study in the influence of Bowie, with his more active compositional style, on Eno.

The whole matter of authorship is complicated in collaborations of this sort. When there is no neat division of roles (composer, arranger, instrumentalist, producer) and several people are active in all these spheres at once, then whose piece it actually is may boil down to who's paying for the studio time, as Eno has suggested. Complex authorial situations arise in many Bowie/Eno tracks from this period. For example, 'Art decade', the composition of which is credited to Bowie, is a piece Eno has claimed responsibility for saving from the out-take pile:

> That started off as a little tune that he [Bowie] played on the piano. Actually, we both played it because it was for four hands, and when we'd finished it he didn't like it very much and sort of forgot about it. But as it happened, during the two days he was gone I . . . dug that out to see if I could do anything with it. I put all those instruments on top of what we had, and then he liked it and realized there was hope for it, and he worked on top of that, adding more instruments.

On numerous occasions and with manifest relish, Fripp has told the story of how, in late July 1977, David Bowie and Brian Eno coaxed him out of contemplative quiescence. One version of the tale goes like this:

> I was in New York and I got a phone call on Saturday night: 'Hello, it's Brian. I'm here in Berlin with David. Hold on, I'll hand you over.' So Mr B came on the line and said, 'We tried playing guitars ourselves; it's not working. Do you think you can come in and play some burning rock-and-roll guitar?' I said, 'Well, I haven't really played guitar for three years . . . but I'll have a go!'

At Bowie's *"Heroes"* sessions in Berlin, Fripp was able, after a long hiatus, to open up musically once again. He enjoyed the freedom Bowie gave him: Bowie would roll a tape he and Eno had been working on and Fripp would simply ad lib straight over the top, with little or no premeditation or planning. The first song on which Fripp played was 'Beauty and the beast', the album's opener, and Fripp describes his contribution as a 'creative high spot' for him: 'I had an opportunity to be what I was with a guitar.' Run through Eno's 'sky saw' treatments, which lend them a sort of digital-age wah-wah sonority, Fripp's licks on 'Beauty and the beast' seethe with educated rock primitivism. Too bad they weren't mixed louder.

Fripp later laid down guitar lines on Bowie's 'Scary monsters' and 'Fashion'. In 1987 he recalled that:

> The solo on Bowie's 'Fashion' happened at 10.30 in the morning after a long drive back from Leeds gigging with the League of Gentlemen. There's nothing you feel less like in the world than turning out a burning solo – fiery rock-and-roll at 10.30 in the morning – just out of a truck. But it doesn't matter much how you feel, you just get on with it.

"Heroes" occupies a special place in Bowie's musical development. Side two in particular shows the chameleon-like poseur at the height of his *musical* experimentation – 'Sense of doubt', 'Moss garden' and 'Neuköln' being among the most *compositionally* interesting instrumentals he has ever produced. Rock music is only partially about musical composition, of course – to use a current phrase, rock is a form in which 'image is everything' – and in subsequent work Bowie was to retreat to more familiar musical territory.

On *"Heroes"*, Eno is listed as being responsible for synthesizers, keyboards and guitar treatments, and is credited as co-composer of four pieces. One is the title track, a rock anthem whose theme – 'We can be heroes . . . just for one day' recalls both Andy Warhol's pop proverb that 'Everyone will be famous for fifteen minutes' and the transsexual character in Lou Reed's 'Walk on the wild side' who 'thought she was James Dean for a day'.

'*"Heroes"*' (the song) possesses a unique sonic character whose identity derives largely from Fripp and Eno's contributions: we hear a magisterially restrained Fripp, the awesomely proficient guitarist making maximum use of a minimal handful of notes, laying down a soul-wrenching, melancholy obligato; and the catalytic *Klangmeister* Eno, whose synthesizer noises sound something like the chugging of an interstellar freight train. Against these hypnotic auditory elements, Bowie's vocal posturings unfold poignantly in all their desperate glory.

Eno was heavily involved in the production of *"Heroes"*, but as with *Low* – side one is again all rock, having a sort of futuristic party-dance atmosphere that Eno's own albums lack. Side two opens and closes with rock numbers, but in between are three instrumental collaborations, leading directly into one another without breaks, on which Eno's influence is palpable.

To discuss these instrumentals, we must delve into one of Eno's most curious inventions, the *Oblique Strategies*, subtitled *Over One Hundred Worthwhile Dilemmas*. A deck of oracle cards which Eno developed and published with his painter friend Peter Schmidt, *Oblique Strategies* is modelled philosophically on the ancient Chinese *I Ching* or *Book of Changes*. While still at art school in the mid-sixties, Eno had taken to formulating aphorisms as aids to the creative process. Each terse proverb was designed to frame a work-in-progress in a fresh perspective when the artist got bogged down in details, unable to maintain a sense of creative options. During the early 1970s, when he was working with Roxy Music, Eno wrote down his aphorisms on cards and placed them in various locations around the recording studio. Random selection of a card and reflection on its message often provided fresh and unexpected resolution of a musical quandary.

These cards, and similar ones authored by Schmidt, evolved into the *Oblique Strategies*, packaged in a handsome black box and sold in limited editions.

The short messages on the cards are varied, evocative and often intentionally cryptic. Some examples, randomly chosen from the deck: 'Would anybody want it?' 'Go slowly all the way round the outside.' 'Don't be afraid of things because they're easy to do.' 'Only a part, not the whole.' 'Retrace your steps.' 'Disconnect from desire.' 'You are an engineer.' 'Turn it upside down.' 'Do we need holes?' 'Is it finished?' 'Don't break the silence.' 'What are you really thinking about just now?' Bowie and Eno used the deck of *Oblique Strategies* extensively in the making of *"Heroes"* and, according to Eno, 'both [of us] worked on all the pieces all the time – almost taking turns.'

'Sense of doubt', one of the Bowie/Eno instrumentals on side two of *"Heroes"*, is a horrific, bleak soundscape with an ominously recurring, deep, slow C, B, B-flat, A piano motif under filtered white-noise swooshings and isolated synthesizer chords in A minor, punctuated occasionally by an evil grating sound that can only be described as the yawn of the dead. When they began work on 'Sense of doubt', Bowie and Eno each pulled out an *Oblique Strategy* card and kept it a secret from the other. As Eno described it:

> It was like a game. We took turns working on it; he'd do one overdub and I'd do the next. The idea was that each was to observe his *Oblique Strategy* as closely as he could. And as it turned out they were entirely opposed to one another. Effectively mine said, 'Try to make everything as similar as possible.' . . . and his said, 'Emphasize differences.'

'Sense of doubt' leads into 'Moss garden', a piece in Eno's full-blown ambient style featuring continuous synthesizer chords, a high jet-plane sound that repeatedly careens across the field of hearing and a koto-like stringed instrument providing plucked melodic fragments. 'Moss garden' revolves around two chords, F-sharp major and G-sharp major, implying but never quite declaiming a tonic of C-sharp.

'Neuköln' is in something like a German expressionist version of the ambient style: dissonant, diminished chords evoking a movie-organ atmosphere, saxophone melodies suggesting gangster life, and some harsh water-like sounds. Again, Eno alone would not – perhaps could not – have come up with a chord sequence like this: the back-and-forth influence is total.

After the delightful, thought-provoking, innovative excursions of *Low* and *"Heroes"*, *Lodger* (1979), the final Bowie/Eno collaboration, shows Bowie retreating into well-worn musical forms. From a purely musical point of view the album is considerably less interesting, stimulating and challenging than the first two. *Lodger* contains merely rock, more rock, and rock until you drop – without so much as a ballad to break up the page. Long stretches of the album sound unedited, as if Bowie did not know when to stop, what to subtract from the frantic mix. Of *Lodger*'s ten tracks, Eno co-wrote six, and is listed in the album credits as providing 'ambient drone', 'prepared piano and cricket menace', synthesizers and guitar treatments, 'horse trumpets', 'Eroica horn' and piano.

Production has always been Eno's strong suit, but *Lodger* is over-produced: in the continuous assault of the rock frenetics, Eno's subtle treatments wind up getting buried. As Eno was later to say, a whole world can be electronically extracted from a single sound; but such delicate wonders are easily lost if the sound input itself – and the surroundings in which it appears – are too ferocious, too complicated. As they made *Lodger*, Eno and Bowie 'argued quite a lot about what was going to happen' on particular tracks, and Eno thought the resolutions were compromises in many cases: 'It started off extremely promising and quite revolutionary and it didn't seem to quite end that way.'[1]

LORNE MURDOCH
Hitting an all-time Low

The three albums of Bowie's 'Berlin trilogy' were not among his most successful in commercial terms, but, although only *"Heroes"* met with widespread critical favour at the time, its predecessor, *Low*, has come to be regarded by many as Bowie's finest achievement.

SPEED OF LIFE

From April 1974 to March 1976 Bowie lived in the USA, first in New York, then in Los Angeles. Some commentators portray these months as an artistic descent (into mainstream dance music) and a physical and spiritual nightmare (worsened by drug abuse and the slide into litigation). Freed from MainMan's protective bubble of hype, Bowie's next few years can be seen as a period of regeneration and purification, an embracing of Old World culture and experimental music – a time of generosity and collaboration.

It is tempting to make this contrast, but the reality is less cut and dried. On the one hand, the process of re-evaluation had begun long before Bowie boarded the boat for Europe. The sequence of artistic, personal and professional changes had commenced within six months of arriving in the States. On the other, it was only after many months on the Continent that his emotional and legal problems were finally resolved.

A NEW CAREER IN A NEW TOWN

If Bowie had started to regain control of his career and reassess his music while still in the States, it took the relocation from America to Europe to complete the process of withdrawal and regeneration. Bowie's first wife, Angie, had set up home for them in Vevey, Switzerland, and it was there that Bowie retreated when not fulfilling dates on the European leg of his Station to Station tour, which ended in May 1976. That summer, Bowie recorded with his friend Iggy Pop at Château d'Herouville, near Paris. As a member of The Stooges, Iggy had been on the MainMan roster earlier in the decade, and Bowie had been one of the few to support him during psychiatric treatment for drug rehabilitation in 1975. Iggy had become Bowie's travelling companion on the Station to Station tour, and the pair co-wrote a number of songs both on the road and at Vevey. In the spring of 1977 Bowie even toured with Iggy, taking a back seat as his keyboards player. While the collaboration allowed Bowie to experiment in advance of his own recording sessions, such apparent generosity of spirit had not been evident during his US stay.

The Idiot was produced and arranged by Bowie, who had a hand in all eight compositions. The recording was completed at Hansa in West Berlin, where the mixing was handled by Tony Visconti, who had last worked with Bowie on the *David Live* album and 'Young Americans' single. In place of the proto-punk metallic assault of The Stooges, Iggy intones or growls his lyrics over slower, repetitive rhythms often underpinned by steamhammer-like percussion. This is not the familiar guitar rock that might have been expected from either Iggy or Bowie, although solos occasionally pass over like a squall and synthesized backing vocals emphasize the impersonal quality of the music. Given Bowie's central role in realizing *The Idiot*, it is not unreasonable to view it as representative of many of his own musical preoccupations. The disembodied, almost mechanical quality had European precedents in the disco productions of Giorgio Moroder and the more experimental approach of groups like Kraftwerk, whose music often dispensed with narrative descriptions of personal relationships to evoke a more general sense of environment.

By August 1976, Bowie was living a life of relative seclusion in West Berlin, seldom approached even when recognized. His interest in European cultures had begun in the States. 'I introduced him to Germany, to expressionism and to Fritz Lang,' claimed singer, model and Bowie-associate Amanda Lear in *Melody Maker* in 1978, 'and he ended up using [Buñuel's] *Un Chien Andalou* on his [Station to Station] tour.' Bowie's thoughts had certainly begun to turn to the Old World by September 1975, when *Station to Station* was being recorded. On its title track, Bowie states that 'the European man is here' and the song is launched by a musical evocation of a train gathering speed. This effect may well have been influenced by Kraftwerk, who had recently enjoyed their US chart breakthrough with 'Autobahn'.

Bowie was attracted to Berlin by its cultural reputation and interdisciplinary possibilities – once again he was consciously seeking a move away from purely musical avenues of self-expression. Berlin was one of the centres of the early twentieth-century expressionist movement in art, literature and music which promoted the expression of emotions over the depiction of externals. In searching for an emotional outlet, Bowie and his friends soon started to frequent the *Brücke* museum of expressionist art: here Erich Heckel's 'Roquairol' provided the model for Iggy's contorted gestures on the cover of *The Idiot*, while Bowie found inspiration for the title track and cover photo of *"Heroes"*.

LOW

> '*I stumble into town just like a sacred cow*
> *Visions of swastikas in my head, plans for everyone*'
> ('China girl' by Iggy Pop and David Bowie)

'That whole period stretching through to '76 was probably the worst year or year and a half of my life in the old re-examination programme', Bowie confided to Angus MacKinnon in *New Musical Express* in 1980. Living in Berlin, where he was instinctively drawn to the artists' community, restored some political equilibrium through exposure to left-wing sympathizers – the reality of Berlin in the seventies helped dispel any romantic sepia visions of thirties decadence – but the process of emotional rehabilitation was inevitably slow. Out of this misery was born perhaps the finest, and certainly the most adventurous, album of his career. Its cover was a profile of Bowie as Thomas Newton in *The Man Who Fell to Earth*, above which appeared the title *Low*: low in profile, low in spirits.

Bowie had been living in Europe for some six months by the time he began recording the album, yet he was still heavily influenced by the two years spent in the States. Participating in Alan Yentob's BBC documentary *Cracked Actor* had held a mirror up to Bowie, and it took time for him to come to terms with the reality he saw there. The character and predicament of Thomas Newton clearly still had resonances, as Bowie adorned his second successive album with an image from the film. Bowie had been under the impression that he would be supplying its musical soundtrack. He had invited Paul Buckmaster out to Los Angeles and developed a number of pieces, but, on learning that the work was out to tender, he declined to submit his own offerings. However, the experience aroused his interest in purely instrumental music. 'The area was one that was suddenly exciting to me', he told MacKinnon. 'And that's when I got the first inkling of trying to work with Eno at some point.'

For the *Low* sessions, Bowie retained Tony Visconti (who was instructed to listen to Kraftwerk and Tangerine Dream albums) and the *Station to Station* musicians Carlos Alomar, George Murray and Dennis Davis, adding guitarist Ricky Gardener and keyboards player Roy Young. All but the last probably constituted the uncredited backing band on *The Idiot*. To a largely familiar brew was added one further ingredient: Brian Eno. An early member of Roxy Music, Eno's subsequent activities had ranged unselfconsciously from rock music to the avant-garde, and he had recently turned towards experimenting with 'ambient' music.

Where Bowie had once been prepared to entrust recording to producers like Visconti and Ken Scott, and the realization of musical arrangements to such figures as Mick Ronson and Mike Garson, he now wanted to exercise control over the whole enterprise. This approach had begun with *Diamond Dogs*, and *The Idiot* provided a dry run for *Low*, where Bowie is credited as arranger and co-producer. Bowie was not looking to Eno as someone who could handle unfamiliar aspects of the recording process with which he felt less than confident, but rather as an imaginative partner for the unorthodox creation of new work. Their creative relationship was reciprocal, with Eno enjoying Bowie's way with words and melodies, and remarking on the unusual speed with which experimental ideas

were put into practice. Sessions again started at Château d'Herouville and were concluded at Hansa. Nine of the album's eleven
tracks were recorded at the Château in difficult circumstances,
made worse by the intrusion of Bowie's legal problems. This dark
atmosphere inevitably pervaded the music – the two instrumental
pieces recorded later in Berlin are lighter in mood.

Low, like its successor *"Heroes"*, is often said to consist of one
side of songs and one side of instrumentals: this is not strictly true
of either album. On *Low*, side one is book-ended by instrumentals,
while side two makes effective use of the voice as an instrument
and, on one track, delivers some lines of invented language. The
instrumental frame of side one, 'Speed of life' and 'A new career in
a new town', might be seen as indicative of Bowie's mental condition at different times. The first suggests a whirlwind lifestyle,
such as he had left behind in New York and Los Angeles; the
second, with its heartbeat-like intro and reprise suggests a revital-
ized European Bowie, with the surprising choice of harmonica as an
instrument adding new warmth and a positive human touch. Both
instrumentals differ from those on the second side, being short
scene-setting themes rather than the longer 'tone poems'. 'Speed of
life' hurries in on side one, serving as a short, succinct musical
manifesto of what is to follow – quite unlike anything else at the
time. While contemporary recordings by The Ramones and other
early punk bands were also startling, it is *Low* that has retained the
power to surprise; it shows no signs of dating. The use of synthesizers and 'treatments' on the first side of the album is extraordinary·
the mechanical 'powerhouse' effect is very striking and, in Eno-
approved fashion, synthesizers are employed not merely to imitate
musical instruments (why bother?) but to create new sounds. Even
when using a string effect on certain tracks, the result is not an
approximation of stringed instruments, but a shimmering, crystal-
line sonority all its own.

In the five 'songs', Bowie's lyrics are rarely less than obscure,
while his embrace of the Burroughs cut-up technique has the
effect of juxtaposing words and images at the expense of narrative.
On *Low*, the traditional verse/chorus construction and narrative concept is virtually absent. This is no radical development for Bowie,
but its persistence throughout these short songs is remarkable.
'Breaking glass' is not so much a song as a snatch of lyric flung
over pulsing music. Brief and unspecific, it seems to offer a glimpse
into some private hell. In contrast, 'What in the world' sounds
almost conventional, re-introducing some of the old tunefulness
but marrying it to a soundscape which shudders and pounds. In

153

'Sound and vision' Bowie is resolved to clear his head and start anew. Again, the tune is conventionally melodic, but the performance brings some startling touches. The instrumental intro is lengthy with more steam-hissing, piston-slamming sounds and icily cascading string-synths. Mary [Hopkin] Visconti's 'do-do do-do-do's and Bowie's saxophone lend a more human touch that hints at the artist reclaiming his soul. The side does not portray an increasingly optimistic Bowie, but rather charts his fluctuating moods: 'Always crashing in the same car' revives the demons of 'Breaking glass' over an other-worldly whispering of swirling 'space synths', courtesy of Eno. 'Be my wife' is a cry for love and support, though whether it should be taken straight or as an ironic look at maudlin sentiments is unclear; given the gaudy honky-tonk piano intro and affected East End accent, the latter seems more likely. 'It was genuinely anguished', he told *Melody Maker*'s Michael Watts in 1978, but added, rather perversely, 'I think it could've been anybody'. Side one ends with 'A new career in a new town', which paves the way for the wordless vistas of side two.

'Warszawa' is Bowie's evocation of the Eastern Bloc city that he had glimpsed on his journey through Poland in April 1976. Officially, it is Bowie and Eno's only joint composition on *Low*; the pace is slow, the mood solemn and brooding. All the instruments are played by Eno, with Bowie's vocal contribution making a spectacular entrance, like the humming of massed monks, subsequently overlaid with Middle-Eastern wailing. The images of the old Jewish ghetto, the city's wartime destruction and the bleakness of the post-war capital are all evoked. But, it is typical of Bowie that the relentless solemnity and vocal exaggeration can also be interpreted as having humorous overtones. Bowie and Eno handle all the instruments on 'Art decade' except for a cello, played by Hansa's engineer. The chugging, jangling sound with its 'pre-arranged percussion' conjures up images that are both industrial and serene. It is reminiscent of Kraftwerk pieces like 'Ananas Symphonie' and 'Kometenmelodie 2', while the wordplay of its title alludes to decay and the locked-in-an-earlier-decade atmosphere of East Berlin.

Also recorded at Hansa, and using the same composing technique as for 'Warszawa', 'Weeping wall' is a solo Bowie performance. Vibes and xylophones create a light, bubbling effect. Bowie uses his voice mixed in with the synths as an instrument; later, after the track has acquired a gentle shuddering quality courtesy of an ARP synthesizer, wordless vocals gradually emerge. The monks return, singing in an invented language on 'Subterraneans', the only piece to be resurrected from Bowie's abandoned soundtrack for

The Man Who Fell to Earth. Spiritually located in East Berlin, 'Subter-raneans' uses underground-dwellers as a symbol for a people going about their lives under a totalitarian regime. Images from Orwell's *1984*, Wells's *The Time Machine* and Lang's *Metropolis* come together as the vocals float away at the end of the track, bringing the album to a close.

AFTER LOW

Low was released in January 1977. In Britain, the initial critical response was bemused if not overtly hostile: here was a major rock star moving into unfamiliar territory. Such bold experimentation unsettled those comfortable with the relatively stagnant Anglo-American rock scene. A few months later, the music press was more receptive to new sounds, with reviewers waking up to the New York sounds and the domestic punk explosion. For the time being, though, the press chose to view *Low* as perpetuating the cold, decadent and politically unsound character they had perceived in the Thin White Duke, little suspecting that the album had pro-vided Bowie with the means to recharge his creative batteries and make it into the eighties with credibility intact.

To those who measure a work's quality and durability by the number of times it is re-recorded, *Low* is a non-starter. No cover versions of either the songs or the tone poems come to mind. Recently though, the 'minimalist' composer Philip Glass has refor-mulated elements of it into a *Low Symphony*, drawing also on the out-take 'Some are'. It's a disconcertingly conventional orchestral interpretation of the material, lacking the adventurousness of the originals, but it points to the fact that the 'works' that comprise *Low* cannot be divorced from their original studio formulations. The instrumentation and recording techniques adopted by Bowie, Eno and Visconti are as integral to the effect as the lyrics and tunes. It is this inspired marriage of elements that is the supreme achieve-ment of *Low*. The songs capture Bowie withdrawing to lick his wounds and take stock of his life; the tone poems find him immersed in his new surroundings. Bowie's bold new music is both the medium for expressing these conditions, and the inspiration to see him through his all-time low.

PATTI SMITH

Heroes: A communiqué

Hit Parader, April 1978

I had the fortunes with me. 10/20. rimbaud's birthday.
I was in koln. so were several young and lusty terrorists.
the tone of the country was meditative, metallic. west
germany had an extreme distaste for overt military
tactics. murder. hi-jack. the need for counter-militia
was an embarrassment for the new middle class as well
as detrimental to the tourist trade.

the customs official found my sunglasses offensive.
italian bodyguard shades. lying on the table with my
keys and kools they seemed to take on the flesh of a
dangerous drug. i refused to part with them and soon
hit the streets with an armed escourt. there was no one around save
servicemen and teenagers. i arrived at
galerie veith turske late greasy and mean.

one of the boys followed us. his name was dominique.
he sat across from me in the music room. i imagined
cradling him. picking him up and drawing him in. he had
all the motion of a twelve-year-old girl. the perverse
sensuality of innocence.

another boy came in. he was older and very cute. maybe
around 22 and very eager. he had an offering in a wax
bag. he said it was the new Bowie album. i was very
happy. i was nervous and alien in this town and the
record was a connection. it was also his contribution
toward the raising of souls in this domestic domain.

i asked dominique to display his drugs. he unrolled
what he had from a piece of grey felt lined in smooth
rubber tubing. it was green devil and very sticky.
he divided the drug. i was given twice as much. i took
this as a token of respect and did not protest. Veith
came in with hash and alcohol. he also brought
an exotic dessert composed of the foam of various
liquors whipped with egg yolk.

boy-2 put side 1 on. i had difficulty focusing. being
among others i was unable to relax and submit into a
groove of total aural adventure. it was also impossible
to glitter and obliterate before a trio of languorous young
men.

i was experiencing a thrill though. since young americans
i have been a quiet yet ecstatic fan. station to station
inspired radio ethiopia. message units are sprayed liberally
between the buds of poppies. when low hit i was in a period
of disgrace. of total immobility. low. the fall and
potential rising of thomas jerome newton. the sound track
of Bowie's escape into film. a backdrop for months of
head-motion. low provided a state of connective id-mutual
non-action. of dream and beyond into creation. a stiff
neck person can indeed inter/enter the wrath of the
creator. and so i was remembering. i was sliding into
the dark backward. revisiting all the carnal landscapes
of the bruised interior.

the boys were discussing Bowie's pronounciations. in
koln heroes is sung in sectioned german. i asked them
what they thought of Bowie's interpretation. they said
it was not rock n roll. it was cabaret.
behind my shades i can imagine him. there in berlin.
in the abandoned section. i imagine him stumbling thru
old boxes and props in the street. i imagine him in
love with the whole world or totally dead.

i imagine the last show of thomas jerome escaping into
life. we are interrupted by a profile. bowie-the-neo-somnambulist
enters the atelier of hugo ball.
he is the angles of kandinsky. he is the incredibly spiritual
phony. a member of a most expiring race – an actor.
specifically designed for the silent screen. one w/the
conceit and innocence of the true silent actor.

in sons of the silent age he is a metropolis valentino –
very mythic very manic and very misunderstood. harmonious
gossip resounds. everyone is murmuring german. i get some
kind of anger/anguish out of blackout. dehumanized speed
of the japanese laborer. we can't compete we just get wiped
out. i think of my mom losing her job in a factory cause

the japs do it faster. i think of transistor you can get
for only seven dollars that really works made in japan.

his new work is not immediately accessible but neither
was exile on main street. beauty and the beast is a shock
that is eventually absorbed into shining acceptance. joe
the lion is startling too and stretched out by some great
guitar. it takes some time to get under the skin.

records sound different in europe. i think the turntables
are faster. theres more treble. i couldn't enter into
V-2 schneider the way i wanted to. not til much later
when i came home. i got off the plane and went downtown
and bought the record. i wanted to keep the feel of being
in transit. new york-koln. i dont usually buy a record
unless i'm in love (stones) or in a state of hot suspense
(idiot).

i listened to the record for 72 hours. day and night.
watching tv and in my sleep. like station to station and
low, heroes is a cryptic product of a high order of
intelligence. committed to survival. the rhythm tracks
are intel-disco. lysis-discos. the disintegration of
brain into lingua into pulse of rhythm. high east
coast wherein all the musicians play w/grace and taste.

the title song is wonderful. it exposes us to our most
precious and private dilemma. he has captured in this
song that desperate moment when one will die for
love. the track is pure. i am waiting for my man.
but i love that song too and what we love we love
repeated. the lyrics are really beautiful. one falls
in love and gets lost in its swirl. one projects far
aware and across the boundaries of space and placement.
we are in dream alive. we are not planets away but
separated by a room or a wall of wire. thats all.

heroes is the theme song for every great movie.
made remade or yet to come. we the living. we are
the girl in a torn wedding dress escaping thru wire
into the crown of a bullet. we are the soldier blowing
kisses from the back of the train. we are drunk and
raging and kneeling in/time in a dead hotel room. we

are the heroes of rimbaud's poem royalty. 2 people
mystically colliding.

En effet ils furent rois toute une matinee . . .

morning in koln, side 2 is still on. sometimes we are
the victim of the senseless anxiety accompanied with
sense of doubt. man desires the immediacy of sense
in/life. he stalks the stars like alien candles.
birthday scars and scars of truth and immortal love.
man desires to drift shamelessly into the realm of
beauty. in the garden the birds chirp. the garden imprisons
an egg which encases the breath of a quivering question.
the question mark becomes the curve of a saxophone.
Bowie is going to bend and pucker and blow like the
pusher (pierre clemente) of steppenwolf. instinctive
as to beauty down and thru a cellar of noise into a
relaxed system of notes and merge with the actor he
truly is.

the boys of koln cut out. the younger stayed longer.
he had a passion for MC5. he was going to quit school and
play guitar all day. secret life came on. i was packing
for america. he was telling me how it felt when he plugged
in and connected with his weapon. he was saying a lot of
stuff and i was thinking about heroes. find them where
they're sleeping. know them where they lie. deep in another
system. deep in the heart and motor of the most despised
cities in the world.

JON SAVAGE

Avant-AOR

Melody Maker, 27 May 1979

Another year, another record. Like Burroughs, David Jones, rootless, looks for unconventional commitment: Burroughs found it in junk, control-systems and predatory homosexuality; Jones found it in a record contract and self-obsessive stardom. One LP a year, no questions asked. A bit of time to write another chapter, a few more Bowiedotes; along the way, he sells millions of records. Usually, it's deserved. The superstructure of analysis erected over this, actively encouraged by the 'artist' – newspaper stories about his 'art' are safer than anything else – is fun for train journeys, but can't be taken too seriously.

Lodger is a nice enough pop record, beautifully played, produced and crafted, and slightly faceless. Is Bowie that interesting?

After unsuccessful commitments to mod and then hippie youthcult, Bowie put his foot on the accelerator and started to reflect styles so fast that he helped define them: by 1974 he'd hustled himself a place in a modern Olympus – pop superstardom.

As modern deities-cum-icons, pop stars live out exaggerated bits of us, parts of our lives amplified which we can then buy in 7- and 12-inch formats. Bowie was that bit in us that didn't want to be what we were – arty, pretentious, posing like crazy – until he went to Los Angeles and found out it was realer than he was.

Since then, the role-playing has become less overt, muted in favour of a more literary approach to popstardom: the role of Renaissance Man, multimedia adept, with a dash of the Garbos. This keeps people interested in what happens next; if they're really into it, they look at what he's reflecting and thus what he's helping to shape. Your reviewer thinks this game is quite fun, up to the point where Bowie's 'legend' becomes top-heavy and obstructive.

So Bowie returns to RCA, rewarded by a personalized catalogue number, with what – playing the significance game – he likes to see as the final part of the *Low*/*"Heroes"* trilogy. Mmmm. The new album appears as a piece of self-plagiarism unmatched since The Seeds: his last eight or so albums are cut up, played backwards and then reassembled. It's a credit to his craft that the end result is still fresh.

Everyone I've talked to hates the cover; I rather like it. It's silly (but when did that ever matter?) like a glossy, exciting advertisement for mouthwash. The lettering isn't very well done, but that's a minor detail: a part of that child-like autistic edge of unease that Bowie likes to keep. The poses at which the cover, shot mimetically, hints are explained inside: a carefully kept baby, a mortuary corpse, a shrouded Christ, a carefully killed Che Guevara. This might be making a point; it might also be a little self-amplifying.

Inside, *Lodger* contains plenty of Bowiedotes – journalistic (some would say voyeuristic) observations converted into music and dance – and absolutely no instrumentals. The synthesized explorations which reached such a powerful, subconscious peak on side two of *"Heroes"* have ceased (just as the genre is getting done to death), to be replaced by ten more conventional song-structures, dominated in turn by Bowie's voice, Carlos Alomar's guitar and Simon House's violin, and within which any exploration is firmly kept. Superficially, the result is a mix of *Station to Station* and the first side of *Low* – avant-AOR.

Illustrating the musical move towards some broader, if not global fusion that Bowie appeared to be aiming for (with the same band) in the curious Earl's Court concert, last summer, most of the songs plunder the world for their material. Some are expressed acutely, with an actor's insight ('African night flight' – the fragmented speech and thought of a European burnt up by African sun), others more romantically and superficially than anything else ('Move on' and 'Red sails' – fairly straight *Neu*), apparently rifling exotica. We turn the world into transient three-minute pop songs! 'Yassassin' escapes a similar fate, that of a Turkish delight ad, through an audacious mix of the 'Fame' riff with some stunning violin from House.

Turning to disco youthcult: 'DJ' is an amusing and sharp look at the fear of instant obsolescence that runs through all media. You could apply the lyric to Bowie, and he's sharp enough to know that.

The single, 'Boys keep swinging', nicks the bass riff from The Beach Boys' 'You're so good to me' in a vaguely homoerotic, Ladybird look at male adolescence. Boys are blue, yes, but what about girls? It's better in place on the album.

The album's only flash – either spontaneous or else so thoroughly practised that it appears spontaneous in comparison with the careful, occasionally stilted face of the rest of the album – is 'Repetition', an understated, circular little song about wife-beating. Built around an eerie rising guitar figure, sickening bass and subliminal synth mumbles, it features one of Bowie's best vocals – clipped, precise, narrative rather than operatic.

Even when playing at superstars, it was always hard to escape the sense of Bowie as tourist. Even on the more emotional pieces on *Low* and *"Heroes"*, it was always at least ambiguous where Bowie stood. Was his investigation of those various states a criticism or celebration?

The influence his precedent as 'artist' has set is spreading like some unavoidable and unpleasant disease among inept imitators – the outdated model of the artist as separate from and superior to the rest of society, sort of divinely chosen.

The inclusion of 'Fantastic voyage' and 'Red money' on the album shows that, publicly at least, he's worried about this: sandwiching the more overtly narrative cuts are two songs, apparently personal, dealing with responsibility and adjustment to imminent collapse. On 'Fantastic voyage', in his nearest approximation to 'Word on a wing' yet, Bowie croons: 'They wipe out an entire race and I've got to write it down . . ./But I'm still getting educated but I've got to write it down'. 'Red money' swipes the 'Sister midnight' riff and tune wholesale, adding a slightly different production and new words: 'Can you hear it fall?/Such responsibility/It's up to you and me.'

So far, so tentative: are we to 'believe' it? Is it not mere commitment-chic? I'm not sure that it matters; even if it is a clever reflection, the ideas of responsibility, of a more realistic adjustment to the outside world, are raised. From the self-absorption of his superstar period to the romantic, pessimistic yet spiritual tone of *"Heroes"*, these latest realizations occur as part of a classic cycle.

Dealers: Bowie has a huge following, expect heavy sales on this return to a more conventional style. Consumers: don't expect another *"Heroes"*. Projection: will the eighties really be this boring?

JEAN ROOK

Bowie reborn

Daily Express, 14 February 1979

He's been all things to a lot of women. And to some men. He admits to a 'more than platonic relationship with drugs'. He's been down to a skeletal eight-and-a-half-stone, and the depths of suicidal despair ('when I thought I was coming to the end of my tether I considered everything as a way out'). He used to dye his hair as scarlet as sin and wear platform-soled women's shoes and one chandelier ear-ring. That was before he caked himself with white Max Factor and tinted his hair tangerine.

David Bowie has rocked a generation of pop fans. But miraculously his flaming mascara'd head hasn't rolled.

Keith Moon and Sid Vicious are dead. But Bowie, at 32, is alive and, at 10 stone, as well as ever he's been in a life that would have killed a far stronger man. Bowie has seen it all and done most of it. When I interviewed him three years ago he was terrifying to look at: chalk-skinned, bloodless and apparently dying, if not un-dead. In 1976 he looked like a cross between a stick insect and Dracula.

Today he looks 17. His undyed hair is pale brown and short-back-and-sides. The unmade-up face is guileless and spotless. In grey flannel bags, grey shirt and tasteful tie he looks like a public schoolboy. Or like Edward before he met Mrs Simpson. And looking like that after all he's been through, Mr Bowie is even more terrifying. Interviewing him is like coming across a daisy in hell. How the hell does he do it, after all he says he's done? And has he really been reborn a brand-new Persil-washed man overnight?

'Not overnight – it's been a struggle,' said the one-time glittering, diamanté, lipsticked superstar. 'I hated the pop lifestyle but it's hard to kick the habits of a lifetime. I'm learning to be happy. To go to bed at night instead of 5 am and get up in the morning instead of halfway through the day. I'm painting pictures nobody wants to buy, but I love it. I've grown my hair back to mouse. I'm even practising walking down the street.'

Doesn't that come naturally?

'Not to me,' said Bowie. 'For years I daren't walk out of my front door alone. I was paranoid about it, terrified. It still takes me courage to walk from A to B and not think, "This person walking down the street is David Bowie and everybody's looking at him." Now I look at other people. I even go into shops and, if somebody talks to me, I chat back. Three years ago I could have no more done that than fly – literally. They couldn't drag me onto an aeroplane screaming, at one time. Now, every day, I get up more nerve and try to be more normal and less insulated against real people.'

Bowie used to be totally lagged against real life. Protected by cars with tinted windows. Guarded by his 'stormtroopers' in black leather pants. He was never seen in public until he appeared like a god – or demon – to lash his thousands of pop concert fans into a foaming frenzy. He's still not that easy to get at. He didn't manifest at the press preview of his new film with Marlene Dietrich, *Just a Gigolo*. And he told me he'd rather face 15,000 pop fans than watch himself, for the first time, at tonight's première of his movie.

I'm the only journalist who knows his hotel and even I don't know his room number. Our undercover meeting took place in a hired private suite, later cleared of any trace of us. Down to the butts of the 60 cigarettes a day on which Mr Bowie is still hooked. How did he drag himself free of the deeper, more dangerous hooks which finally tore apart Moon and Vicious?

'I don't really know what happened to them – their deaths were terrible. If I really knew that, I'd be one of them. I nearly was. I realized just in time that I was destroying myself,' said the man-god who claims he shocked himself even more than he electrified his audiences.

'I loathed the pop scene – I never wanted to be a pop star. I was David Jones from Brixton who wanted to do something artistically worthwhile. But I hadn't the courage to face an audience as myself. It takes tremendous courage to face up to the adulation, the pressure, without cracking. That's why some of us crack. I was the first pop star to invent masks to hide behind. I played at being Ziggy Stardust. That was fine until I became Ziggy, and Ziggy became a monster who nearly destroyed me. Then I played at being the Thin White Duke. Now, I think I've got rid of him.

'Making films has helped. It's taught me that you can be a character and stop being him when they finish the movie. As a rock star I couldn't stop – I went on playing the bizarre people I'd invented on and off stage. I honestly believe that what you see now is myself.'

Now that the real David Bowie is standing up – however unsteadily – what manner of man is he? A modern rock poet. A chronicler of his disturbed times. A probable genius. The nearest thing to Christopher Isherwood, whom Bowie idolizes. And the furthest from a lesser pop light like Moon or a flashy little star like Vicious. Though, to be more generous to Vicious than I am, Bowie maintains: 'Punk was absolutely necessary. A sort of musical enema. I think they honestly believed it was a new wave, a new school of music. And maybe it was until they started selling one another out.'

Stripped of his paint, powder, drugs, dyed hair, ear-rings, boy-friends and false eyelashes, Bowie sees himself as 'a very conservative man'. Now that his world-rocking marriage to Angie Bowie, who prides herself on her bisexuality, is nearing divorce, he's fanatically protective of his son, Zowie, pushing eight and 'already overly fond of playing his drums'.

'I want him to be a real person,' said the man who's pushed himself to the limits of unreality. 'Thank God he doesn't associate me with the awesome thing he sees on stage. He thinks of that as just the way Daddy makes his money. He doesn't take much interest in what I do. To him I'm Dad – the man in the next bedroom who has breakfast with him every morning. For me, that's being real people.'

Real people grow old, lose their hair, whatever colour it's dyed. Die undramatically in the next bedroom. How will David Bowie face up to his unmasked, lined face at 50?

'I shall welcome it, Lord yes,' he said. 'Pop stars are capable of growing old. Mick Jagger at 50 will be marvellous – a battered old roué – I can just see him. An ageing rock star doesn't have to opt out of life. When I'm 50, I'll prove it.'

GORDON BURN

Bowie holds court

Sunday Times Magazine, 30 November 1980

We had seen the dress rehearsals of *The Elephant Man* and *The Elephant Man* itself. We had played our complimentary copies of *Scary Monsters*, David's new record, paying particular attention to the words ('Put a bullet in my brain/And it makes all the papers' – not many of us had missed that). We'd digested our press kits and our photocopy raves of David's Broadway debut – 'shockingly good' (*New York Post*), 'preternaturally wise' (*New York Times*), 'piercing and haunted' (*Daily News*) – and been suitably impressed. We'd put our hands up and received handsomely packed pictures of David's paintings, and we'd watched the videos where we'd seen David playing Glenda Jackson playing Stevie Smith singing a song called 'Boys keep swinging' ('When you're a boy, you can wear a uniform/When you're a boy, other boys check you out.') We'd turned up to interview David on Tuesday only to be told he was indisposed until Thursday. We'd come back on Thursday and now here he was. Here, too, was the PR person from his record company; Mr and Mrs de Witt, who handle his personal PR; his personal make-up lady and personal photographer plus assistant, and a technical adviser whose job it also was to pull the plugs on any crew overrunning their allotted 15 minutes.

Not that anybody would get a chance to overrun their allotted 15 minutes with Mr and Mrs de Witt around. There were five TV interviews to do for five European stations whose separate camera set-ups around the hall – a studio, in fact, in the RCA building on Sixth Avenue – made it look like the Electrical and Allied Trades Exhibition.

165

Like clockwork, one crew was ushered in by Mr de Witt as his wife hustled the previous one out and David had the perspiration blotted away. This was the schedule before lunch. 'Printed media' he'd take on after. In the evening, he'd be bundled through the police barriers and uniformed security at the Booth Theatre to change into a nappy and play the Elephant Man.

In the course of their briefing, each country had been handed a chart and invited to choose a colour for the 'No-seam' stiffened paper the interview would take place in front of. France, who were second in after the Italians, had opted for the black, a choice that wasn't lost on David. 'This is so Left Bank. And theirs was so Milan,' he said, while the camera was being reloaded. 'What's Germany got?'

The French interviewer had kicked off with the question everybody would kick off with – 'Why do you play ze Elephant Man on Broadway?' – and he'd got the stock answer: (a) 'because somebody asked me to go "legit" and I'd always been meaning to try it', and (b) 'because I've always had a thing about freaks and isolationists and alienated people'. Then, very quickly, the Frenchman had got metaphysical. 'Are you ze last rock star?' Panicky looks from the de Witts.

'In my family, certainly.'

Laughter. Relief. But the Frenchman was pressing on, regardless. 'What is your idea on ze beauty?'

This was more up David's street. He looked eager, the way contestants often do on quiz shows when they think they've got the answer: 'I think it was Dame Edith Evans when she went to Los Angeles for the first time. She went to the observatory, to the same one that was in *Rebel Without a Cause* as a matter of fact, where she was taken into the depths, led along these dark, doomy corridors by the curator. At last they stopped in front of a refrigerator and from it the curator removed two pieces of glass between which was a snowflake. "This snowflake," he said, "fell on Los Angeles in 1935." I think *that* is beauty.'

David was wearing a cowl-neck sweater, possibly a lady's, jeans and brown leather shoes with odd little zips up the front. Nothing fancy. And yet, even without any of the props he has used in the past to 'reinvent' himself, he was effortlessly and unsettlingly androgynous, suggesting both Lauren Bacall, say, and Johan Cruyff, caught in a sort of flicker-frame. Sworn off the drugs he feels nearly did for him in California in the early seventies when he reached what he calls 'the low-point of a tormented lifestyle', he chain-smoked Marlboros and, to start with at least, seemed very nervous. By the time the Austrians were wheeled in, though, he had found his stride.

He crouched in the chair with both feet under him, in his padded-cell pose, one of his favourites, and faced the long-haired young man from *Apropos Music* who wanted to know all about the flirtation with Nazi ideology – 'infantile,' admitted David. 'That was quickly blown away by meeting members of the far Left while I was living in Berlin' – and whether he still intended playing Egon Schiele in a film. He also wanted to draw him out on why being just a rock star had obviously proved in the end to be so frustrating.

'Being a paragon of rock-and-roll intensity proved to be not quite as fulfilling as one might have hoped,' David set off, ploughing a familiar furrow. 'I make a point now of going for the most unlikely things that come along. If I know the vocabulary of what I'm doing too well, I . . .' The camera had started to make belching noises and it was distracting him. He called a halt until it was corrected. The de Witts fiddled with their watches.

'I've just had the most coruscating interview with a woman from *Stern*. All she did was attack me about my "decadent" audiences.' It was after lunch and David had been transported to a hotel suite uptown full of artistically arranged rent-a-blooms. This was no less a set than the 'No-seam' had been. The impression that we were on stage was reinforced by the knowledge that there were people lurking in the 'wings'. The de Witts were hovering in the bathroom, and the make-up girl must have been on the scene somewhere because, although the armpits of David's sweater were dark with perspiration, his forehead was freshly powdered and dry. He was on his third packet of Marlboros.

After all the exhaustive priming and the morning's mini-marathon there seemed only one question left to ask him: 'Why?' Why, after years of relative seclusion, had he suddenly been made so available? Two answers, of course, had already suggested themselves. David Lynch's film version of *The Elephant Man*, the by now well-known story of a Victorian freak, John Merrick, sometimes said to have been the ugliest man ever, was opening that week in Manhattan, and the Bowie blitz would minimize the effectiveness of all their 'promo'. Second, after a string of albums that had had him experimenting with electronics and 'difficult' *neumusik*, *Scary Monsters* was regarded by RCA records as a return to the mainstream and they were going to milk it for all it was worth.

'I keep telling myself every time I finish one of these forays into the public eye, never again. Because I feel fettered by cliché all the time, and become quite parrot-like. I don't help myself at all.'

His manner, as it had been in one or two of the television interviews, is flirtatious. He breaks out of 'character' all the time to crack a smile that is amused but rather chilling. His eyes are what he gives as his distinguishing feature, but he's wrong. His mouth is. He has eye-teeth like fangs.

'Tomorrow belongs to those who can hear it coming' is the slogan David coined to promote one of his albums, and nobody has ever been able to accuse him of not keeping his ear to the ground. His problem, however, is that he has always wanted to have a genius for more than just keeping one step ahead. He has always wanted to be part of the international avant-garde. Coming from Beckenham is, as he is the first to acknowledge, what goes on keeping him out. He has talked in the past about 'the ball-and-chain of middle-classness' that he is doomed to trail around, and agrees now, although it at first raises a giggle, that a good word to describe him might be 'sensible'. Even while discussing the reasons why he'll never be what he would most like to be, which is another Duchamp, most modern of the moderns, who chose to produce nothing in his last forty years, David's background – or maybe just his Englishness – trips him up. 'I could never play chess like Duchamp, so that rules me out.' Said with all the conviction of a guest at one of Robert Robinson's excruciating dinner-parties-without-dinner on Radio 4.

'Oh I know. I *know*. Don't tell me. That always happens to me in conversation.' Again he's laughing, but it's possible that it has struck a nerve. 'I have so many streaks of sensibleness that it's frightening. I keep getting drawn back to such a logical, conservative me, but it wears me out trying to fight it. And fighting it used to lead me into that very rough, drug-oriented, *forceful* kind of lifestyle which makes one on edge all the time. Now, having beaten that back, I'm confronted with the basic facts of where I came from and who I am. I'm not playing a part constantly any more, the way I used to. I used to be very protective – *very* protective – of what I considered to be my "real" self. I would dress it up or disguise it to the point where I was beginning to lose it myself. At the minute I'm trying to deal as best I can with that *and* present my awkward perception of the small part of the world that I know. But I am still, as you can see, fighting.'

David is far too big these days for London, where he still has 'that peculiar sort of following one gets in those kinds of cities', meaning the acolytes now half his age who, brought up on the sexual ambiguity and Weimar 'camp' he pioneered, mobilize themselves into an entourage that he can't shake off. In America, of course, he is no less a celebrity, as the 'A list' turnout – Isherwood, Hockney, Radziwell, Warhol, Aaron Copland, Diana Vreeland, etc. – for his first night of

The Elephant Man had proved. The difference is that, in America, he is nobody's patron saint.

Even so, after a hundred performances of *The Elephant Man* and three months in New York, he'd be off, to the Far East again, or Africa, anywhere where he can be 'an anonymous presence'. He has no permanent address and keeps on the move so that he never again becomes cocooned – 'what happens when a rock star gets surrounded by that particular killing kind of sycophancy' – the way he once was in Los Angeles.

But Tim Rice and the BBC, who were next on, were waiting. Twice Mrs de Witt had approached purposefully from the bathroom, and twice David had prevailed on her for a few minutes more. This time, though, Mr de Witt appeared simultaneously from the bedroom. This time they meant business. Mrs de Witt broke into the conversation as elegantly as possible; her husband led me firmly by the elbow to the door. A backward glance seemed to confirm that people were coming out of the woodwork now, seeing to it that David got through this very busy day.

JOHN ROCKWELL

A revolution with Bowie

New York Times, 25 December 1980

Only a few years ago, 'rock opera' seemed on the verge of taking over not just the musical theatre, but perhaps even our opera houses as well, what with *Hair* and *Jesus Christ Superstar* on Broadway and *Tommy* at the Metropolitan Opera. But the form never really caught on. Ultimately, the rock idiom proved too limited to adapt to the long-lined expressive demands of conventional opera, and both Broadway and the operatic world itself turned out to be too hidebound to foster such a revolutionary evolution in the first place.

Now, however, rock has found its own form of theatrical expression – quite apart from the operatic theatrics of a singular performer like Bruce Springsteen. That form is the video vignette. Right now, New York's hippest dance-rock clubs are caught up in the video revolution;

they compete in the lavishness of their video installations and in the acquisition of the latest video software, which may then be seen flickering on the omnipresent monitors and giant projection screens.

These efforts – which are also shown as promotional shorts on rock television programmes and will one day soon be made available on videodiscs – are mostly unimaginative, commercially calculated affairs that all too perfectly match the music they illustrate. Or – when the clubs turn to unsynchronized showings of Japanese monster movies and decadent-looking European high-fashion commercials – the video explosion looks like an eighties update of sixties psychedelic lightshows.

But the new video shorts are far better than that, and really quite extraordinary. Devo made some fine ones a couple of years ago (they were films, actually), and The Boomtown Rats contributed nobly to the cause as well. But the real hero of the rock video revolution so far is that perennial pioneer David Bowie.

Mr Bowie made three video illustrations of songs from his penultimate album, and has done two more from his latest, *Scary Monsters*. The footage for his song 'Ashes to ashes' is a surrealist collage, full of continually intercut images: Mr Bowie as a forlorn clown wandering along an ink-black sea (and talking at the end to an earnestly chatty old British mum), as a spaceman, a deep-sea diver, and so forth. The other, for his song 'Fashion', alternates a bizarre assortment of folk standing in a soup-kitchen line, a dance class, various characters who look as if they had stepped from fifties British commercials and Mr Bowie in performance.

What is remarkable about these spots is not so much the images as the brilliant way they are edited and how they expand on the music itself, rather than merely accompanying it or even contradicting it. These little shorts are genuine music theatre in a new and modern guise, and they deserve to be seen by anyone interested in either rock or opera.

JON SAVAGE

The gender bender

The Face, November 1980

> *'What do you want to be when you grow up, David?' 'Mum, I want to be an Artist, even a Star.'*

And so it was. Most pop stars are transient moths to the flame; David Bowie has lasted. To the public he's beyond Pop Star – he's Star Artist. On a plateau untouchable and mysterious.

His influence has been huge, and not always healthy. You can see it on any high street, in any disco, in any gay club, on any record sleeve, in every kid who 'works at Woolies and wants to be a star'. Worst, you can see it in the current crop of 'art' bands. Mary Harron remarked disparagingly about the recent Futurama Festival that Siouxsie and The Banshees 'taught a whole generation to pose without humour'. But who taught *them*?

'They shared lovers of both sexes, freely and openly . . . they shaved their eyebrows and dyed their hair outlandish colours . . .' So ran the intro to Angie Bowie's kiss-and-tell memoirs from Two Goose Ranch. This is exactly what most people want to know – you can always rely on the *Sun* to give the public what it wants – about David Bowie, Star: a bit of futurism, a bit of make-up, but best, lots of Gender Confusion.

This, just as much as the 'art', is the key component to the Bowie monolith: Ziggy, you see, hit home. The great public only ever likes to keep one thing in its head about people: just as Bowie's massive contribution to fashion was in the fact that you can *still* see the glam uniform of baggies, tank-top and platforms on provincial streets, so the spice in his image was gayness. Ultimately, if Bowie has invented a whole language of 'art' posing, he's invented more specifically *the* language to express gender confusion. It still hasn't been superseded.

Only last summer a group was to be seen on the stage of a more liberal Manchester club; called Spurtz, they featured two girls who knew what they were doing and one chap who didn't really. They weren't much – noisy and atonal – but what struck me was that the lead singer, banging around in a lurex mini-dress, was drawing entirely from a vocabulary invented by Bowie. And people stood and took it.

These days Bowie is beyond such open campery, as he's beyond open doom-peddling and glam: that's just to say that he's more subtle

171

about it. Angie panders to the great public's view, whereas 'Ashes to ashes' – his first number one for ages – pandered perfectly to the pop public's view of Bowie: now taking his place as a 'mature' artist.

David Mallett's brilliant video packed in the usual elements – space, madness and lots of blurred gender – in three minutes that seemed pregnant with meaning; once examined, of course, it was at best expressionist and haunting, at worst hooey, but that's irrelevant. It dazzled, it sold. For that one time you saw it on *Top of the Pops*, it was everything.

Ultimately Bowie is still worth watching, if not for the actual performances, many of which have been perfunctory over the last three years, but because of the dreams that reside in him; not as a stylist now, but as a totem. If all his costumes were sold, like Judy Garland's in the MGM lot, what kink would wear them?

What the hell is wrong with me?
I'm not what I want to be!

Bowie's real success (after all, any tart can bang around the stage in a skirt) is in tapping that perennial teen equation – which, so protected have we been, has carried over into the twenties. Teenage isn't a very nice age – most people who tell you so are lying – and it's one of the immutable facts that the pop biz is staffed by 20- and 30-year olds reliving the teenhood they never had in recreating it for consumption by teens.

David Bowie came out properly in a blaze of obvious self re-creation – from Terry Nelhams through Andy Warhol – and it touched every suburban heart. You don't need to be you: you can change your clothes and your name and your hair and be an entirely new person!

Where Bowie upped and out was in changing this on *every* album. That is the promise, the premise of pop and teen fashion: overnight, you can be transformed into something superhuman. Not very pretty, but, to date, necessary. Bowie is the agent of that transformation made manifest and perennial: 'Every man and woman is a star.'

David Bowie started as Davy Jones, a dedicated follower of fashion: from sharp mod to fuzzy hippie. 'Space oddity' caught the end of hippie idealism perfectly. It was too fragile, but it crystallized one aspect of the myth – futurism. The breakthrough came later. Along with Mark Feld – another mod re-creation – Bowie reacted sharply against the supposed 'authenticity' of hippiedom.

The sleeves of *The Man Who Sold the World* and *Hunky Dory* set the correct note of ambiguity (at the time, so shocking that the sleeve to the former was changed so as not to sully clean-cut American youth) and *Ziggy*, a truly plastic piece of posing worthy of Paul Gadd, cracked it. All Bowie did was release a catchy 'Over the rainbow' steal in 'Starman', say 'Hi! I'm bi!' in the *Melody Maker* and hey presto! – Glam!

This really was news. Homosexuality, if not bisexuality, had always been part of pop, both in the process (managers picking up potential singers) and the appeal. Film stars like Montgomery Clift had killed themselves in a previous age trying to deny it, but this was the first time, five years after legalization, that any star came right out and *said it*.

People might have nudged each other about Cliff, would have made jokes about The Beatles if Lennon hadn't been such an obvious thug, might have suspected Ray Davies, but the only heavy ones were The Stones and The Velvet Underground. Even in their case, it was only the icing on the cake of outrage: for The Stones (in particular Jagger and Jones) it was part of their package of anarchic assault, while The Velvets just used it as sleaze – homo mixed with heroin, drag with S & M.

Bowie acknowledged the debt by recording 'White light' and 'Queen bitch' – the one that got everybody going with the glitter eyeliner – finally paying tribute on 'Let's spend the night together', a version that made full use of any possible ambiguities. John, I'm only *dancing*.

What he did, then, was to open Pandora's box: by making *homosex attractive* (rather than a snigger) he liberated and brought into the mainstream a whole range of fantasies which had hitherto been repressed. Naturally they came out with great force.

Make-up definitely beat dope as the thing to shock your parents with. It must have taken a degree of courage – although Bowie had the distancing effect of the Ziggy superstructure – but in a way it was inevitable. Some of the results were OK, others awful. At best it was a healthy reaction against gender stereotypes, puritanism, and gave people a chance to move out of whatever closet, but at worst it was Jobriath.

Naturally the puritan hangover still bit; homosexuality had to be perceived as part of some greater decadence. Bowie's gently pessimistic futurism had gradually been replaced by a harsher, apocalyptic view. Distorted as all pop messages are, it read: if it's all ending, anything goes. As such, it was rationalized and easier to cope with: homosex became so pop that it even entered the puritan world of Richard Allen's *Skinhead* series, in his peerless *Glam* – whose cover is an exactly inept copy of *Aladdin Sane*. In the book, his descriptions of faggy glam rockers conform absolutely to public stereotype.

If he wanted to avoid becoming a sharper, futurist John Inman, Bowie had to move fast. He was already outgrowing glam and its restrictions, while the public was celebrating Slade and Sweet – brickies dressed up as rent-boys. It'd been good to him: the homosex angle had provided the scandal on which any sound teen career is based (and had opened the floodgates for such as Elton John) and glam had handed him a generation on a plate. Increasingly he pushed at the limits, offering himself as Artist, a generalist adopting different roles over a series of brilliant, yet reactive and reflexive albums.

Each had a high-profile, visual identity that went with the product: these identities Bowie would live out for the duration of the product's life, to such an extent that the albums seemed to have more life than he did – possession in reverse. However dangerous, it was a shield, and gave the advantages of being an Artist rather than an Entertainer: a more permissibly aloof stance, a greater deal of privacy, a greater ability to chop and change. Ultimately, it was that distancing inherent in Ziggy – avoiding the effects of being a pop star by adopting it as a *role* – amplified.

All this time he was being watched. And copied. Having taught a whole generation to pose, they weren't about to give up: they just got arty as well.

To fit the artist image he began to steal from, and model himself on, specifically literary sources: particularly William Burroughs and Christopher Isherwood. Both are more or less specifically homosex authors, both deal with smut and totalitarian control as *part* of a slightly more complicated world view that Bowie seemed to transmit. Pop will never leave anything alone, and automatically trashes literary models; either way, Bowie's dilettante fancy flashed on the most obvious elements of both.

From Burroughs he took cut-ups (now translated as 'random' or 'planned accidents') and control paranoia, *1984*-style. From Isherwood the physical spirit of society in decay, pushing the Weimar parallels – the dyed blond, ambiguous dandy, the Thin White Duke. All this was at best stylish and illustrative, particularly when coupled with some good torch songs like 'Win' and 'Golden years', at worst silly and dangerous, not only generally – in reinforcing the role of the Artist as divine, separate from society and responsible only to himself – but personally. Role assumption became loss of identity: crack baby crack.

By this time Bowie was reaping the rewards of what he'd sown. Punk professed to take *Diamond Dogs* seriously. In a fit of cultural Stalinism, it ignored homosex and concentrated on decay and *1984*: true to its roots as an Art Movement (rather than a True Expression of Working Class Revolt) it was fascinated by Bowie as Artist, as Art object, in an orgy of self-re-creation. Remember those wacky pseudonyms?

The man himself had meantime Come Down to Earth and side-stepped into withdrawal, away from any sharply defined image: always at his best when writing for kids ('Kooks'), Bowie introduced a note of autism into the next two albums, *Low* and *"Heroes"*, as well as several electronic pieces that had the power to disturb dreams. True to form, this mode was discontinued.

As Bowie marked time for two unproductive years, his electronic pieces were copied endlessly and became Moderne. He spent the rest of his time appearing in a silly 'decadent' movie and endorsing various people on the sillier end of arty pop: with the exception of Talking Heads, he was to give his direct or indirect approval to Eno, Human League, Devo and Siouxsie and The Banshees. His approval meant they were all taken *very* seriously.

Most revealingly, he made heavy use of Steve Strange in the 'Ashes to ashes' video – the most recent, the most absurd, yet *the* most magnificent, exponent of the Suburban Pose which never dies.

At the time of writing, what was once irritating and daft is fast becoming a bleat of defiance; *Scary Monsters* arrives in a climate which is hard on both Bowie and his chosen children.

In the face of increasing hardship and political polarization, arty posing and homosex – inextricably linked too often thanks to Bowie's example – are definitely seen to be *out*: the former as a childish luxury, the latter as a definite social disadvantage as dog eats dog.

The new album attempts to come to terms with this: angry, disturbed singing over harsh distorted noises laid on a familiar Bowie beat. A careful mix of the familiar and the novel, some of it is impressive, all of it beautifully crafted, while two tracks – 'Scary monsters', and 'Scream like a baby' – are equal to anything he's done.

Bowie would like to sound worried, and he no doubt is: at least three of the tracks contain a futurism that is only a small projection from present trends, call it Alternative Present if you will.

'Fashion', always an acrostic of fascism and passion, accurately catches the soldier talk coming from the middle classes, while 'Scream like a baby' makes it quite clear that if you're gay or socially at all divergent then they'll come for *you*. He even appears to give the lie to his own position on 'Teenage wildlife': 'I feel like a group of one'. AAAaaah.

And yet the record arrives in a typically frittery sleeve. In the same week the press is full of glowing reports of *The Elephant Man* as Bowie keeps his options out of pop, out of Europe. You can't teach an old dilettante new tricks.

Each new album raises the question of his relevance: this one even more so, as Bowie backs up against the wall of his futurism. What was once projection is now fact. But each time, his relevance is reaffirmed: not necessarily because of musical or pop merit, or even brand loyalty, but because it touches on the concerns that are expected.

No one has surpassed Bowie as gender bender, not even the Village People, although macho styles have taken over in the gay discos, parodying the world outside. Tom Robinson's committed model didn't last either. Nor has anyone surpassed him as Artist model, not even Eno. Even though he's due for supersession on both counts, the mystique is still deadly strong. Why? Because David Bowie has entered British life as the model for every kid who says 'I wish I was . . .'. He's the creation of that need, and as long as it remains, so will he. Will it be for ever?

SIMON FRITH

The art of posing

New Society, 23 April 1981

When I first came to Coventry, in 1972, I used to see them at the bus stop: the boys with green hair, the Bowie Boys, their style shifting with the record sleeves. There were a handful of Bowie Boys in every provincial town and I thought them the bravest of all the youth cults: everything they did was determined by their pose, and every youth pose since has owed something to them.

British pop fans have always liked to dress up like the stars, but the Bowie Boys didn't just get ready on their nights out. Bowieism was a way of life – style as meaning – and no other idol has had such an intense influence on his fans as David Bowie. His example of self-creation was serious and playful – image as art as image, and his tastes, the selves he created, were impeccably suburban: he read romantic literature; he was obsessively, narcissistically, self-effacing. Bowie wasn't sexy like most pop idols. His voice and body were aesthetic not sensual objects; he expressed semi-detached bedroom fantasies, boys' arty dreams; there were few Bowie Girls. Bowie was youth culture not as collective hedonism, but as an individual grace that showed up everyone else as clods.

In the event, then, it was ironic that punk became such a cloddish music, because it was the Bowie Boys' intense concentration on style that inspired Malcolm McLaren (The Sex Pistols' inventor) to make his move from clothes to music fashion. McLaren, like several other professional image-sellers, was fascinated by the Bowie nights which were a feature of London life from about 1975 – David's records on the turntable, his styles on the dance floor, private desires gone public.

Punk fashion soon went the way of all youth subcultures (routinized, uniformed, dulled) but the Bowie Boys stayed locked into their original dreams. By 1978 the most stylish Bowie night was Tuesday at Billy's. Rusty Egan (then in a pop-punk band, The Rich Kids) was the disc jockey; Steve Strange, a long-standing punk club parasite, was the doorman, the arbiter (the idea was taken from New York's Studio 54) of who was smart enough to be allowed in.

By 1979 these Bowie nights had moved to the Blitz and there were as many photographers present as there were posers, as many professional designers as amateurs. The Bowie fixation had been diluted into an art college ball, and as the Blitz style became an academic exercise (come dressed as the Weimar Republic), as Blitz music became the standard electric sound of the 'futurist' disco, so the Blitz pose became a very self-conscious, media-aimed affair. Everyone was calculating the commercial possibilities of a national Blitz culture – hence Spandau Ballet, four boys, a manager and graphicist from the Blitz dance floor; hence Visage, the band put together by Rusty Egan for Steve Strange.

Visage and Spandau Ballet have had such an instant pop success that the Blitz kids, new romantics or punk peacocks, are now a full-scale, media-charted 'movement'. Most of its observers don't much approve. Since punk, the sociological assumption has been that British youth is living in a state of mental siege. Music is expected to express the consequences, whether through the collective muddle of The Clash or in the raincoated despair of Joy Division. From this perspective the new-romantic approach seems straightforwardly decadent.

This is to take the Blitz kids at their own pose value. Much of what's going on, in fact, is a punk reshuffle – new, more melodramatic versions of old McLaren themes (tartan bondage trews, face paint), as punk's musical failures now relievedly follow the imperatives of pre-Pistols pop: look flash, gob first, make money!

The most successful pop group in 1981 is Adam and The Ants. Adam wasn't a Bowie Boy, but he was a punk failure and every day there's a picture of him somewhere in the *Sun* or the *Mirror*. The style of his success is a clue to the meaning of the whole 'new romantic' scam: Adam is a teenybop idol, a cross between Gary Glitter and Marc

Bolan; and Spandau Ballet are obviously Sweet – big lads dolled up, red faced, for a camp issue of *Vogue*.

There was a noisy group of girls behind me in the newsagent the other week, 11- and 12-year-olds arguing about the cover of *The Face* magazine. 'If that's Adam,' said one girl disgustedly, eyeing a nice-looking boy with a Dirk Bogarde quiff, 'then I'm Debbie Harry.' She wasn't, it wasn't – rather, Martin Kemp of Spandau Ballet. Adam is on the cover of this month's *Face*, holding a rose like a social democrat, ribbons in his hair. His appeal is more solid than Kemp's; he is the ageing juvenile lead in a low-budget children's swashbuckler. But both Adam and Kemp have the asexual, pinned-up looks of the authentic teenybop star; both are too well groomed to suggest anything . . . messy.

The Face is an interesting music paper. It is an independent monthly with a brave advertising policy (never more than eight pages out of 64) which has, remarkably, survived for a year now, getting better all the time. It is published and edited by Nick Logan, who edited the *New Musical Express* in its readable days. But it reflects, more obviously, Logan's experience with *Smash Hits*, a teenybop lyric magazine which he turned into a bestseller. *The Face* is, essentially, a picture paper; it has the best musician photos there have ever been and it has flourished (luckily? presciently?) on the recent emphasis on style.

There is, in fact, an odd disjunction between the cultural claims of the new pop stars themselves and the reality of their *Face* appeal. The official Blitz-kid mythologist, Robert Elms (bright and banal as a button), writes in the magazine about the electric dance floor and organizes loving fashion spreads for his mates' clothes-makers, but the pictures, which are all anyone reads, have a different reference point – those poster mags (appearing in the shops again) that flourished in the days of T Rex and The Osmonds. Blitz clothes look nice enough pinned up on the bedroom wall, but most people who buy *The Face* dress like Sheena Easton.

Cult fashions in Britain have always tended to the tacky. The images may be neat, but the reality has to be cheap clothes, badly made, ill-fitting; these fashions aren't chain-stored (like mainstream mod) and most young people can't afford their own costumers. Some youth styles, like skinhead and punk, have turned their tackiness into an aspect of the look itself; other styles – the 1967 summer of love, for instance – always looked better in the colour supplements.

The new romantics, precisely because of their elaboration, are particularly tacky, and it is ironic that the Bowie Boys, who were genuinely elegant (using simple clothes: their effort went into hair styling and make-up), should have given birth to such a clumsy fashion montage. These clothes (see *The Face*) are merely costumes: sewn on for the performance, seams showing from the back and sides. The point of Blitz posing is less the night itself than the pictures in the papers that follow; the Blitz kids don't wear clothes but model them.

There is now a fashion fanzine, *i-D*, which articulates this ideology of style. The *i-D* staff go into the streets and use passers-by as their dummies, snapping them as fashion plates, documenting their details. (Where did this come from? How much did it cost?) The argument is that we are what we dress ourselves up to be, and everybody is dressed up to be something. But the sociological implication is different: despite *i-D*'s selective tastes, the magazine mostly turns up people not *inventing* ways to express themselves but making do with what they can get.

i-D documents a street fashion which is essentially second-hand. The *i-D* models are not part of a new subculture (romantic or not) but draw eclectically on late hippie (the clothes stalls in Kensington market are lively again), mid-period punk (short hair and streaks and badges) and the 1970s feminist anti-feminine look (baggy, primary colours, prepubescent). *i-D*'s models share only a non-fashion fashion that takes its stylistic signs from wherever it can find them; these clothes are worn, and in taking them out of their daily routine, posing them, *i-D* undermines its own fashion-trade assumption – such unself-conscious coats and blouses are more emotional, more expressive, than anything drawn by the new-romantic designers. They're working clothes; they've earned their right to be tatty.

The art college theorists, of course, are fascinated by the idea of the Blitz. In her magazine ZG, Rosetta Brooks interprets posing as a performance art in which subcultural signs are deliberately jumbled up and thus made ambiguous, brought into question. She rightly points to the nostalgic elements of posing – the stylistic allusions are to past youth styles, to a lost community of 'innocent' male fun. Much of the so-called 'futurist' concern with style is, in fact, deeply reaction-ary. At the same time, the treatment of youth style as performance art makes for an immense condescension to the youth cultures involved: the history of rock-and-roll is trawled for the poses it can yield; the implication is that the music had no substance at all.

The new romantics, for all their clever ideas, end up with a conventional teenybop appeal – they've got a detached, entrepreneu-rial concern to get the formulas right. Their art of posing is still defined by the middle page of *Jackie*, and Adam's teeny-fans have the right response to all this – they laugh at him.

The only new pop person with an interesting idea is Malcolm McLaren, who encouraged Adam to dress up and go 'tribal' and has been explicitly pursuing teenybop sales with his own group, Bow Wow Wow. McLaren (who with The Sex Pistols drew loosely on situationism) is drawing loosely now on autonomism – the concept of the young as an American Indian tribe, for example, was developed by the youth movement in Zurich. The message of the latest Bow Wow Wow single, 'W.O.R.K.', is plain enough: Demolition of the Work Ethic takes us to the Age of the Primitive!

'T-E-K Technology is DEMOLITION OF DADDY is A-U-T Autonomy,' sings Annabella, 'There's no need to work ever!'

Bow Wow Wow's records have not yet swept the nation. McLaren's scheme has foundered, as always, on bohemian arrogance, on the assumption that he is an expert on other people's fun. He continues to treat pop style both too seriously and not seriously enough. If the vast majority of fans (punks, Blitz kids and Antpeople alike) dress up just for a laugh and do not follow McLaren's general arguments at all, for the stylish minority dressing up is not a matter of fun even to start with. The art of posing, as the Bowie Boys discovered, is a matter of commitment: the problem is not to turn work into play, but to turn play into a precise, disciplined work.

Notes

1. See also the following sources:
   Allan Jones, 'Riding on the dynamic of disaster', *Melody Maker* (28 April 1979), p. 19.
   Kurt Loder, 'Eno', *Synapse* (January/February 1979).
   Glen O'Brien, 'Eno at the edge of rock', *Interview*, 12 (September 1982), p. 32.
   Charles Amirkhanian, 'Eno at KPFA', unpublished typescript from 2/2/80 radio interview, transcribed by S. Stone.
   Anthony DeCurtis, 'Fripp, lord of discipline', *Record*, 3 (May 1984), p. 20.
   John Diliberto, 'Zen and the art of Fripp's guitar', *Electronic Musician* (June 1987), p. 48.

SIX

Fame

ANNE RICE

David Bowie and the end of gender

Vogue, November 1983

Whirling on the very edge of the culture, the great rock singers of our time personify our laments, our fears and our dreams. They are the fantasy figures of the romantic artistic vision, set free to evolve on record and in live performance exactly as they please.

In a technological society obsessed with the redefinition of masculine/feminine, they shatter conventional notions of sexual charisma – male singers plastered with lipstick and rouge as they gyrate like belly-dancers, female singers packed into metal and leather armour as they abandon the natural soprano for the guttural chest voice.

Looking at this stunning confluence of creativity and power, one can't help but wonder why so few of these rock stars have made electrifying transitions to the screen. Experts tell us that record audiences and movie audiences are almost exactly the same: young people to whom change isn't so much frightening as essential, the most willingly experimental class of consumers who transmit the major changes in costume, style and ideas. One senses a loss of energy somewhere, a connection misunderstood.

One magnificent exception, however, is glitter rock star David Bowie, who rose to fame in the seventies with his flamboyant concert performances and freakish theatrical personae – Ziggy Stardust, the Thin White Duke. Bowie, who has always promised the end of gender in his elegant and feline guises, not only is fascinating as an actor but amplifies in his films the lithe androgynous beauty underlying his ever-powerful rock-singer appeal.

As the sublimely gentle extraterrestrial in Nicolas Roeg's *The Man Who Fell to Earth*, Bowie gave fragility and passivity a new integrity. And as the decaying vampire John Blaycock in Tony Scott's *The Hunger*, he gave the picture – almost entirely through the exquisitely modulated delivery of his lines – its only real hint of tragic depth.

These films, coming seven years apart, are amazingly similar in the way they use Bowie's aura of vulnerability: he is a wounded and doomed monster in both.

And now, in his latest picture, Nagisa Oshima's *Merry Christmas, Mr Lawrence*, Bowie plays Major Staffer Jack Celliers, a British prisoner in a Japanese war camp, the victim of overwhelming forces once again. But in this picture he is also the hero, with an irrepressible vigour alien to the unearthly stranger and the languishing vampire he played before.

Something new is happening with Bowie, and it bears examination. Each of these three films was made by a different creative team – writer, director, producer. Yet it is impossible not to see *Merry Christmas, Mr Lawrence* as deliberately playing with the sexual ambiguity that surrounds Bowie in his earlier roles. How can one escape noticing, for example, that in both *The Man Who Fell to Earth* and *The Hunger*, Bowie is so physically weak at one point that he has to be carried by the female lead. (Candy Clark, his marvellously mundane girlfriend, carries him down a hotel hallway in the former film, and Catherine Deneuve, his seemingly immortal vampire lover, lugs Bowie all the way to the attic of her Manhattan townhouse in the latter.) Yet in *Merry Christmas, Mr Lawrence*, it is Bowie who does the carrying – of the badly beaten British officer (played by Tom Conti) in the very same manner that Bowie himself was carried.

And how can we not observe that in *The Man Who Fell to Earth*, Bowie, the impotent alien, fails to bring water back to his dying planet. But in *Merry Christmas, Mr Lawrence*, he is the one who brings nourishment to the hungry English prisoners to whom the Japanese have denied food.

In *The Man Who Fell to Earth*, Bowie horrifies Candy Clark when he reveals his reptilian appearance to her. She climbs out of the bed and runs. And in *The Hunger*, when the immortal Catherine Deneuve kisses the decrepit and decaying Bowie who has aged three hundred years in one day, it is a moment of true horror because we know the revulsion she feels. But in *Merry Christmas, Mr Lawrence*, Bowie never ceases to be, even in martyrdom, the unquestioned object of the Japanese camp commander's fascination and desire.

The most amazing thing about his new film is that through all these inversions and reversals, Bowie as the courageous British soldier never loses his androgynous allure. Even battered and soiled, he is a golden blaze of lissome gesture, seraphic facial expression, satin hair. No matter what the action demands of him, there is an entrancing rhythm to his movements. And in bringing food to the starved British prisoners, he also gathers basketfuls of red flowers, which he defiantly munches on before the Japanese guards. In the film's vivid flashbacks, he is intimately connected to his younger brother, seen twice in a garden of breathtaking beauty, who sings in an almost magical male soprano, the true pre-gender voice.

And finally it is through the sexually charged gesture of kissing the Japanese captain (Ryuichi Sakamoto) before the whole camp that Bowie manages to draw the man's anger away from the British commander who is about to be killed.

Bowie, in this film, is the saviour and the hero he wasn't in the others, but it's a hero of his own unique design. He redefines his androgyny rather than renouncing it for the simpler, more brittle masculinity a less confident actor might have brought to the role. Or maybe Bowie is simply expanding on what he has been doing with androgyny all along.

We never doubt the goodness of Newton, the alien, in *The Man Who Fell to Earth*, or that he possesses his own brand of enormous strength. His fragility and generosity of spirit have nothing to do with the sophisticated renunciation of gender that we may associate with some rock singers or with the reckless, sneering (and extremely talented) he/she star of the recent film *Liquid Sky*, who, at one point in the film, looks right at the camera and tells us she is as androgynous as David Bowie. Newton's helplessness isn't the impotence of the transvestite or transsexual whose defiance of gender may be his or her only creative act. Rather, it is a harkening back to the pre-adolescent androgyny we have all known, a wise innocence that embraces the power of both sexes and uses it effortlessly before adult gender distinctions clamp down.

If we can see Bowie's three film roles as creating a real film personality – like the personality of a Bogart or a Fonda – Bowie is telling us in *Merry Christmas, Mr Lawrence* that this early androgynous wisdom is a greater reservoir of energy than we believe, and that a figure of immense magnetism and courage can be created without surrendering it, one equalling the Fondas and the Bogarts of the past.

The end of gender isn't the abolition of the masculine/feminine. Rather, it is the abolition of the gender tyranny that would divide us into armed camps. And this film, more completely than *The Man Who Fell to Earth*, tells us that if we can preserve that earlier complexity, that mingling of masculine and feminine we hear so exquisitely in the boy soprano, we can have the endless possibility of it all.

In sum, Bowie has expanded his range while sacrificing nothing of his old charm. The eyes (one cobalt, one grey), the flawless skin, the almost preternatural shimmer, continue to distract and disarm.

That *The Man Who Fell to Earth* was not followed by a string of Bowie films is a mystery. But this is a new decade, and it is obvious that the star once totally associated with the sexual and psychedelic obsessions of the seventies is as vital as ever as he pursues his unique vision in the world of Mel Gibson, Richard Gere, and other rough-edged screen heroes whose allure is rooted in the past. Simple virility may never become outdated any more than robust wines or log fires. But in a time when both men and women are becoming more and more androgynous to meet the demands of love, career, and family, it is Bowie, through the alchemy of his subtle strength and yielding beauty, who emerges as the new and thoroughly contemporary star.

LAURA FISSINGER

As I write this letter . . .

Creem, July 1983

Dear David,

Welcome to panic in Detroit.

Next to Bruce Springsteen and Bob Dylan, you are the mythical demi-god of rock. Next to Bob and Bruce, you've been written about the most, which is way too much. Now we're doing this special issue on New Rock and it's the day before press-time and I'm stuck. I'm writing this letter because (a) I've got to do something to fill the pages and (b) maybe you'll be enchanted with my cleverness and penchant for public humiliation, and write me a letter. Then we can go out for lunch. You'll tell me some great stories and then I'll write this earth-shattering feature which *Creem* or maybe *Psychology Today* will pay thousands of dollars for. Yeah? Only talking to you could provide a writer with things that haven't already been said.

Then! Then we'll go to some *really* great parties. (You won't think they're great because you've probably been to weirder parties than I could ever imagine. But my reactions will be amusing enough for an hour or two.) Then we'll be pals. So what makes me different from any other Bowie fan in the universe if that's what I want? Don't they all want that? Doesn't every fanatic want to be born again as the shoehorn of their idol?

Not me, buster. I've interviewed the guys in *Kansas*; celebrity holds no sway for me. Hey, this is the New Rock, and idols are against the religion. Thou shalt (overtly) take no idols, false or otherwise. Pagan, even.

Actually, that's part of what you tried to do for us lemmings when you split LA in 1976, sent Ziggy Stardust to space for ever and did the Berlin trilogy of *Low*, *"Heroes"* and *Lodger*. Not that brown hair means a person is being *themselves* or something, but as you dismantled the characters with bronze blush-on and platform shoes, I think people got a chance to see a process of growing up that was instructive, to say the least.

I can feel my language becoming academic here; God knows *Creem* has no love for four-syllable words and commas and stuff. I just don't know a funny or indirect way to say I think you've done things for pop music and culture as important as anything that Springsteen or Dylan have done. If I get too serious here, you'll never take me to those parties, I just know. It's a hell of a bind. Not only has too much been written about you, too much *serious* stuff has been written about you. And who needs a treatise on your link with New Rock? Your paw prints are all over it. From Blondie to PiL, fans *know* Bowie is not one of the hated dinosaurs.

This may be the most convoluted l-u-v note you've ever received.

Well, maybe not. I've met more than a few of your big fans. Not the ones that dye their whole bodies orange and really think they're Martians, but the more 'normal' ones. Again, like Bob and Bruce, you inspire this devotion. You become mirror, catalyst, precursor, sex object, therapist, role model, fashion director, etc.

In some of those *seeerrrious* essays, writers blather on about 'the mercurial, ever-changing Mr Bowie'. Hey – if changin' clothes is all the deal is, we could pitch tents in front of Macy's. Here is my theory of your charm: most people feel like they have no power to transform themselves. Going through life seems only to be about getting old, not getting different. Via music and visuals, you have implied that self-transformation is *possible*. Move over, Dr Joyce Brothers!

OK, sure, you've been an idol for some of these people. That's just it. If you were really the psychotic swish from space, no schlubs who drink beer and drive vans would ever have loved you. The great amorphous hoard of consumers is stupid . . . and yet *not* stupid. If they didn't smell a person inside the fashion spectacle and musical melodrama, you would have been declared a dead lizard years ago. Even pre-Berlin, in all those 'I am a freak of nature' interviews, the fans *knew*.

So anyway, now we hear you're taking a break from film and *Elephant Man* stage triumphs and all that and recording again. Well shit, let's get out the dancing shoes. Welcome back. You always used to say in interviews how you weren't really a musician, that music was just a way to make money and work on the large artistic ideas on a feasible scale. For not being a musician, you're not bad, dad!

So, David. Thanks for the hair that sticks out on the top, hair that sticks out at the crown, androgyny, creative pillaging from rock's past, the love of Brian Eno, feeling hot and playing it cool. More than anything, thanks for lasting. You'll be my idol through the next fifty waves. Lunch or not.

DEBORAH ELIZABETH FINN

Moon and gloom: David Bowie's frustrated messianism

Commonweal, 9 September 1983

Almost fifteen years after his first hit single, David Bowie can still market best-selling records and fill Madison Square Garden at will. Perhaps it is time to think very seriously about his rhetoric.

Mr Bowie is an important indicator of trends of thought and musical genre in popular culture. Although he has often made disclaimers of any didactic intentions whatsoever (while pausing for breath between bombastic philosophical pronouncements), he has led the way in popular music to the exploration of the themes of alienation and technology through folk music (*Space Oddity*), sexualized mysticism through heavy metal (*The Man Who Sold the World*), messianism and apocalypticism through blues-based rock-and-roll (*Ziggy Stardust, Diamond Dogs*), the American Dream and totalitarianism through soul and disco (*Young Americans, Station to Station*), solipsism in tension with global consciousness through avant-garde expressionism (*Low, "Heroes", Lodger*) – and of late has signalled a return to rock-and-roll and R & B in order to confront modernity (*Scary Monsters, Let's Dance*).

Let's Dance is a strange and difficult album; the music consists of breathtaking and very nearly seamless exercises in several popular music sub-genres, with lyrics that are disturbing in their expression of an ambivalent religiosity. In the keynote song, 'Modern love', we are told that 'There's no sign of life/It's just the power to charm'; evidently life has been supplanted by something known as modern love. The narrator tells us that he will never fall for modern love, but that it 'gets me to the church on time', which 'terrifies me . . . makes me party . . . puts my trust in God and Man', which in turn means 'no confession . . . no religion'.

'No religion' seems to be a cry of denial that echoes throughout the album; Mr Bowie, who in fifteen years of songwriting has seldom missed an opportunity to articulate the theme of naive but grandiose messianic aspirations, is not entirely successful in abandoning his preoccupation. In his latest work, the 'sound of the devil breaking parole' ('Ricochet') is very much in evidence.

Although 'Modern love' establishes the album's evasiveness on the subject of religion, it also represents an explicit attempt to come to grips with the problem of love, which, in Mr Bowie's world of modernity, is a disease of addiction. This theme persists throughout the album: 'I'm a mess without my little China girl' ('China girl'); 'I love you . . . what would I do' ('Without you'); 'my love for you would break my heart in two' ('Let's dance'); 'you wouldn't believe what I've been through . . . it's been so long' ('Cat people'). It is a theme closely associated with a sense of anomie and despair; Mr Bowie tells us: 'I feel like a sailboat adrift on the sea . . . I'm feeling disconnected' ('Shake it'); 'I feel a wreck . . . I feel tragic . . . I'm a mess' ('China girl'); 'I'm ready to throw in my hand . . . I'm willing to call it a day . . . I won't take another chance' ('Without you'). Love is a drug that sometimes brings relief, but often the side effects are quite as severe as the initial pain. 'Cat people', a new arrangement of the 1982 movie theme song with lyrics by Mr Bowie, is a track that conveys the rawness of emotion associated with addictive love. He has never been more apt in his description of the self-sustaining nature of obsession: 'I've been putting out fire with gasoline'.

Mr Bowie's songwriting has often suggested that the potential for intimacy and connectedness is pitted against a desire for supremacy. In 'China girl', the narrator has 'visions of swastikas in my head/Plans for everyone'. He warns her that he is 'a man who wants to rule the world'. But when he gets excited by the grandiosity of his vision, it is the China girl who soothes away the tension, substituting sexual release for the fulfilment of his global plans. It is love as methadone.

The album's title song is in many ways an extended meditation on the transience of this kind of love: 'Let's dance for fear your grace should fall/Let's dance for fear tonight is all'. It is not grace at all, but temporary relief that the narrator finds 'under the moonlight, the serious moonlight' ('Let's dance').

By the end of the album, love has been denatured and recreated as a transient dance floor phenomenon; any other manifestation would constitute too serious a spiritual threat. In the final song, 'Shake it', the narrator recognizes the potential for seeking heaven or hell, but opts instead for a more familiar destination: the discotheques of New York City. This reflects a pattern that is repeated throughout the album: crucial moral issues pertaining to religion and love are confronted; each time they prove to be too shattering to resolve, and solace is sought in whatever gratifications are available.

Let's Dance is a disturbing failure – if it is an attempt to trivialize what Mr Bowie has called (in the 1981 single, 'Under pressure') 'the terror of knowing what this world is about'. A song from the *Scary Monsters* album ('Because you're young') may offer us a clue as to Mr Bowie's artistic intentions: 'These pieces are broken/Hope I'm wrong but I know . . . and it makes me sad/So I'll dance my life away'. He offers what is ultimately an unsatisfactory antidote to the tensions of secularized modernity: 'Turn the holy pictures so they face the wall' ('Ricochet') and 'Let's dance to the song they're playing on the radio' ('Let's dance'). And in fact, the music has an exuberance that contrasts sharply with the anomie and fragmentation expressed by the lyrics. David Bowie has not merely enjoined us to dance; he has also provided some of the most exciting R & B-based dance music in years.

DEBORAH H. HOLDSTEIN

Put on your red shoes and dance the blues*

Jump/Cut, February 1984

The video to David Bowie's 'Let's dance' merges several interesting structures and categories: while not as indebted to the traditional musical as most pop videos, Bowie's tries to make a political statement about the permeation of capitalism, particularly as it both seduces and then rejects those outside the mainstream of society, people for whom there may never be a place, with or without the American Express card featured in the narrative. Atypically, 'Let's dance' does not create

* Part of a longer article, 'Music videos: messages and structures'.

its visuals from the lyrics of the song. If anything, the visuals completely contradict the deceptively simplistic words:

Let's dance.
Put on your red shoes and dance the blues
Let's dance
To the song they're playing on the radio
Let's sway
While colour lights up your face

The setting is Australia, presumably outside Sydney. Bowie, the performer/narrator of this apparently political video, performs in a bar filled mostly with Aborigines, people who haven't had a share in Australian culture or its financial spoils. The red shoes prove to be the video's central symbol of capitalism and White culture: as a young Aborigine man and woman dance in the bar, we cross-cut to the same couple with friends or family. They find the red shoes in the dirt on a mountaintop overlooking the city. She puts them on, and they begin to dance, accepting the material seduction of capitalism and the promise of a 'better life if one works hard'.

Out of these come images that reinforce exactly what the red shoes mean to the narrative. The young man is suddenly a factory worker, as Bowie, in the guise of the manager, walks in with a woman associate who's wearing the red shoes. Bowie evidently speaks harshly to the young man; the woman's red shoes visually represent capitalism and its oppression of the young man's people. We next cross-cut to the young woman, scrubbing the front porch of a wealthy White woman, who walks by the young woman wearing – what else – the red shoes, as the Aborigine woman looks after her longingly. Alternating surreal images of the young man pulling heavy machinery through Sydney traffic, and the young woman trying to scrub clean the city's streets, Bowie undercuts his own stardom, his own capitalism, his own success: these images tell us not only of the Aborigines' oppression at the hands of people like Bowie, but also that their desire to give in to the seduction of capitalism and the promise of a more comfortable existence won't work.

Bowie illustrates this with yet another example. The young man and woman are now in a shopping centre in Sydney where they purchase things – a necklace, a fancy dinner – with an American Express card, probably the most visible worldwide symbol of the dominant culture. After they've had this fling, however, we have reason to both applaud the Aborigines and hate ourselves for oppressing them: the young woman takes off the red shoes and stomps them in the dirt, a decision to reject that dominant culture and to preserve her own.

Unfortunately, however, this rejection keeps the Aborigines at the fringes of a world they deserve to share: a final series of shots places them high atop a mountain overlooking the city, distant from the life they can't have. The final shot is three-part in nature. With Bowie at the centre, the Aborigine couple at the left, and visions of elegant Sydney on the right, the rock star visually and narratively becomes the 'bridge' between the dominant and oppressed cultures, partly with the capitalists, partly with the oppressed. He reveals the multilayered complexities of keeping one's culture while participating in another, and the essential problem of the Aborigines being able to participate *at all* in a White-dominated world.

Bowie deserves credit for participating in the oppressive side of the video's action. A performer known for taking risks, he doesn't pretend that 'Let's dance' can represent a panacea for all the world, in the way that the dances in Michael Jackson's 'Beat it' pretend to resolve all social conflict. While he acts as the instrument through which the 'problem' is presented, he doesn't pretend that he alone can or will solve it. He is both the musician in the Aborigine bar and the capitalist-industrialist who, however indirectly, helps to oppress people. While the final image might appear to 'detach' Bowie, in the way that Donna Summer's detachment throughout her 'She works hard for the money' video undercuts her pretence of participation, Bowie has kept the structure and purpose of the narrative valid through his own appearance in a variety of roles. For David Bowie, there are no simple solutions; we can't solve the problems of the world in a six-minute video, but Bowie's one of the only performers who appears willing to acknowledge this.

MICK FARREN

Surface noise:
The trouble with Bowie

Trouser Press, December 1983/January 1984

It's not without a certain irony that we find ourselves sliding into 1984 with David Bowie the biggest thing in pop this side of Michael Jackson. It's not just that Bowie has survived to experience a date he once sang about. His current dazzling success tends to defy common wisdom about popular culture.

Bowie's been in this game for close to twenty years. He is well past the age when Mick Jagger was first called a boring old has-been. His radical changes of style would have totally alienated the fans of most other artists. Yet you hear few unkind words about David Bowie. He is one of a handful of pop stars who even the most vitriolic icon-busting critics seem unwilling to attack – either as man or as legend. Jim Morrison is one who enjoys such a hands-off situation, and Morrison has been securely dead for over a dozen years. Bowie, however, remains quite visible, hopping from one foot to the other, continuing a career.

Don't get me wrong, I am not a Bowie-hater. (I already feel some of you reaching for your poison pens or worse.) I have huge reserves of admiration for David Bowie, both as an entertainer and as a technician. He is without doubt one of the most consistently bright and innovative rock practitioners – and, unlike virtually any of his rivals, he has managed to parlay pop stardom into a credible career as an actor. The trouble I experience with Bowie? Whenever he comes under discussion and the folks around the bar start to get rapturous, a small voice pipes up in the back of my mind to remind me: this is the man who recorded 'The laughing gnome'.

There are a number of moments like this in Bowie's career. Together, they make me less than secure about his ambitions and motivations. Of course, everybody makes mistakes. With Bowie, it's the *quality* of his mistakes that gives pause. For example, let's go back to the very start, when he'd just ceased to be David Jones: one minute he wanted to be [Yardbird] Keith Relf, the next, Anthony Newley. *Anthony Newley?* What lurked in the psyche of the young David that wanted to be Anthony Newley?

Not just the young David either. A few weeks ago I saw Newley himself on the *Tonight* show. He was promoting some dumb musical he'd written based on the life of Charlie Chaplin. He sang. It was the first time I'd witnessed this not terribly attractive business in many years. I'd pretty much forgotten what he sounded like. It was chilling. Bowie still has that delivery. Through all these years, and all the way to Mars and back, Bowie still carries the Newley legacy.

I had misgivings when I first heard about the Ziggy Stardust concept. Bowie was clearly very eager to succeed, and there was nothing wrong with the music, but so much of the story seemed to have been a melange of H.P. Lovecraft and Robert Heinlein's *Stranger in a Strange Land*. I was certain someone would call him out for plagiarism. Nobody did. Ziggy drove the youth of the world bananas (and would-be bisexual). Since then, many have felt they owed Bowie a debt of gratitude for starting the first craze they could remember that had absolutely nothing to do with the sixties.

What made Ziggy run? Aspects of Bowie's behaviour could be explained only by an overwhelming desire for public acceptance. Far from having a burning desire to say something, he seemed willing, particularly in the early stages of his career, to say anything if he thought that was what the crowd wanted to hear. I started to think that maybe his major talents were the abilities to borrow and synthesize; he could also predict, at times with uncanny accuracy, the moods and needs of his audience. He was more like a shrewd politician than a driven artist. As with many shrewd politicians, it's hard to tell exactly what Bowie's politics – beliefs, if you like – actually are. His songs are clever but always oblique. It was never clear which goon squad was coming to town, and whether Bowie stood for or against them.

I recall him making an overtly political statement only once. During a bout of what was reputed to be cocaine psychosis, Bowie announced that Britain would do well to become a fascist dictatorship, with himself in the Hitler role. Apologists pointed out that this was a naive and addled statement made by someone attracted by the trappings and charisma of fascism, but who was definitely not a death camp enthusiast. I didn't buy it. As far as I was concerned, it was one of the man's most dubious statements. That everybody else forgave and forgot filled me with total amazement. Bob Dylan deep-sixed his career by becoming a born-again Christian; when Bowie announced he'd like to be a Nazi, everyone was extremely understanding.

The most popular aid to understanding David Bowie has always been the celebrated reptile theory: at regular intervals Bowie sheds his entire creative personality to reveal a new one formed beneath the old. I can't quite come to grips with this either. The cracked actor flitting from role to role may explain Bowie the performer/interpreter, but not the creator/innovator. To be able to drop a concept or 'personality' at a moment's notice indicates a shallowness of thought. This fatal trendiness may inspire my doubts about Bowie. The shallowness, if it exists, hasn't done Bowie any harm. He is the leading White pop star, with many millions stashed in the bank (Swiss, no doubt). His current image is upright if not totally straight. In traditional superstar manner, his name appears in the gossip columns, linked with Susan Sarandon. The uncut version of the 'China girl' video shows his current image to be decidedly heterosexual. More importantly, Bowie is making a smooth transition from pop star to movie idol – a transition that has eluded most aspiring rockers, particularly Mick Jagger.

David Bowie is riding so high that his thoughts must now, at least part of the time, be focused on a place in history. He has yet to have what you'd call an enormous hit movie, and he has yet to explore the possibility of directing or anything approaching serious writing. He has conquered most other worlds. Once again, I admit my admiration for the man. But, from Anthony Newley on, I still have all these unanswered questions. There are more. Are the native Australians in the 'Let's dance' video objects of compassion, social comment or just Pacific chic?

Far be it for me to trigger a Bowie backlash. I don't need the hate mail. Let's just say that the hottest item of 1984 is a mass of questions that haven't been answered satisfactorily for two decades. That must say something about the times we live in.

PATRICIA MACKAY
Serious – and stunning – moonlight
Theatre Crafts, January 1984

David Bowie. Polished and elegant. In suit and tie. Albeit very special suits and ties with high-waisted, pleated trousers and very short jackets. Egg-yolk yellow for one set and baby-blue for the second. And on stage throughout the Serious Moonlight concert tour he uses every gimmick such seemingly traditional garb provides. Carefully timing the removal of his jacket. Selecting the right moment to casually roll up the sleeves of his shirt. Nonchalantly loosening his tie. In earlier rock eras, these moves might have been in the heat of the moment. But not now. Not for Bowie. He's in control. This is a performance choreographed, rehearsed and blocked. Serious Moonlight is an arena-scale, one-man show. His first in the United States in five years. And eagerly awaited.

The 18,000-plus crowd, filling Madison Square Garden, was ready for a performance. And a performance they got. There, on a stage set with designer Mark Ravitz's neo-classical lintels and pediments, backed by a band clothed (by Peter Hall) in the multi-ethnicity befitting crossroads Hong Kong, the singer was pinpointed in beams of light designed by Allen Branton. Light that constantly swept and changed.

195

Colouring the space with unexpected depth. Branton's plot put 40 Vari-Lites (plus other conventional instruments) on stage, overhead, on either side of the performance area. The Vari-Lites swept up, down, over the audience, around, back and forth, catching Bowie in the beams. Suspending him in a colour-saturated space. And then in a flash, changing one powerful hue to another. It was as if a thousand individually hand-controlled follow-spots, with a limitless array of colours, had been choreographed with the precision of The Rockettes. Now wide. Now narrow. Now a cluster of pin beams. White to turquoise to green. Some in red while others criss-cross in yellow. Jerky, stark-white for 'Fame'. Hot reds and yellow for 'Red sails'. Creepy green for 'Scary monsters'. Seemingly endless variations.

The look – seamless and flawless – did not get that way by accident. This tour was carefully planned. The finished set was shipped to a soundstage in Dallas. There Bowie, Branton, and three guys who were going to be the principal lighting staff, Bowie's two lead musicians, and dancer/choreographer Chris Dunbar rehearsed daily for about two weeks. Here's where Branton and Bowie worked out the colour and the coordination of lights and music. Says Branton, 'I've never worked as far ahead, as effectively. Bowie was very serious about doing something polished and he had a clear sense of what he wanted the total product to be.'

Practise makes perfect – that old dogged adage – is seldom heard in the halls of the touring rock concert world. But it is that very old-fashioned ethic that, according to Branton, made Serious Moonlight so special. Practise, rehearsals and collaboration all coalesced into a special evening. While Branton sheepishly admits that it seems a bit silly to be marvelling over something so fundamental, he continues, 'but it seems rare in this kind of show. It's funny – a lot of the bigger acts will spend the money Bowie has to prepare and mount the show, but they'll spend it on toys – staging and special effects. They'd be better off spending half their money on hardware and more on gathering the whole team and talking about it for a week or so and seeing what they are going to do and why. Again, it sounds silly – but it is so fundamental and so rare.'

Sitting with Branton the morning after the New York Bowie première, he is already thinking about his next gig – Diana Ross in Central Park. Looking at the young – very early 30s – busy and professional concert lighting designer, you're very aware that this is no longer the seventies – the age of the big, wide, outrageous tours and all that went with it. Branton, a slim red-haired chap with a bent toward conservative, almost preppy dressing, hails from Little Rock, Arkansas . . . Branton was on the road with Ross when he got the phone call from Bowie. 'We talked for a few minutes. I told him I wanted to see lighting be more atmospheric than rock-show-tricksy-and-flashy. He said he wanted German expressionism. And I went and bought all the books.'

From the beginning they all knew that lighting was going to be the major element in the show's design. Says Branton, 'Given the state of technology today, that's probably the most efficient, cost-effective way to do a show. Sure you could spend millions on scenery and special effects. Flying David on a wire. Setting the band on fire. All that translates into construction costs and truck space. Lighting is what it is. Everybody said we want this to be really special; nobody knew what that meant.'

Strangely, in a passing shot at modesty, Branton at first denies that the use of the Vari-Lites is as special as it appears. With a little warming-up he confesses he knew that he wanted to push them to the limit and tried things that hadn't been done before. 'Every show thus far, including mine, generally has hung them in the same horizontal plane, on the overhead light grid. I wanted them on different planes. Turned on 90 degrees. Stretching their physical parameters.' The designer had started with heavy interpretation of David Bowie as a tragic figure. Then came the Dallas rehearsals. 'He turned out to be too much fun and not all that serious about being a tragic figure any more. It was so tempting to turn the whole thing into *Saturday Night Live*.'

So the stark white, Albert Speer shafts of light, the mysterious old German movies that Branton thought would form the backbone of the design gave way to a more diversified and colourful look. Branton pauses, finding the words for the final look, 'Fellini, Ziegfeld and Steven Spielberg would all be proud of us. It's got all those elements.' Branton admits to resisting the first draft of a plot saying, 'that means I've made up my mind. Once I zoom in there I feel this is what I've got to stick with. So I always try to inflate the first draft about ten to fifteen percent so that I've got options. For Serious Moonlight, my original version was sort of drawn on the back of a room service tray. The next version was the one we ordered equipment from. The third was the one the vendor drew so that it would make sense to him. And then there's the next one.'

Much like all designers who are not academically trained, Branton professes not to be very concerned with the tech-jock details of lighting equipment. He does, however, know his stuff – or at least as much as a designer needs to. 'It's silly, but it drives me nuts. The first question people always ask is, how many lights? That's not the point.' When Branton designs he first asks how many people, what are they going to do, what's the general content. Then, 'I keep drawing until I've got all the bases covered and then say, "This is what I want. How much?" I fight tooth and nail for the best equipment – exactly what I need.'

The positive collaboration Branton experienced with the Bowie Serious Moonlight tour is one that he hopes to recreate on future tour gigs. He's not exactly sure how you manage to create the atmosphere and get the people working together but, as he ruminates over a cup of coffee in a New York hotel, he says, 'I think you just chip away at it. From the time you get the first call, you start dropping hints that if you're calling me expecting certain results then part of the ground rules for getting those results is that I need x amount of time and I need to have certain questions answered. Not demanding, but gradually laying out the groundwork. And, if they buy into that, fine. Hopefully the other people they're hiring are saying the same things – if they're hiring the right people.'

Struck by the realities of the rock tour business, he shrugs, 'And maybe they won't. I don't know. These things are really so random. But it is very satisfying to work in a collaborative environment. It also has its practical aspects. If you want to do good work, and you want to be thought of as doing good work, then you come to realize that you don't do your best work in rotten situations. You try to avoid those. Just out of the survival instinct.'

KURT LODER

Tonight

Rolling Stone, 8 November 1984

This album is a throwaway, and David Bowie knows it. 'Blue Jean', the first single, sounds like a reject from *Diamond Dogs*; 'Don't look down' and 'Neighbourhood threat', two of the three Iggy Pop updates, are pointless travesties; and the gobs-of-sobs cover of The Beach Boys' 'God only knows' is the most embarrassing thing Bowie has committed to record since 'The laughing gnome'. Still, even when he's just going through the motions, Bowie is able to come up with something of interest, and the title cut – an inspired and blessedly spare reworking of an old Iggy-and-Ziggy collaboration from Pop's 1977 LP, *Lust for Life* – is one of the most vibrantly beautiful tracks he's ever recorded. Built on a bedrock reggae arrangement, with guest duettist Tina Turner adding grit and sinew, 'Tonight' displays Bowie's voice at its sweetest and most human. Having lopped off Pop's original explicit introduction – the song is addressed to a dying girlfriend – Bowie intones the text as a simple, if rather ambiguous, romance: 'Everything will be all right tonight/No one moves/No one talks/No one thinks/No one walks/Tonight.' By the end, after a lilting marimba solo, when Bowie sings, 'I will love you till I die/I will see you in the sky', and you realize the tonight he's talking about is actually the Big Sleep, the hook is in – this song's a hit.

Maybe 'Loving the alien' is too. Although declaimed in Bowie's quasi-operatic, belting-to-the-box-seats mode – a style overused throughout the LP – 'Alien' explicitly sticks it to today's hard-core religious bores ('Believing the strangest things . . . loving the alien'). Also appealing is the version of Leiber and Stoller's 'I keep forgetting', although Bowie, a big horn man these days, perversely replaces the stark horn break on Chuck Jackson's original version with a guitar solo. 'Tumble and twirl' and 'Dancing with the big boys' are overwhelmed by their busy, blaring arrangements: it would be nice to hear what's actually buried under all that storm-and-clang. Considering what Bowie is capable of, *Tonight* is an uninspired disappointment. But the title track, at least, proves that he *is* still capable – and perhaps of even more than we've previously realized.

PHILIP NORMAN

Beginner's luck

Vanity Fair, January 1986

> *Yes, I tell you, it had real savage splendour in the days when we found that no one couldn't sit on our faces any more because we'd loot to spend at last, and our world was to be our world, the one we wanted and not standing on the doorstep of someone else's waiting for honey, perhaps.*
>
> Colin MacInnes, *Absolute Beginner*

The pity of it is that no one managed to film Colin MacInnes's *Absolute Beginners* twenty years ago. Then there would have been only one choice to portray the novel's teenage hero, strutting the London streets in 'mock croc' shoes and Italian jacket, looking about him with eyes quick and bright as computer digits . . . Who else could it possibly have been but the teenage David Bowie?

The grown-up Bowie, instead, steals this musical *Absolute Beginners* in a character part revealing still further unexpected sides of his endlessly unpredictable talents. Having won acceptance as an actor in realms of the eerie and inscrutable, he clearly has decided it is time to let us start loving the alien. As Vendice Partners, the wicked adman, Bowie is funny, and he tap-dances. In his 'That's motivation' number – mesmerizing the street kid who might so easily have been his own younger self – he does an Astaire-style routine through a mirror, over a giant typewriter, and on top of a world globe. The Man Who Fell to Earth could not have foreseen ending thus.

Absolute Beginners is the first pop-trivia musical. That its trivia is predominantly and peculiarly British will not deter those many Americans whose study of old import-record jackets has familiarized them with such period Anglicisms as teddy boys, Vespa motor scooters, skiffle groups and the 2 I's coffee bar. Mid-fifties Britain in pop culture has assumed the idyllic nature of Julie Andrews's Alps or the barnyard in *Oklahoma!* So it is rendered here by a young director and an even younger producer, both steeped in rock-and-roll yet equally in love with the Technicolor extravaganzas of Stanley Donen and Vincente Minnelli. *Absolute Beginners* is an avowedly 'old-fashioned' musical, the kind Hollywood has been too nervous to produce for almost two decades. It also is utterly of its moment in containing enough cross-hatched stylistic references to make a new best-selling board game. Mixed up in it, for the trivia hound to disentangle, are progenitors as crazily unalike as *Guys and Dolls*, Jack Kerouac, Cliff Richard and The Sex Pistols.

Colin MacInnes published *Absolute Beginners* in 1959. He was himself a fascinating literary puzzle: son of the novelist Angela Thirkell, homosexual, depressive, a patrician pub crawler who, in deep middle-age, suddenly spoke for youth with the inspired empathy of a Kerouac. *Absolute Beginners* catches London precisely at its mid-fifties turning point from ancient to modern, bound in Victorian torpor yet trembling with the energy of a fresh-minted generation it had barely yet noticed. MacInnes was first to comprehend this new species, unleavened by war, indifferent to age-old British customs of class and manners, and just now taking its first espresso-froth sips of economic power. Teenagers are the 'absolute beginners', beginning their crusade to an era that would give them everything. MacInnes's sharp-faced, sharp-shod 19-year-old, with his ferocious dedication to 'kicks and fantasy', is their front-line skirmisher.

The novel has long enticed filmmakers with its neon-buzz vividness and pinball-busy pace, its cast of Runyonesque fellow-plotters in the teenage underworld – Dean Swift, Hoplite, Mr Cool, the Misery Kid. There is still no better sense of how it feels to be an absolute beginner, that perpetual, unknowing ecstasy, ricocheting from moment to moment, able to invest a lifetime in a kiss or coffee cup. The narrator's 'teenage dream' is, if anything, more potent now that the crusade is lost; their licence has been withdrawn from youth, and power rests, once more, in the grip of middle age.

The musical *Absolute Beginners* derives its major impact from the celebrated old-timers it features in surprising and irony-laden character parts. The young hero's sentimental dad is played, à la 'Come dancing', by Ray Davies of The Kinks. His mother is played by Mandy Rice-Davies, a principal in the Profumo sex scandal that toppled Britain's Tory Government in 1963. James Fox – whose first pop picture, *Performance*, contributed to his giving up films and joining a religious sect – plays Henley, the archetypal fifties smoothy. These Golden Oldies are set about by dollops of necessary mid-eighties youth, just as mid-eighties music augments the book's original modern-jazz background. Sade appears as Athene Duncannon, torch singer at the Chez Nobody club. With Bowie's and Ray Davies' original songs, there are soundtrack contributions from Nick Lowe, Animal Nightlife and Paul Weller's Style Council.

The whole enterprise is proof of the vastly healthier state Britain's movie industry has achieved since its seventies slump, thanks to new stimuli emanating from its supposed enemies, television and pop music. *Absolute Beginners* is financed jointly by Richard Branson's Virgin empire and Goldcrest, the London based film and TV company that, in 1984, scored massive international success with *The Killing Fields*. Both, to their credit, stuck by the aim of producer Steve Woolley and director Julien Temple to make an old-fashioned musical, taking no shortcuts even after its costs had proved – by British standards – enormous. The production, shot at Shepperton Studios outside London, involved an interior recreation of mid-fifties Soho and a back lot transformed into 'Napoli', as MacInnes's hero romantically dubs decrepit Notting Hill. Shooting was plagued by a summer of almost ceaseless rain. As a result, a budget fixed at $8.5 million ended up at more than $11 million.

Julien Temple, a saturnine 31-year-old, in his Giorgio Armani tweeds, is an unlikely heir to Vincente Minnelli. Son of a travel agent from Marylebone, North London, he studied history and architecture at Cambridge University, switched to the National Film School, and so found his true milieu in 1976, when London shimmered under

Saharan heat and shuddered at what then seemed a barely human new rock band called The Sex Pistols. Temple became The Pistols' personal filmmaker, writing and directing their apotheosis-cum-epitaph, *The Great Rock 'n' Roll Swindle*.

Steve Woolley, 28 and ponytailed, started in film from the bottom, working as an usher and ice-cream salesman at the Screen on the Green, a London art cinema that adventurously showed Julien Temple's earlier punk *cinéma vérité, Sex Pistols No. 1*. Punk and The Pistols inspired Woolley to quit his ice-cream booth and eventually to co-found Palace, a distribution company whose inventory reflected his own highly uninhibited tastes. Palace distributed *Diva* and *Paris, Texas*, as well as *The Evil Dead*, and was prescient enough to acquire British rights in David Bowie's much acclaimed *Merry Christmas, Mr Lawrence*. In 1983, Woolley teamed with Chris Brown, a respected young producer from mainstream British cinema. Brown's experience allied to Woolley's daring resulted in *The Company of Wolves*, a major British box-office success in 1984.

Julien Temple stumbled on *Absolute Beginners* in 1981 while researching a TV film on fifties style. He acquired the rights for a modest sum, but then ran into script difficulties that held the project over through the hot summer of 1984. The credits list three writers, not to mention obvious input from Temple, Woolley, Brown, executives at Virgin and Goldcrest, and the US distributor, Orion. There is also – *pace* P. G. Wodehouse – a 'writer of additional dialogue'.

By comparison, persuading the big names to play character roles proved relatively easy. Temple had already directed pop videos for Bowie and Ray Davies and won their esteem by using them as actors, not merely glorifying them in humdrum MTV style. Bowie was enthusiastic about the chance to develop his otherworldly screen aura into something more like David Bowie used to be on the rock stage. 'Everyone was keen to do it – and not for that much, either,' Woolley says. 'They all feel involved in the idea that it's about London, it's making London a big thing again.' His last outstanding objective was to persuade Keith Richards, a closet vaudeville fan, to appear as a seedy music hall comedian.

The action is set in 1958, in a London heat wave which did not actually occur that year but, rather, reflects the punk fantasia Woolley and Temple both remember fondly from '76. 'London in long spells of hot weather becomes quite different . . . almost magical,' Julien Temple says. 'I got a worm's-eye view of it in 1958, looking up at all the teddy boys. Even then, I don't think there were the extraordinary characters around that you saw in 1976. I remember those long sunsets down Oxford Street, when you'd see a girl with nothing on but a polka-dot mac walking into the 100 Club.'

The affinity of punk with late-fifties pop folklore and ephemera has made period details in the movie that much more obsessively exact. Some, indeed, may be over the heads of even British audiences. A pop promoter, Harry Charms, is seen ogling his latest discovery, with a Boy Scout manual on his desk. You would have to have read my book *Shout!* to know the significance of that. When Bowie offers a cigarette, he says, 'You're never alone with a Strand', quoting a famously disastrous TV advertising slogan that actually made people shun the brand for fear of being lonely. 'David had a very good memory for all that kind of thing,' Julien Temple says. 'Like knowing the jackets he wore shouldn't be padded. And E-Type Jaguars were an important part of the period for him.'

Bowie, in fact, surprised everyone with his straightforward professionalism, his memory for detail, and his intuitive comic gift. 'The character he plays really represents the whole change of Britain in the fifties,' Temple says. 'The frozen food, the cars with fins. David knew just how to get the right mid-Atlantic accent for an adman trying to be so slick and American but every so often slipping back into cockney.'

Colin MacInnes, who died broke in punk's *annus mirabilis*, would find piquancy in the $11 million now tied up in his prose. Temple and Woolley, he might be glad to see, face their budget overrun with the aplomb of true absolute beginners. 'Whatever we spent,' Steve Woolley says, giving the ghost of a Sex Pistol shrug, 'it's all up there on the screen.'

SEVEN

Rock 'n' Roll Suicide?

DAVID BUCKLEY
Political animal

The Tin Machine project has re-opened the question of just where David Bowie stands on political and social issues. In his twenty-five-year career, the man has adopted and rejected a succession of political and religious creeds, from his flirtation with Buddhism in the late sixties, through his fascination with German romanticism and German fascism, to his social and humanitarian concerns in the 1990s. Superficially, Bowie's development has been from far right to soft left, though it has always been extremely difficult to pin him down on single issues. Any distinction between Bowie's lyrics and what can be gleaned from interviews is complicated by his deliberate manipulation of image. One must always bear in mind that Bowie's lyrics, by their very nature, are a creative outlet open to influences which deflect and play with any political truths he might wish to put across. In general, those lyrics (certainly until Tin Machine) have not been simplistically didactic – they don't purport to moralize or to provide a plan of action. As Bowie commented in an interview with DJ Simon Bates in January 1990:

> An artist isn't there to be morally right, politically right or spiritually right. If he does put himself in that position then he's either aligned himself with the government or he's paid to do that – he's an artist for the state or he's working for a dictator . . . I mean, we are up there to scream and shout about ourselves and at the world, and you make the best of it you can.

We might not expect to extrapolate a coherent philosophy from a set of highly impressionistic lyrics, but Bowie's interviews, particularly those of the early and mid-seventies, were subject to a remarkably similar blend of theatricality and truth. Bowie admits that he would read something he hadn't actually said in the papers, and adopt that false viewpoint in interviews to create a third response. With these complications in mind, let's make of him what we can.

Probably the earliest Bowie track to be inspired by a politico-philosophical creed is 'The Supermen' (1970), which places him very much in the tradition of nineteenth-century romanticism. Bowie commented in 1976:

> I was still going through the thing when I was pretending I understood Nietzsche . . . A lot of that came out of trying to simplify books that I had read . . . And I had tried to translate it into my terms to understand it, so 'Supermen' came out of that . . . It's pre-fascist.[1]

This fascination with the superhuman potential and God-like qualities of the human condition was one that was to stay with Bowie until the *Station to Station* period. The rather lightweight instrumentation of *Hunky Dory*, for example, disguises the fact that much of the lyrical matter is very heavy meat indeed. 'Quicksand' is of obvious relevance here:

> I'm not a prophet or a stone-age man
> Just a mortal with potential of a superman

'Oh! You pretty things', covered with bizarre inappropriateness by Peter Noone, carried the message:

> Let me make it plain
> You gotta make way for the *Homo superior*

Ziggy Stardust was both the archetypal 'needing people' rock-and-roller and a Christ figure. The brilliant *Diamond Dogs*, based in part on Orwell's *1984*, again returns to the idea of the deification of the human condition, though now in the guise of totalitarianism. 'Big Brother', with its references to a nation needing a 'saviour', 'someone to follow' and 'some brave Apollo', reiterates this central theme.

By 1975, Bowie's interest in German romanticism had developed into a fixation with fascism. He appeared to be a man totally lost in his own circle of mysticism. *Station to Station* saw the creation of the pure, Aryan, monarchical Thin White Duke possessed with the power to 'bend sound' and obsessed with 'making sure white stains'. 'White stains' carried with it both a political and a sexual connotation while gesturing to a book of poems by Aleister Crowley, the self-styled 'wickedest man in the world', whose ideas also attracted Jimmy Page of Led Zeppelin.

Station to Station was a great album, but the eighteen-month addiction to cocaine was beginning to take its toll on Bowie's already fragmented mind. In an interview in 1975, Bowie commented, 'I think

that morals should be straightened up for a start. They're disgusting.'
He added:

> There will be a political figure in the not-too-distant future who'll sweep
> through this part of the world like early rock-and-roll did. You probably
> hope I'm not right, but I am . . . You've got to have an extreme right
> front come up and sweep everything off its feet and tidy everything up.
> Then you can get a new form of liberalism.[2]

During 1976 Bowie also stated that he wanted to become prime
minister, gave what looked like a Nazi salute at Victoria Station,
allegedly visited Hitler's bunker and was in trouble with the authorities
on the Russian/Finnish border when fascist 'research materials' were
confiscated. Bowie saw in Hitler all the attributes which made rock
stars tick:

> Adolf Hiter was one of the first rock stars. Look at some of the films and
> see how he moved. I think he was quite as good as Jagger . . . He [Hitler]
> was no politician. He was a media artist himself. He used politics and
> theatrics and created this thing that governed and controlled the show
> for those twelve years. The world will never see his like again. He staged
> a country.[3]

What do we make of all this? By 1977, Bowie had back-tracked:

> I am totally apolitical . . . It is not my position for the kind of artist I am,
> who tries to capture the rate of change, to adopt any given policy or
> stance politically because my job is an observer of what is happening and
> any statements made in that direction [*vis-à-vis* fascism] were a general
> reaction and a theatrical observation of what I could see happening in
> England.[4]

Bowie thus explained his comments as a piece of imaginative theatre –
another pose to be adopted for the purpose of his art. In 1992,
Morrissey engendered a tirade of abuse and criticism from press and
public alike for his politically ambiguous stance and his use of the
Union Jack on stage as signifier for a perceived loss of true national
identity. The ironic use of such potentially distasteful political symbols
invites criticism from those unwilling to accept their adoption as
theatrically expedient. In Bowie's case, it seems clear that he was
mentally unbalanced when he made these statements (he was also
storing his own urine in a refrigerator, if one biography is to be
believed!).[5] He was flirting with the symbols of fascism in a very
dangerous way – and at a dangerous time, given the social and
political unrest of the late seventies, the rise in Britain of the National
Front, and the beginnings of severe economic decline and the consequent disillusionment of youth.

However, the year of punk's most public, communal and vocal

demonstrations against the status quo found Bowie at his most detached from the outside world with *Low* and *"Heroes"*. As Jon Savage put it:

> Framing 1977, both records had a huge impact. For every person who saw the necessity of getting *into* the world, of becoming politically active and thus translating the original commitment of punk into a fierce, organized protest campaign, there was another who wanted to get *out* of this world: to disengage, to sort out the turmoil within their own heads . . . [6]

Bowie provided the ultimate example – wholly obsessed with self. From this high tide of solipsism, Bowie slowly opened his music up to show more awareness of social and political issues. 'Fantastic voyage', the big, quasi-balladic opening to *Lodger*, used the threat of nuclear war as subject matter, commenting on the cold war mentality of our leaders:

> Dignity is valuable, but our lives are valuable too.
> We're learning to live with somebody's depression

Scary Monsters, possibly Bowie's masterpiece, included the first clear statement from Bowie distancing himself from his mid-seventies fascist proclamations ('To be insulted by these fascists, it's so degrading')[7] amid a roar of angry, disorientating musical images.

It was not until the mid-eighties that Bowie could emerge with any credibility as a rational political and social observer. The switch can definitely be attributed to his relationship with his son, which assumed overriding significance, as the pop star on auto-destruct *circa* 1975 became the concerned and protective father a decade later. His altruistic concerns included patronage of the Brixton Community Centre, his manifest (over?) enthusiasm for Live Aid (Bowie had wanted to make it an annual event!) and his championing of the Aboriginal cause in the 'Let's dance' video. All these can be viewed as traditional showbiz alignments with good works and charities. Yet Bowie has been selective in his support and, in interviews, has resisted the overtly sermonizing tone of some of his peers. His commitment to causes has remained typically ambiguous; pop's most adroit moving target refuses to settle for long.

It is against this fluid attitude that the 'political' stance of Tin Machine must be viewed. In the mid-eighties, when Bowie appeared to have lost much of his thirst for innovative music, he was wont to describe himself as a 'populist entertainer', leaving direct social comment to others. A change in musical aesthetic around 1988, with his involvement with Edouard Lock, Reeves Gabrels and La La La Human Steps, appears to have a disaffection with contemporary society. In an interview in July 1989, on the TV programme *Rapido*, he predicted that his son's teenage years could see a collapse of values:

> What is the purpose of daily life? It doesn't seem any more to have any values that mean a thing. It's very hard for him to understand the structure because, in fact, I think the structure is decaying rapidly.

Bowie was revisiting the themes of apocalyptic disintegration that made *Diamond Dogs* so compelling. This time the material was fired at us straight, not refracted through the ironizing prism of his art.

On the first Tin Machine album, redolent with kamikaze guitar burn-outs and hastily composed lyrics screamed out over the top, songs which seem to end as if beheaded mid-verse none the less demonstrate a concern to present disaffection in a more didactic way than before. The two most overtly political songs, 'Under the god', a direct denunciation of neo-Nazis, and 'Crack city', a tirade against drug dealers and a warning against drug use, are both extremely simple lyrically, and deliberately so. Bowie commented:

> I don't wanna go on preaching but I've only heard a couple of anti-drug songs. Frankly, I don't think many people are writing them, but I've not heard one that's effective because they're all intellectual, they're all literate, and they're written for other writers.[8]

Of 'Under the god', he said:

> I wanted something that had the same simplistic, naive, radical, laying it down about the emergence of a new Nazi so that people could not mistake what the song was about.[9]

Of the two, 'Crack city' works much better, mainly because it retains a parodic element. Bowie starts in uncustomary, schoolmasterly mode:

> Oh come on all you children
> Don't grab that scabby hand
> It belongs to mister sniff and tell
> It belongs to the candy man

and there's no sympathy for the devil-pusher:

> May all your vilest nightmares
> Consume your shrunken head
> May the ho-ho-hounds of paranoia
> Dance upon your stinking bed

This is Bowie at his most lyrically direct, but the song works all the better for a touch of his old penchant for intertextuality. He deliberately rips off the riff from The Troggs' 'Wild thing' (subsequently covered by Jimi Hendrix) and, in musically recreating the persona of

Hendrix, presents us with one of the most resonant paradigms of pop star death through drug abuse.

Throughout the album the tone is engaged, if not positively sermonizing in tone. All this is pretty hard to take from pop's primary psychic disappearing act. 'Shopping for girls' on the second Tin Machine album eschews the swagger and posturing of, say, 'Under the god' through the readoption of some narrative distance. The images of child prostitution are described with the narrator disengaged from events, depicting, surveying – but not judging:

> These are children riding naked on the tourist pals while the
>   hollows that pass for eyes swell from withdrawal . . .
> Between the dull cold eyes and the mind unstable
>   No one over here reads the papers pal

Whatever tactic he adopts, one must question whether Bowie could ever effectively reposition his music along more didactic lines: it has always been underpinned by disengagement, with the listener never being sure whether what is *sung* is really *felt*.

Those with a penchant for dialectics have proposed that pop sensibilities fall broadly into two categories – the Apollonian (connoting reason, order, and moral and political engagement) and the Dionysian (concerned with the pleasures of the body, with irrationality and disorder). So, for example, Paul Weller, Elvis Costello and Bob Dylan would fall into the former category; The Stones, The Sex Pistols and The Happy Mondays into the latter. In *Blissed Out: The Raptures of Rock*, Simon Reynolds spoke for all those who championed the Dionysian view of pop, those – to use Barthes' distinction – who prized *jouissance* over *plaisir*. The language of order, principle and rationality was fine for everyday interaction, but successful art championed the disruptive, was fundamentally anti-meaning. Thus the eighties crop of entryist performers, those who sought to make political points subversively by their incorporation into conventional pop songs, were contrasted unfavourably with those groups, such as The Cocteau Twins and The Sugarcubes, who prized a language of non-sense, whose work functions as a sonic recreation of the self, a cartography of the mind. Reynolds argued:

> Me, I find myself steadily drifting back to the unfashionable conviction that radical meanings are betrayed by conventional forms; that if melodies, key changes and vocal cadences follow expected paths they can only reinforce commonsense perceptions . . . Instead of 'subversion', the cunning interpolation of irregular meanings into pop's circuitry, I'm more interested in a more literal upturning – topsy-turviness, the vaporization of meaning itself.[10]

With Bowie too, his most telling moments come when he is at his most disruptive. His mid-eighties creative nadir coincided with a lame attempt to make 'useful', emotionally engaged music. His period of brilliance came when he was synthesizing styles and strategies from Eno or William Burroughs, challenging how art could be codified, playing around with the formal conventions. When meaning is made too literal, the musical codes too obvious, and when the ironizing Bowie bleeds into the moralizing version, the results are, at best, uneven.

Perhaps the mock-political Tin Machine songs are a public exercise in purging himself of his own guilt, of pressing the erase button on the mid-seventies. With that particular operation over, perhaps we shall see a return to a less ordered, less worldly style of writing and performing. In the seventies, Bowie's sexual politics, his admission of bisexuality in the famous Michael Watts interview of January 1972,[11] aligned him immediately with forces in society which were pro-change and anti-Establishment. Bowie, with typical ambivalence, disdained the role of freedom fighter for sexual liberation and thus avoided the acrimony meted out to Lennon for his championing of radical issues. Nevertheless, this initial association with the gay cause provided the space for more vocally supportive stars like Tom Robinson later in the decade. When Bowie remade himself in the guise of peroxide all-round entertainer *circa* 1983, he threw away the trappings of bisexuality and thus removed a vital component from his creative armoury – who could ever forget the 'psychosexual apocalypse'[12] of Bowie in drag for the video of 'Boys keep swinging'? He lost that quality of sexual ambivalence and downright kinkiness that Madonna and Prince have exploited with such conspicuous success.

While many would find a broad measure of agreement with Bowie's recent social pronouncements, his best art has always been individualistic and he has shied away from any subscription to a programme for social change. Bowie's vast hinterland of narcissistic grandeur is the territory many hope he will inhabit again.

DAVID WILD

Bowie's wedding album

Rolling Stone, 21 January 1993

'Welcome to Spock's place,' says a chipper David Bowie as he ushers a visitor into Studio B at the Hit Factory Studios, in midtown Manhattan. The room bears a passing resemblance to the starship *Enterprise*, but what's more striking is the fact that the star trekking behind the boards is none other than Major Tom himself.

It's early on a crisp fall morning, and Bowie – looking fit and unsurprisingly stylish in black jeans and a grey sweater – is anxious to get to work on the mixing for his upcoming album, his first solo effort in six years. 'I'm so proud of this record,' says Bowie, breaking into a little tap-dance of excitement. 'At the risk of blowing my own horn, I don't think I've hit this peak before as a performer and a writer.'

In fact, Bowie blows his own horn – saxophone, to be precise – all over the new album, the title of which he wishes to keep secret for the time being. That's just one surprise that comes from a sneak preview of some of the new material Bowie selects to play this morning. The album – to be released by the new BMG-distributed Savage label in March – finds Bowie reteaming with producer and Chic mastermind Nile Rodgers, with whom he collaborated on *Let's Dance*, the 1983 soul-inflected smash that remains the biggest album of Bowie's career. It's also the first new Bowie offering since he signed up with Tin Machine, in 1988; publicly retired his old song book on the 1990 Sound + Vision tour; and married Iman, the model, actress and, most recently, outspoken advocate for Somalian relief, in 1992.

Combining some deeply personal, almost confessional writing with an eclectic musical approach – touching on both funk and jazz and featuring appearances from old pals like Mick Ronson and new ones like Al B. Sure! – the intriguing new music sounds worlds away from the aggressive guitar rock Bowie's been making with Tin Machine. It's also no *Let's Dance* rehash.

'If Nile and I wanted to do *Let's Dance II*,' Bowie says, 'we would have done it years ago, when, perhaps, it would have made some sense. Working together again, we avoided falling into that trap at all costs.' If anything, Bowie says, the music he and Rodgers are making reminds him more of his experimental work with Brian Eno during the seventies.

'For us to repeat ourselves would be about as exciting as a director making *Friday the 13th Part VII* or something,' says Nile Rodgers, arriving from work in another studio. 'Half the fun of working with David is that you never know *what* the fuck he's going to come up with.'

After *Let's Dance*, Bowie drifted through much of the mid-eighties. He says his subsequent experiences with Tin Machine got him back on course creatively. And though the public has failed to embrace the band, Bowie reports that the group is 'still alive and well, living in various parts of America'. He also reports he's not desperate for a hit. 'Frankly, I've made a lot of money over the years,' he says. 'If I want to make music outside the mainstream, I can't expect massive sales, so there's no self-pitying to go on.'

The new album features a unique, dramatically different approach, with guitar largely taking a back seat to Bowie's own sax stylings (many of which are electronically treated) and the trumpet, cornet and flugelhorn work of the distinguished jazzman Lester Bowie. 'The Fabulous Bowie Brothers together again for the first time', Bowie says with a chuckle. Both Bowie and Rodgers were interested in exploring music with elements of jazz but without the elitist jazz sensibility they both find deadly.

Asked to rank himself as a sax player, Bowie offers Tin Machine guitarist Reeves Gabrels's description: 'the Neil Young of the saxophone', an instinctive, not technical, talent. Contacted later, Lester Bowie gives a different comparison: 'David's a saxophonist kind of like Bill Clinton is', he says with a laugh, 'but it works. The music is really good.'

As Bowie cheerfully bounces around the studio, it seems clear marriage is agreeing with him. 'I have someone who loves me for me,' he announces in a mock-cockney accent. 'Seriously, it *really* helps.' Two songs inspired by his marriage to Iman frame the new album. 'The wedding' – which opens the record – is a joyous instrumental complete with church bells that Bowie wrote for his nuptials, then reworked in less dreamy, funkier form for public consumption. The album-closing 'Wedding song' – an ultraromantic number that finds Bowie crooning to his 'angel for life' – sounds, according to the singer, 'every bit as saccharine as you might want it to be'.

Decidedly less celebratory, is 'Jump, they say', an intense yet infectious track that features a backward sax solo, which lends the song an eerie Middle Eastern tone. Bowie confesses that the haunting song is loosely autobiographical in that it deals with the suicide of his step-brother. 'It's the first time I've felt capable of addressing it,' he says.

Bowie's Spiders From Mars-era sidekick Mick Ronson – with whom he's stayed in touch – offers an inspired guitar solo on another track, a wild, funked-up cover of a well-known sixties FM chestnut, 'I feel free'. 'The dear old thing plays great,' Bowie says of Ronson, who has been battling cancer recently.[13] 'He's got the will-power of all time.' Bowie was impressed with Ronson's production of Morrissey's recent release, *Your Arsenal*, so he also recorded 'a *totally* camp' cover of 'I know it's gonna happen someday' from that album. 'It's me singing Morrissey singing me,' says a grinning Bowie, adding that the result sounds like an *Aladdin Sane* outtake.

Also joining the core band – the Bowies, Rodgers on rhythm guitar, Sterling Campbell on drums, Barry Campbell on bass, Philippe Saisse on keyboards and Richard Hilton on synthesizer – is former Bowie pianist Mike Garson. Gabrels, meanwhile, appears on 'You've been around', a powerful rocker he and Bowie co-wrote.

One potent track sure to attract attention is 'Black tie, white noise', a complex, Marvin Gaye-influenced duet with Al B. Sure! inspired by the Los Angeles riots. 'Iman and I arrived in LA from Europe the day the [Rodney King] decision came in,' Bowie says. 'The whole thing felt like nothing less than a prison riot by people who had been caged up for too long with no reason.' The song has a tough, edgy quality that Bowie wanted. 'I didn't want it to turn into an "Ebony and Ivory" for the nineties,' he says.

Bowie says he has no regrets about retiring his old hits and no plans to tour behind his new album or take on any new acting roles. After completing the album, he'll spend time with his wife and get ready to record with Tin Machine later in 1993. Still, asked if he ever has a hankering to return to the days when every record meant a new persona, Bowie admits: 'It has been gnawing at me, the idea of one more time developing a character. I do love the theatrical side of the thing – not only do I enjoy it, I also think I'm quite good at it. But for the time being I'm *quite* happy being me.'

MICHAEL BRACEWELL
Dedicated followers of Bowie
Guardian, 16 April 1990

At around about the time that punk rock hit Guildford and people who wouldn't know a dole card if it bit them were beginning to drop their aitches when they talked about their records, an advert appeared in the music press. It said: 'There is old wave, there is new wave, and there is David Bowie . . .'

It was the kind of slogan one could imagine being intoned by a man with a husky voice during the trailer for a horror film, and it seemed (on first reading) to be quite impressive. Various people I know cut out this ad and stuck it on their bedroom wall ('Jeremy! I hope you're using Blu-tack . . .') as a kind of token of respect towards the last rock 'superstar' whom it was still all right to like now that we were all born-again urchins with A-levels.

Most young people of the punk rock generation had cut their teeth on the androgynous excesses of David Bowie (even though in later years they would claim they'd been listening to Motown all along), and it suddenly seemed (now that the Thin White Duke himself was doing vaguely punkish things in that frightfully punk city, Berlin) that they needn't drop their hero after all. Indeed, now that Bowie had toned down his image (we are talking late seventies here), it was much easier to look like him without being told to change or having to endure embarrassing conversations about the nature of one's sexuality.

But it wasn't always like that, oh dear no. There was a time when David Bowie's 'look' (or 'mask' if you are intellectual) came across as both significant and dangerous. From a dubious underground incubator in which bisexuality had mingled with a host of eclectic cultural influences (most of which were later researched at length to spawn industrial quantities of dull art-student dissertations), a beautiful monster called Ziggy Stardust emerged. Though obviously a stranger to the dentist, he was the nearest thing to heaven on earth that a generation of pasty European and American teenagers had ever seen. And that's when the fun began.

We can laugh about it now (as we gaze pityingly at Brosettes or sneer at the Clanger-like tribes of short people who say 'Aceed' for no apparent reason as they lollop down the high street pretending to be Black), but do you remember the state of those early Bowie audiences? Of course you do. They were Tony and Kev, their fat little faces caked with foundation as they twirled their pearls and discussed the smell of Boots' henna. And there were Jane, Trish and Judy, each with carefully drawn lightning flashes zooming across their noses and fingering their *one earring*. Not until new romantics were the youth of Britain destined to look so silly. But it seemed so good at the time. There is many an estate agent joining the Wine Society now who was once slave to a style that involved crossing Aubrey Beardsley with Flash Gordon to look like Joe 90 in drag.

But Bowie (as we constantly reminded one another) was always one step ahead. Just when we'd all worked out how to put on nail varnish without looking as though we'd had a nasty accident with a tinopener, Bowie appeared on the front of *Diamond Dogs* wearing nothing at all, with paws, and this defeated everyone. (I gather that in Idaho there was someone who removed to a kennel for the duration, but if this is true then it is too heart-breaking to dwell upon.) By now David Bowie was an International Legend, and while the cloning levelled off a little, the world held its breath to see what the next image would be.

Well, would you credit it? Nice trousers, a fringe, just a hint of clear nail polish and a loose grey shirt. The girls went loopy with lust and Croydon found its place on the map as a place to listen to the White soul that *Young Americans* pumped into the suburbs. The cosmetics bar at Miss Selfridge was mercifully freed from the male contingent among its customers, and it appeared that Bowie wannabees had been released from fashion demands that endangered their personal safety.

Not for long, however. It was dinner suits and white shirts (minus jackets) next, causing the proceeds of Oxfam to rocket, and then it was baggy white trousers with about twenty pleats which (no matter how hard one tried) would never have the cool elegance of those that The Master wore.

Although the shock factor in the Bowie look had been reduced to enter the opulent eighties, not many of the fans (now, let's face it, getting a little too old to copy their idol verbatim) could *afford* these new looks. Exquisite suits, Platonically perfect leather jackets, Japanese shirts – it was all too much for a 20-year-old trying to make a start in advertising or pay off a bill from Mothercare that made the Bolivian national debt look manageable. The chain-stores took over, and fashion did whatever it is that fashion does when nobody's particularly interested in clothes for a while. But Bowie had one more card to play . . .

I know hardened merchant bankers who cannot resist the urge to weep when they see the 'Ashes to ashes' video. To the depths of their index-linked souls they feel that it is *their* youth that wanders off down that beach at the end, a curious pierrot, a Peter Pan left behind in

Never-Never Land to be lost and frightened, bewildered and sad. If David Bowie is (or was) a genius (and I use the term with caution), then it is the 'Ashes to ashes' pierrot that affirms his status. We all know that he should have retired then, and God knows what the poor man must have suffered in the subsequent years of mediocrity, but if you ever get the chance to watch that video again, do – it is as touching and poignant as anything any of our best young artists have ever created.

Notes

1. Interviewed by Stuart Grundy for *The David Bowie Story*, broadcast on BBC Radio 1, May 1976.

2. Quoted in Anthony O'Grady, 'Dictatorship: The next step?', *New Musical Express* (23 August 1975), pp. 5–6.

3. Quoted in Barry Miles (ed.), *Bowie in His Own Words*, London, Omnibus Press, 1980, p. 124.

4. German TV interview to promote *"Heroes"*, 1977.

5. Tony Zanetta and Henry Edwards, *Stardust: The life and times of David Bowie*, London, Michael Joseph, 1986, p. 261.

6. Jon Savage, *England's Dreaming*, London, Faber & Faber, 1991, p. 421.

7. From 'It's no game'.

8. Steve Sutherland, 'Tin Machine: Metal gurus', *Melody Maker* (1 July 1989), p. 29.

9. *Idem.*

10. Simon Reynolds, *Blissed Out: The raptures of rock*, London, Serpent's Tail, 1990, p. 98.

11. See p. 47. Twenty years later, in 1992, Brett Anderson, lead singer with Suede, pulled exactly the same stunt with his 'I'm a bisexual man who's never had a homosexual experience' claim.

12. Thanks to Simon Reynolds for this phrase.

13. Mick Ronson died on 29 April 1993.

Selective bibliography

A plus sign following a page number indicates that the article continues on unspecified pages later in the volume or issue. Items marked with an asterisk are represented in this book.

Ahrens, Susan, 'David Bowie', *Modern Hi-Fi* (June/July 1976), pp. 49–53

Alterman, Lorraine, 'Bye, bye, Bowie', *Melody Maker* (23 December 1972), p. 37

Altman, Billy, 'Bowie on the brink: Waiting for the gift of sound and vision', *Creem* (April 1977), p. 58

Appleyard, Bryan, 'How Ziggy fell to earth', *Times* (18 June 1987), p. 16

Aronowitz, Al, 'The super pop event', *New York Post* (29 September 1972), p. 32

Arthur, J., 'Hard rockin' Mr Bowie', *Record Mirror* (9 September 1972)

Ashes [periodical], 1983–

Atkinson, Rick, 'All that glitters', *Disc* (20 January 1972)

Bailey, Andrew, 'Tears as Bowie bows out', *Evening Standard* (4 July 1973)

—— and Gambaccini, Paul, 'Big private party caps Bowie's final night on stage', *Rolling Stone* (16 August 1973), p. 8

Balaam, Dean, 'David Bowie: Claridge's to *Twin Peaks*', *Record Collector* (May 1992), pp. 3–9

Balfour, Lewis, 'David Bowie live', *Record Collector* (September 1988), pp. 3–6

Balm, Trixie A., 'Diamond wog', *Creem* (June 1975), pp. 62–3

—— 'Persona non grata ad astra', *Creem* (September 1976), pp. 54–5

—— 'Heroes', *Creem* (February 1978), p. 59

Bangs, Lester, 'Iggy and The Stooges: The apotheosis of every parental nightmare', *Stereo Review* (July 1973)

*—— 'Swan dive into the mung', *Creem* (August 1974), p. 68

*—— 'Johnny Ray's better whirlpool: The new living Bowie', *Creem* (January

1975), pp. 38–40, 76; reprinted in *Psychotic Reactions and Carburetor Dung*, London, Heinemann, 1988, pp. 146–50

*—— 'Chicken head comes home to roost', *Creem* (April 1976), pp. 58–9; reprinted in *Psychotic Reactions and Carburetor Dung, op. cit.*, pp. 161–4

—— 'Iggy Pop: Blowtorch in bondage', *Village Voice* (28 March 1977), p. 49

Bashe, Philip, 'David Bowie, man of ch-ch-changes', *Circus* (31 August 1983), pp. 62–4

Bell, Max, 'The man who fell into Sinatra's suit', *New Musical Express* (15 May 1976), pp. 17, 46

Blair, Iain, 'Black and white minstrel', *Rock CD* (1/10), pp. 21–4

Blake, John, 'Back from Russia with love', *Evening News* (12 May 1973)

—— 'Kinky king of rock', *Evening News* (12 May 1973)

Blight, Cyril, 'Bowie plays Baal', *Creem* (September 1982), p. 46

Bloom, Howard, 'Bowie foresees the States in flames', *Circus* (July 1973), pp. 61–5

Bohn, Chris, 'The Rise and Fall of Ziggy Stardust and The Spiders From Mars', *Melody Maker* (19 November 1979), p. 36

—— 'Merry Christmas Mr Bowie', *New Musical Express* (16 April 1983), pp. 27, 30, 49

*Bolan, Marc, 'Music-hall humorist', *Melody Maker* (12 March 1977), p. 14

Boser, Volker, '[Roof-garden music from a charlatan]', *Abendzeitung* (1 September 1992)

Bosworth, P., 'Bowie: Is it all for a lark?', *Melody Maker* (6 January 1973), p. 35

Bowie, Angie, *Free Spirit*, London, Mushroom Publishing, 1981

—— *Backstage Passes*, London, Orion, 1993

*[Bowie, David], 'A Message to London from Dave', *Melody Maker* (26 February 1966), p. 13

*Bracewell, Michael, 'Dedicated followers of Bowie', *Guardian* (16 April 1990), p. 8

Brazier, Chris, 'Bowie: Beauty before outrage', *Melody Maker* (4 September 1976), pp. 17, 38

—— 'From idealism to alienation', in *Melody Maker Book of Bowie* [tour souvenir issue], 1978, pp. 33–9

—— 'Seriously, it's Bowie', *Melody Maker* (24 June 1978), p. 13

—— 'Stage', *Melody Maker* (30 September 1978), p. 18

Brown, Mick, 'This man taught David Bowie his moves', *Crawdaddy* (September 1974), pp. 28–9

Brown, Tina, 'The Bowie odyssey', *Sunday Times Magazine* (20 July 1975), pp. 8, 10–12

Buckley, C. T., 'David Bowie: The musician's Indonesian – style refuge on Mustique', *Architectural Digest* (September 1992), pp. 100–11

[*Bulldog*], 'White European dance music', *Bulldog* (November/December 1981)

*Burn, Gordon, 'Bowie holds court', *Sunday Times Magazine* (30 November 1980), pp. 48+

Campbell, Jackie, 'Rock star Bowie convincing as elephant man', *Rocky Mountain News* (31 July 1980), p. 79

Cann, Kevin, *David Bowie: A chronology*, London, Vermilion Books, 1983

Carr, Roy, and Murray, Charles Shaar, *David Bowie: An Illustrated Record*, London, Eel Pie, 1981; New York, Avon, 1981

Carson, T., 'Riffs: David Bowie looks back in horror', *Village Voice* (8 October 1980), p. 75

Case, Brian, 'The cracked image', *Melody Maker* (10 December 1983), pp. 24–5

*Chambers, Iain, *Urban Rhythms*, London, Macmillan, 1985

*Chapman, Don, 'Miming promise', *Oxford Mail* (29 December 1967)

Charlesworth, Chris, 'Bowie gets the Spector sound', *Melody Maker* (11 May 1974), p. 3

—— 'Bowie, birth of the new rock theatre', *Melody Maker* (22 June 1974), p. 3

—— 'Bowie: Ringing the ch-ch-changes', *Melody Maker* (13 March 1976), pp. 16–17, 47

—— *David Bowie: Profile*, London and New York, Proteus, 1981

Childers, Lee Black, 'On tour with David Bowie', *Hit Parader* (December 1974)

Chin, Brian, 'Bowie sprinkles stardust at the Garden', *New York Post* (27 July 1983), p. 25

*Christgau, Robert, 'Growing up grim with Mott The Hoople', *Newsday* (December 1972); reprinted in *Any Old Way You Choose It*, Baltimore, Penguin, 1973, pp. 283–90

Claire, Vivian. *David Bowie*, New York, Putnam, 1977; London, Flash Books, 1977

Clark, David, 'Bowie the cosmic yob', *Sounds* (6 January 1973), p. 30

Clarke, Peter, 'A lad insane', *Hi Fi News & Record Review* (March 1985), pp. 89–93

Cocks, Jay, 'David Bowie rockets onward', *Time* (18 July 1983), pp. 46–51

Cohen, Debra Rae, 'David Bowie eats his young', *Rolling Stone* (25 December 1980/8 January 1981), p. 102

—— 'David Bowie takes on the challenge of being himself', *New York Times* (15 May 1983), II, p. 27

Coleman, M., 'Riffs: David Bowie's tube-age daydream', *Village Voice* (9 October 1984), p. 77

223

Selective Bibliography

*Coleman, Ray, 'A star is born', *Melody Maker* (15 July 1972), p. 43

Connolly, Ray, 'Wowie, Bowie', *Evening Standard* (3 February 1973), p. 13

Cook, Richard, 'Ziggy popped', *Punch* (23 March 1990), pp. 38–9

Cooper, B. L., 'Image of the outsider in contemporary lyrics', *Journal of Popular Culture*, **12** (Summer 1978), pp. 168–78

Cooper, C., 'Licks: Serious Bowie', *Village Voice* (9 August 1983), p. 66

*Copetas, Craig, 'Beat godfather meets glitter Mainman', *Rolling Stone* (28 February 1974), pp. 14–17

Craig, James, 'Bowie goes north', *Record Mirror* (26 May 1973), p. 9

[*Crawdaddy*], 'Hunky Dory', *Crawdaddy* (20 February 1972), p. 15

—— 'The Rise and fall of Ziggy Stardust and The Spiders From Mars' *Crawdaddy* (August 1972), p. 20

—— 'Pinups', *Crawdaddy* (February 1974), pp. 72+

—— 'Young Americans', *Crawdaddy* (June 1975), p. 73

—— 'Low', *Crawdaddy* (April 1977), p. 97

—— '"Heroes"', *Crawdaddy* (January 1978), pp. 70–1

Cromelin, Richard, 'The Rise and Fall of Ziggy Stardust and The Spiders From Mars', *Rolling Stone* (20 July 1972), p. 54

—— 'Bowie: Time for another ch-ch-change', *Rolling Stone* (10 October 1974), p. 6

—— 'David Bowie', *Circus* (2 March 1976), pp. 24–7

Crowe, Cameron, 'Bowie to tour: No gimmickry', *Rolling Stone* (15 January 1976), p. 12

—— 'Ground control to Davy Jones', *Rolling Stone* (12 February 1976), pp. 29–33

—— 'Space face changes the station: David Bowie pulls a Lazarus', *Creem* (May 1976), pp. 38–41, 82–3

Currie, David (ed), *The Starzone Interviews*, London, Omnibus, 1985

—— *David Bowie: Glass Idol*, London, Omnibus, 1987

Curry, John, 'Play: Bowie in Elephant', *New York Times* (29 September 1980), C, p. 15

Curtis, A., 'It's not only rock 'n' roll', *New Statesman* (19 November 1976), p. 710

Curtis, Jim, *Rock Eras: Interpretations of Music and Society 1954–84*, Bowling Green, Ohio, Bowling Green State University Popular Press, 1987

[*Daily Mirror*], 'Row over Davy's hair', *Daily Mirror* (4 March 1965), p. 2

Damsker, Matt, 'Philly stopover: Fans and funk', *Rolling Stone* (10 October 1974), pp. 10–11

224

Davies, S., 'Performance: Radio City Music Hall', *Rolling Stone* (29 March 1972), p. 16

Davis, Michael, 'Let's dance', *Creem* (August 1983), p. 54

Deevoy, Adrian, 'Golden years', *Q* (May 1993), pp. 74–84

De La Parra, Pimm Jall, *The David Bowie Concert Tapes*, Amsterdam, Pimm Jall De La Parra, 1983

Delingpole, James, 'Half as minimal as he used to be', *Daily Telegraph* (20 March 1993) p. xiv

Demorest, Steve, 'Bowie salutes the sixties stars', *Circus* (December 1973), pp. 4–9

Denisoff, R. Serge, 'Music videos: Serious Moolight', *Popular Music and Society*, 10/1 (1985), p. 74

Detheridge, D., 'Caught in the act', *Melody Maker* (18 October 1969), p. 6

Di Perna, Alan, 'Tin Machine: They're a garage band . . . only Bowie's the singer', *Creem* (special issue 1991)

Doggett, Peter, 'David Bowie's UK singles', *Record Collector* (November 1984), pp. 3–9

Douglas, David, *Presenting David Bowie*, New York, Pinnacle, 1975

[*Downbeat*], 'Low', *Downbeat* (19 May 1977), p. 33

Downing, David, *Future Rock*, St Albans, Panther, 1976

Drummond, Keith, 'The EMI reissues 69–78', *Rock CD*, 1/1 (1992), pp. 58, 60

Duncan, Robert, 'Anthropomorphosis was never like this. Or is David Bowie really Billy Carter?', *Creem* (February 1978), pp. 36–7, 65–6

Edmonds, Ben, 'Bowie meets the press', *Circus* (27 April 1976), pp. 24–9

Edwards, Henry, 'The rise of Ziggy Stardust', *After Dark* (October 1972)

—— 'A growing boy who gets better and better', *After Dark* (October 1973), p. 39

—— 'Rock and rouge', *Hi Fidelity/Musical America* (October 1973), pp. 95–7

—— 'Bowie's back but the glitter's gone', *New York Times* (21 March 1976), p. 1

Eggen, T. and Haugland, G., 'You can't say no to the beauty and the beast', *Ballade Tidsskrift for Ny Musikk* (Oslo) 7/4 (1983), pp. 14–22

Emerson, Ken, 'New Bowie: A dog', *Rolling Stone* (1 August 1974), pp. 35–6

Evans, Paul, 'Bowie 93: Soul to soul', *Rolling Stone* (29 April 1993), pp. 59, 61

Fallowell, Duncan, 'Twinkle twinkle superstar', *Records & Recordings* (August 1972), pp. 36–7

Fandray, David F., 'David Bowie: Diamond Dogs', *Popular Music and Society*, 3/4 (1974), p. 345

Farber, Jim, 'Return of the dudes', *Village Voice* (3 January 1984), p. 54

225

Selective Bibliography

—— 'Glass Spider', *Rolling Stone* (11 August 1988), p. 87

Farren, Mick, 'Mr Bowie has left the theatre', *New Musical Express* (16 November 1974), pp. 5–6

*—— 'Surface noise: The trouble with Bowie', *Trouser Press* (December 1983/ January 1984), p. 55

Feiden, Robert, 'David Bowie brings back style to rock and roll', *Record World* (3 March 1973)

Fernbacher, Joe, 'Scary Monsters', *Creem* (January 1981), p. 56

*Ferris, Timothy, 'David Bowie in America', *Rolling Stone* (9 November 1972), pp. 38+; reprinted in *What's That Sound?*, ed. Ben Fong-Torres, New York, Anchor, 1976, pp. 126–35

Fielder, Hugh, 'Fans phone in song requests for Bowie tour', *Billboard* (3 February 1990), p. 90

*Finn, Deborah Elizabeth, 'Moon and gloom: David Bowie's frustrated messianism', *Commonweal*, 110 (9 September 1983), pp. 467–8

*Fissinger, Laura, 'David Bowie: As I write this letter', *Creem Close-Up* (July 1983), p. 25

Fletcher, David Jeffrey, *David Robert Jones Bowie: The discography of a generalist 1962–79*, Chicago, F. Fergeson Productions, 1980

Flippo, Chet, *David Bowie Serious Moonlight*, New York, Doubleday, 1984; London, Sidgwick & Jackson, 1984

Fowler, Pete, 'Fighting off the Martians', *Let it Rock* (October 1975), pp. 22–3

Fox-Cumming, Ray, 'Bowie bows out', *New Musical Express* (14 July 1973)

Fricke, David, 'David Bowie', *Musician* [US] (December 1984), pp. 46–52+

—— 'Live! Twenty concerts that changed rock 'n' roll: David Bowie and The Spiders From Mars US Tour', *Rolling Stone* (4 June 1987), pp. 72, 139–40

—— 'The dark soul of a new machine', *Rolling Stone* (15 June 1989), pp. 137–9

Fried, Stephen, 'The fans who fell to earth', *Gentleman's Quarterly* [US] (February 1990), pp. 101–2, 112

Frith, Simon, 'How Low can you get?', *Creem* (May 1977), pp. 56, 80

*—— 'The art of posing', *New Society* (23 April 1981), pp. 146–7; reprinted in *Music For Pleasure*, Cambridge, Polity Press, 1988, pp. 176–9

—— 'Only dancing – David Bowie flirts with the issues', *Mother Jones* (August 1983), pp3+; reprinted in *Zoot Suits and Second-hand Dresses*, ed. Angela McRobbie, London, Macmillan, 1989, pp. 132–40

—— 'Confessions of a rock critic', *New Statesman* (23 August 1985), pp. 21–3; reprinted in *Music For Pleasure, op. cit.*, pp. 163–8

—— 'Art versus technology: the strange case of popular music', *Media Culture and Society*, 8 (1986), pp. 263–79

—— *Facing the Music*, London, Mandarin, 1990

—— and Horne, Howard, *Art into Pop*, London, Methuen, 1987

Gaines, Steve, 'Bowie divines doom in Moscow', *Circus* (August 1973), pp. 30–2, 41–3

Gerson, Ben, 'Bowie's Martian Spiders spin new world', *Boston Phoenix* (17 October 1972), pp. 1, 28–31

*—— 'Aladdin Sane', *Rolling Stone* (19 July 1973), p. 44

Gett, Steve, 'David Bowie', *Melody Maker* (23 November 1985), p. 39

—— *David Bowie*, Port Chester, New York, Cherry Lane Books, 1985

Giangrande, Mark, 'Take David Bowie for instance: A collector's tale', *Stereo Review* (March 1976), pp. 74–5

Gill, Andy, 'And the bride came too', *Independent* (1 April 1993) p. 17

Gillman, Peter and Leni, *Alias David Bowie*, London, Hodder & Stoughton, 1986

Goddard, Peter, *David Bowie: Out of the Cool*, London, Virgin, 1983

Goldstein, T., 'David Bowie: The glass spider tour', *Video* (September 1988), p. 128

Goodwin, Andrew, 'Popular music and post modern theory', *Cultural Studies*, 5/2 (May 1991), pp. 174–90

Gross, Michael, 'David Bowie's Diamond Dogs', *Circus* (July 1974), pp. 62–7

Grossberg, Lawrence, 'Rock, territorialization and power', *Cultural Studies*, 5/3 (October 1991), pp. 358–67

Gussow, Mel, 'Roeg: The man behind The Man Who Fell to Earth', *New York Times* (22 August 1976), D, p. 11

Guterman, Jimmy, 'The wooing of David Bowie', *Rolling Stone* (18 May 1989), p. 28

—— 'Sound + Vision', *Rolling Stone* (19 October 1989), p. 85

Haddad, M. George, 'Bowie: No Ziggy or Iggy ... just a gigolo', *Creem* (September 1978), pp. 38–41, 66

Harrington, Richard, 'The fall and rise of David Bowie', *Washington Post* (2 May 1983), B, pp. 1, 17

Harris, John, 'Value added tux', *New Musical Express* (3 April 1993), p. 28

Hatch, David and Millward, Stephen, *From Blues to Rock*, Manchester, Manchester University Press, 1987

Hauptfuhrer, Fred, 'Rock's space oddity David Bowie falls to earth and lands his feet in film', *People* (6 September 1976), p. 57

Hayman, Martin, 'Life and times of David Bowie', *Sounds* (26 May 1973)

—— 'Farewell to the genie!', *Sounds* (14 July 1973), p. 7

—— 'David Bowie – In search of lost time', *Sounds* (4 August 1973), pp. 10–11

Hebdige, Dick, *Subculture: The Meaning of Style*, London, Methuen, 1979

Selective Bibliography

[*Hello*] 'The Wedding of David Bowie and Iman', *Hello* (12 June 1992), pp. 36+

Hibbert, Tom, 'The most preposterous David Bowie interview ever!', *Smash Hits* (17 June 1977), pp. 72–4

Hilburn, Robert, 'David Bowie rocks in Santa Monica', *Los Angeles Times* (23 October 1972)

—— 'Second Bowie concert for overflow crowd', *Los Angeles Times* (3 March 1973)

—— 'Rock theatre of David Bowie at Long Beach', *Los Angeles Times* (12 March 1973)

—— 'Aladdin Sane features a broader Bowie', *Los Angeles Times* (3 June 1973)

—— 'Pop poll points to new leadership', *Los Angeles Times* (6 October 1973)

—— 'Bowie finds his voice', *Melody Maker* (14 September 1974), pp. 8–9

—— 'Bowie: Now I'm a businessman', *Melody Maker* (28 February 1976), pp. 9–10

—— 'David Bowie has dropped his disguises', *Los Angeles Times* (29 May 1983), C, p. 50

Hill, Dave, 'The boy keeps swinging', *GQ* (October 1991), pp. 134–7

Hisama, Ellie M., 'Post-colonialism on the make: the music of John Mellencamp, David Bowie and John Zorn', *Popular Music* 12/2 (May 1993), pp. 91–104

Hoare, Ian, 'You're so wonderful, gimme your hands', *Let It Rock* (October 1972), pp. 6–8

Hoberman, J., 'Rockers', *Village Voice* (6 September 1983), p. 48

—— 'Scanners: Bowie to go', *Village Voice* (30 April 1985), p. 36

Hodenfield, Chris, 'Bad boys in Berlin', *Rolling Stone* (4 October 1979), pp. 41–5

Hoggard, Stuart, *Bowie Changes*, New York, Putnam, 1980

—— *David Bowie: An Illustrated Discography*, London, Omnibus, 1980

Holdship, Bill, 'Ziggy no Biggie', *Creem* (December 1984), p. 52

*Holdstein, Deborah H., 'Music videos: Messages and structures', *Jump/Cut*, **29** (February 1984), pp. 1, 13, 14

Hollingworth, Roy, 'Can Bowie save New York from boredom?', *Melody Maker* (7 October 1972), p. 38

—— 'Ch-ch-ch-changes – A journey with Aladdin', *Melody Maker* (12 May 1973), pp. 9–11

—— 'Drive out Saturday', *Melody Maker* (19 May 1973), pp. 20-1

—— and Benton, Michael, 'Is Bowie really quitting?', *Melody Maker* (14 July 1973), pp. 8–9

Holloway, Danny, 'David Bowie – I'm not ashamed of wearing dresses', *New Musical Express* (29 January 1972)

*Holmes, Peter, 'Gay rock – David Bowie in concert at the Royal Festival Hall', *Gay News* 5 (July 1972), p. 7

Hopkins, Jerry, *Bowie*, London, Elm Tree, 1985

Horkins, Tony, 'Control zone', *Melody Maker* (14 April 1990), p. 46

—— 'The man in the machine', *Melody Maker* (9 November 1991), pp. 48–9

—— 'Bowie's golden years', *Rock CD*, 1/1 (1992), pp. 56–8

*Hughes, Tim, 'Bowie for a song', *Jeremy* (January 1970)

Hull, R. A., 'David Live', *Creem* (January 1975), p. 69

Humphries, Patrick, 'Scary Monsters', *Melody Maker* (20 September 1980), p. 32

—— 'David's Baal of confusion', *Melody Maker* (6 March 1982), p. 4

Hunter, J., 'Licks: White cat moan', *Village Voice* (4 May 1982), p. 80

Hustwitt, Mark, 'Sure feels like heaven to me: Considerations on promotional videos', *IASPM [International Association for the Study of Popular Music] Working Paper* 6, IASPM, 1985

[*Independent*], 'Space oddity comes back to earth', *Independent* (24 March 1990), p. 18

Inhoffen, Matthias, 'Pop-CDs Spezial: David Bowie', *Stereoplay* (Stuttgart) (April 1985), p. 145

—— 'Geldgieriges genie', *Stereoplay* (Stuttgart) (June 1987), pp. 120–1

Isler, S., 'David Bowie opens up – a little', *Musician* [US] (August 1987), pp. 60–4

Jackson, Richard, 'David Bowie: The early years', *Record Collector* (September 1986), pp. 3–7

Jarman, Marshall, 'David Bowie: Rare picture sleeve singles 1967–71', *Record Collector* (September 1987), pp. 3–6

[*Jazz Magazine*], 'Echoes d'ecran (bande originale du film The Falcon and the Snowman), *Jazz Magazine* (Paris) (7 June 1985), p. 7

Jerome, Jim, 'A Session with David Bowie', *Life* (December 1992), pp. 90–2

*Jewell, Derek, 'Bowie and Bassey', *Sunday Times* (9 May 1976), p. 35; reprinted in *The Popular Voice*, London, Sphere, 1981, pp. 105–6

Johnson, Brian D., 'Golden years', *Macleans* (12 March 1980), pp. 62–4

Johnson, Derek, 'Final Bowie gig filmed', *New Musical Express* (14 July 1973)

Jones, Allan, 'Ronson: I'd like to kick sense into Bowie', *Melody Maker* (5 April 1975), pp. 29+

—— 'Bowie stands alone', *Melody Maker* (24 January 1976), p. 26

—— 'The David Bowie story', *Melody Maker* (1 May 1976), pp. 36–7

—— 'Space oddities', *Melody Maker* (15 May 1976), p. 13

Selective Bibliography

—— 'Bowie's raw power', *Melody Maker* (22 May 1976), p. 13

—— '"Heroes"', *Melody Maker* (1 October 1977), p. 23

—— 'Goodbye to Ziggy and all that', *Melody Maker* (29 October 1977), pp. 8–11

—— 'Man, myth and music', *Melody Maker Book of Bowie* [tour souvenir issue], 1978, pp. 5–18

—— 'Bowie: It's a blackout', *Melody Maker* (3 June 1978), p. 10

—— 'The Great White Hope versus The Thin White Duke', *Melody Maker* (21 April 1979), p. 9

Juby, Kerry, *David Bowie*, Tunbridge Wells, Midas Books, 1982

—— (ed), *In Other Words: David Bowie*, London, Omnibus, 1986

*Kael, Pauline, 'Notes on evolving heroes, morals, audiences', *New Yorker* (8 November 1976), pp. 136–45; reprinted in *When The Lights Go Down*, London, Marion Boyars, 1980, pp. 195–204

Kamin, Philip and Goddard, Peter, *David Bowie: Out of the Cool*, New York, Beaufort Books, 1983; reprinted as *David Bowie Live*, London, Virgin Books, 1984

Kelleher, Ed, *David Bowie: A Biography in Words and Pictures*, New York, Sire Books, 1977

Kent, Nick 'David Bowie: Best dressed Mainman at the Twilight Zone Ball', *Creem* (August 1973), pp. 41–5, 75

King, Arthur, 'David Bowie: The Ziggy Stardust years', *Record Collector* (February 1987), pp. 3–8

Kresh, Paul, 'Rock person's guide to Peter and the Wolf', *Stereo Review* (July 1978), p. 85

Kubernik, Harvey, 'Fame at last for soulful Bowie', *Melody Maker* (25 October 1975)

Laing, Dave, *One Chord Wonders*, Milton Keynes, Open University Press, 1985

*—— and Frith, Simon, 'Bowie Zowie: Two views of the glitter prince of rock', *Let It Rock* (June 1973), pp. 34–5

Lake, Steve, 'Bowie: Serious Moonlight', *Melody Maker* (28 May 1983) pp. 23–6

—— 'Crock and roller', *Guardian* (11 April 1987), p. 11

Lane, L. M., and Berry, Y. C., 'Has there been a sexual revolution', *Journal of Popular Culture*, **15** (Winter 1981), pp. 155–64

Lester, Paul, 'Low/Heroes/Lodger', *Melody Maker* (14 September 1991)

Levy, J., 'I'm with the band', *Spin* (July 1989), pp. 35–6

Lewis, George H., 'Positive deviance: A labelling approach to the star syndrome in popular music', *Popular Music and Society*, **8/2** (1982), pp. 73–83

—— 'Uncertain truths: The promotion of popular culture', *Journal of Popular Culture*, **20/3** (Winter 1986), pp. 31–44

Lifflander, John, and Shroyer, Stephan, 'David Bowie: Spaced out in the desert', *Creem* (December 1975), pp. 43–6, 75–6

—— and —— 'Nick Roeg . . . and the man who fell to earth', *Andy Warhol's Interview*, **3** (March 1976), pp. 34–6

Lisle, Tim de, 'Sound and vision', *Independent on Sunday* (2 August 1992), pp. 18–19, 21

Livingstone, David, 'An exquisite legend in his own time', *Macleans* (19 September 1983), p. 54

Loder, Kurt, 'Scary monster on Broadway', *Rolling Stone* (13 November 1980), pp. 8–11

—— 'Straight time', *Rolling Stone* (12 May 1983), pp. 22–8, 81

—— 'Iggy Pop: Bowie's Main Man', *Rolling Stone* (25 October 1984), p. 17

*—— 'Tonight', *Rolling Stone* (8 November 1984), pp. 71, 73

—— 'Stardust memories', *Rolling Stone* (23 April 1987), pp. 74–7+; reprinted in *Rolling Stone: The Interviews 1967–92* (15 October 1992), pp. 141–2

Loeffler, Mark, 'Designer remedies for Bowie's theatre bug', *Theatre Crafts*, **21** (November 1987), pp. 38–41, 80–1

Lycett, Andrew, 'David Bowie: A rock oddity', *Creem* (November 1971), pp. 16–17, 51–2

Lynch, Kate, *David Bowie: A Rock and Roll Odyssey*, London and New York, Proteus, 1984

Mabbs, Val, 'Ziggy's back', *Record Mirror* (19 May 1983)

McCormick, Ruth, 'Let's act', *American Film*, **8** (September 1983), p. 29

MacDonald, Ian, 'The revolution is here . . . doesn't anybody want it?', *New Musical Express* (17 March 1973)

—— 'A boy and his dog', *New Musical Express* (11 May 1974), p. 5

*MacKay, Patricia, 'Serious – and stunning – moonlight', *Theatre Crafts*, **18** (January 1984), pp. 17–19, 66, 68–71

MacKinnon, Angus, 'The future isn't what it used to be', *New Musical Express* (13 September 1980), pp. 31–2, 35, 37, 39, 61

Mantle, Jonathan, 'David Bowie: A really strange kettle of poissons', *Vogue* (September 1978), pp. 192–5

Marcus, Greil, 'The incomplete David Bowie', *Rolling Stone* (9 August 1979), pp. 53–4

Marsh, Dave, 'The incredible story of Iggy and The Stooges', *Creem* (May 1970)

Martin, Linda and Segrave, Kerry, *Anti-Rock*, Hamden, Connecticut, Archon Books, 1988

Maslin, Jane, 'A rock singer takes off as a movie star', *New York Times* (29 May 1983), II, pp. 16, 20

—— 'Making movies – the long jump from MTV', *Record* (September 1985), pp. 21–4

Matthew-Walker, Robert, *David Bowie: Theatre of Music*, Bourne End, Kensal, 1985

[*Melody Maker*], 'Rock and roll suicide?', *Melody Maker* (9 June 1973), pp. 12–13

—— 'Bowie fan dies', *Melody Maker* (18 July 1987), p. 3

—— 'The 80s: A vinyl documentary', *Melody Maker* (4 February 1989), pp. 28–9

—— 'Live! NEC Birmingham', *Melody Maker* (31 March 1990), p. 20

Mendelsohn, John, 'The Man Who Sold the World', *Rolling Stone* (18 February 1971), p. 45

*—— 'David Bowie? Pantomime rock?', *Rolling Stone* (1 April 1971), p. 16

—— 'Hunky Dory', *Rolling Stone* (6 January 1972), pp. 43–4

—— 'David Bowie and Dee Snider: The bizarre passions they can't control', *Creem* (March 1985), pp. 49, 60

—— 'Absolute beginners', *Creem* (September 1986), pp. 18–19

Meredith, L., 'Bowie jazzin' ', *Stereo Review* (February 1985), p. 83

Miles, Barry, *The David Bowie Black Book*, London, Omnibus Press, 1981; New York, Quick Fox, 1981

—— (ed), *Bowie in His Own Words*, London, Omnibus Press, 1980; London, W. H. Allen, 1982

Miles, Milo, 'Stardust', *New York Times Book Review* (24 August 1986), p. 19

Miller, Jim, 'David Bowie's new look', *Newsweek* (18 July 1983), pp. 76–8

Millman, J., 'The concert – video shell game', *High Fidelity/Musical America* (November 1984), pp. 86–7

Milne, Tom, 'The man who fell to earth', *Sight & Sound*, **45** (Summer 1976), pp. 145–7

Milward, John, 'Low', *Rolling Stone* (21 April 1977), p. 88

—— 'David Bowie: Man of many phases', *Rolling Stone* (15 June 1978), p. 116

Missing Link [periodical] 1984–

Morgan, Jeffrey, 'Stage', *Creem* (January 1979), p. 78

Moris, Teri, 'Station to Station', *Rolling Stone* (25 March 1976), pp. 34–5

Morley, Paul, 'Thoughts of a coriander king', *Guardian* (22 July 1992), p. 38

Mower, Sarah, 'Fashion takes a Bowie', *Harpers & Queen* (May 1993), pp. 42–5

Murray, Charles Shaar, 'David at the Dorchester', *New Musical Express* (22 July 1972)

—— 'Back at the Dorchester', *New Musical Express* (29 July 1972)

—— 'Goodbye Ziggy and a big hello to Aladdin Sane', *New Musical Express* (27 January 1973), pp. 5–6, 54

—— 'Gay guerrillas and private movies', *New Musical Express* (24 February 1973), pp. 16–17

—— 'Aladdin Seine', *New Musical Express* (12 May 1973), p. 5

—— 'Total sensory overload', *New Musical Express* (26 May 1973), pp. 10–11

—— 'David Bowie: Pin Ups', *Oz*, **48** (1973), p. 52; reprinted in *Shots From The Hip*, London, Penguin, 1991, pp. 39–41

—— 'Angie: Life with David, or when will those clouds all disappear?', *Creem* (June 1974), pp. 38–41, 76–7

—— 'Won't you come home David Bowie?', *Creem* (March 1976), pp. 22, 66

—— 'Glam rock remembered', *New Musical Express* (8 October 1977); reprinted in *Shots From The Hip*, *op. cit.*, pp. 222–7

—— 'David Bowie: Who was that (un)masked man?', *New Musical Express* (12 November 1977); reprinted in *Shots From The Hip*, *op. cit.*, pp. 227–38

—— 'Let's talk', *Rolling Stone* (25 October 1984), pp. 14–15, 18, 74

—— 'On the set with Bowie', *Record* (December 1984), pp. 23–5

—— 'And the singer's called Dave', *Q* (October 1991), pp. 56–64

—— 'The man who fell to earth?' *Arena* (May/June 1993), pp. 80–2

[*Musician*], 'Sound & Vision', *Musician* [US] (21 November 1990), pp. 120–21

Nelson, Paul, 'Preview: The Man Who Fell to Earth', *Circus* (December 1975), pp. 8–9

—— 'Bowie film falls flat: Too much of nothing', *Rolling Stone* (15 July 1976), p. 22

Nigro, D., 'Death and suicide in modern lyrics', *Suicide*, 5/4 (1975), pp. 232–45

*Norman, Philip, 'Beginner's luck', *Vanity Fair* [US] (January 1986), pp. 58–65

O'Grady, Anthony, 'Dictatorship: The next step', *New Musical Express* (23 August 1975), pp. 5–6

Orman, John, *The Politics of Rock Music*, Chicago, Nelson Hall, 1984

Owen, Frank, 'Fans, fantasy and Bowie', *New Musical Express* (31 October 1987), p. 13

Palmer, Robert, 'David Bowie', *Penthouse* (November 1983), p. 118

*Palmer, Tony, 'Up-to-date minstrel', *Observer* (7 December 1969), p. 29

—— *All You Need Is Love*, London, Weidenfeld & Nicolson, 1976

Pareles, Jon, 'Lodger', *Creem*, (September 1979), p. 53

—— 'Eno uncaged', *Village Voice* (4 May 1982), p. 77

—— 'The rock and roles of David Bowie', *Harper's Bazaar* (May 1983), pp. 163+

—— 'David Bowie ponders his new-found popularity', *New York Times* (4 November 1984), II, pp. 25–6

—— 'David Bowie ch-ch-ch-changes his tune', *Mademoiselle* (July 1987), p. 44

Parsons, Tony, 'The Tin Man', *Arena* (November 1991), pp. 86–91

—— 'Bowie by Bowie', *Arena* (May/June 1993) pp. 60–79

Pattison, Robert, *The Triumph of Vulgarity*, New York, Oxford University Press, 1987

Paytress, Mark, 'Bowie plastic soul to Scary Monsters', *Record Collector* (May 1991), pp. 3–10

—— 'David Bowie at the Beeb/David Bowie and British R & B', *Record Collector* (November 1991), pp. 3–9

Peacock, Steve, 'Confessions of a disillusioned old rocker', *Sounds* (14 August 1971), p. 11

—— 'Rock on Ziggy', *Sounds* (17 June 1972)

—— 'Under the image', *Sounds* (21 October 1972)

Peel, M., 'David Bowie's next big thing', *Stereo Review* (July 1983), p. 86

Petrie, Gavin, 'Bowie is end of an era', *Disc* (23 September 1972)

—— 'Ziggy Stardust', *Disc* (23 September 1972)

Philbin, Peter Jay, 'In Long Beach: David Bowie sings', *Los Angeles Free Press* (23 March 1973)

Piccarella, J., 'Riffs: Iggy transformed', *Village Voice* (17 October 1977), p. 65

—— 'Riffs: David Bowie moves on', *Village Voice* (2 July 1979), p. 49

Pitt, Kenneth, *Bowie: The Pitt Report*, London, Design Music, 1983; London, Omnibus, 1985; New York, Putnam, 1985

Pond, Steve, 'Never say never', *Rolling Stone* (4 June 1987), pp. 129–30

Pulin, Chuck, 'Ziggy in NYC', *Sounds* (7 October 1972)

Puterbaugh, P., 'Bowie's Tin Machine', *Stereo Review* (September 1989), p. 129

Ratcliff, C., 'David Bowie's survival', *Artforum*, 21 (January 1983), pp. 39–45

Ressner, J., 'Bowie's bicoastal blitz', *Rolling Stone* (10 August 1989), p. 24

*Rice, Anne, 'David Bowie and the end of gender', *Vogue* [US] (November 1983), pp. 432–4, 498

Riegel, Richard, 'Tonight', *Creem* (January 1985), p. 50

Roberts, Chris, 'Never let me down', *Melody Maker* (18 April 1987), p. 29

—— 'ChangesBowie', *Melody Maker* (17 March 1990), p. 37

—— 'Tin Machine', *Melody Maker* (7 September 1991), pp. 10–11

Robinson, Lisa, 'David's the darling of the city', *Disc* (7 October 1972), p. 11

—— 'Cracked actor zaps Cannock thespians', *New Musical Express* (29 June 1974), pp. 14–15

—— 'David Bowie has left the theatre', *New Musical Express* (27 July 1974), pp. 18–19

—— 'Clockwork Orange in black and white', *Creem* (May 1976), pp. 48–9

—— 'Mick and Patti and David and Iggy and Brian', *Hit Parader* (September 1977)

—— 'David Bowie', *Andy Warhol's Interview*, (8 June 1978), pp. 28–9

—— 'A cracked actor makes repairs', *Times* (14 March 1983), p. 8

Rock, Mick, 'David Bowie is just not serious', *Rolling Stone* (8 June 1972), p. 14

—— *Ziggy Stardust: David Bowie 1972–3*, New York, St Martin's Press, 1985

Rockwell, John, 'Hunter/Ronson at the Felt Forum', *New York Times* (3 May 1975)

*—— 'A revolution with Bowie', *New York Times* (25 December 1980), p. 15

*Rogan, Johnny, *Starmakers and Svengalis*, London, Queen Anne Press, 1988

[*Rolling Stone*], 'Stage', *Rolling Stone* (30 November 1978), p. 66

—— 'The top 100: Let's dance', *Rolling Stone* (16 November 1989)

*Rook, Jean, 'Waiting for Bowie – and finding a genius who insists he's really a clown', *Daily Express* (5 May 1976), p. 5

*—— 'Bowie reborn', *Daily Express* (14 February 1979), p. 7

Rose, Cynthia, 'Letter from Britain: Stayin' hungry', *Creem* (July 1983), pp. 43, 71

Rose, Frank, 'Four conversations with Brian Eno', *Village Voice* (28 March 1977), p. 69

—— 'After the Wall', *Playboy* (July 1983), p. 26

—— 'Is David Bowie coming to earth?', *Mademoiselle* (October 1983), pp. 72–3+

Ross, Ron, 'David Bowie's glamorous career', *Phonograph Record Magazine* (October 1972)

—— 'David Live: Bowie throws a bone to his Dog fans', *Circus* (December 1976), pp. 70–3

Roxon, Lilian, 'A rock happening: David's debut', *Sunday News* [NY] (8 October 1972), p. 9

Russell, Rosalind, 'David Bowie – Bent on success', *Disc* (6 May 1972)

—— 'Bowie's back-up men', *Disc* (15 July 1972)

—— 'David Bowie, the man who saved the music world', *Disc* (23 September 1972)

Ryback, Timothy W., *Rock Around The Bloc*, New York, Oxford University Press, 1990

Saal, Hubert, 'The stardust kid', *Newsweek* (9 October 1972), p. 115

Salamon, Julie, 'David Bowie confronts Japan: the twain don't meet', *Wall Street Journal* (15 September 1983), p. 24

Selective Bibliography

Salierno, Rick, 'David Bowie: a guide to collectibles', *Goldmine* (December 1983), pp. 180, 182–4, 186

Salvo, Patrick William, 'Changing face of David Bowie', *Sounds* (2 December 1972), p. 12

Sandall, Robert, 'A last bow to the gallery', *Sunday Times* (25 March 1990), E, p. 1

—— 'Just one of the boys in the band', *Sunday Times* (11 August 1991), pp. 5, 12–13

Savage, Jay, 'A whirlwind ride to . . . er, where?' *Western Mail* (South Africa) (25–31 July 1986)

*Savage, Jon, 'Bowie: Avant-AOR', *Melody Maker* (27 May 1979), p. 28

*—— 'The gender bender', *The Face* (November 1980), pp. 16–20

—— 'The age of plunder', *The Face* (January 1983), pp. 44–9; reprinted in McRobbie, *Zoot Suits and Second-hand Dresses*, pp. 169–80

—— 'Tainted love' in *Consumption, Identity and Style*, ed. Alan Tomlinson, London, Routledge, 1990, pp. 153–71

—— *England's Dreaming*, London, Faber & Faber, 1991

Schaffner, Nicholas, *The British Invasion*, New York, McGraw-Hill, 1983

Scoppa, B., 'New faces', *Senior Scholastic*, 102 (29 January 1973), pp. 28+

Scott, Steve, 'David Bowie: The songs he gave away, the records he produced and the sessions he played from 1966 to the present', *Record Collector* (August 1983), pp. 8–11

Seideman, T., 'Bowie/Jagger vidclip heads for movie screens', *Billboard* (24 August 1985), pp. 1+

Shinfield, Barry, 'The prettiest star', *Beckenham & Penge Advertiser* (28 June 1973)

Simels, Steve, 'David Bowie: No honey, it's not one of those', *Stereo Review* (January 1973), p. 90

—— 'Bowie and Hoople and Reed', *Stereo Review* (February 1973), p. 92

—— 'Bowie: three ways, no way', *Stereo Review* (February 1975), pp. 52, 54

—— 'He lost me (again) at the movies', *Stereo Review* (September 1976), p. 56

—— 'Stagey Bowie', *Stereo Review* (January 1979), p. 122

Simmons, Doug, 'David Bowie: Straight up', *Village Voice* (27 June 1989), pp. 79–80

Sinclair, David, 'Ziggy just wants to be a revived 45', *Times* (2 September 1991), p. 13

—— 'Credible', *Q* (May 1993), p. 88

—— 'Station to station', *Rolling Stone* (10 June 1993), pp. 56–8, 60, 62, 64, 80

Smith, A., 'The Tin Machine', *Melody Maker* (20 May 1989), p. 19

Smith, Joe, *Off The Record*, London, Sidgwick & Jackson, 1989

Smith, Mat, 'David Bowie', *Melody Maker* (28 March 1987), p. 3

*Smith, Patti, 'Heroes – A communiqué', *Hit Parader* (April 1978), pp. 26–8

Sparn, E., 'Now more mellow, less glitter', *Senior Scholastic*, 105 (12 December 1974), pp. 25–7

[*Spearhead*], 'Don't condemn pop', *Spearhead*, 150 (April 1981)

Spencer, Neil, 'At last, the man himself', *Observer* (4 April 1993), p. 55

[*Spin*], 'Now here it comes again: David Bowie and Rolling Stones reunion', *Spin* (December 1989), p. 28

Starzone: The International Magazine of David Bowie [periodical, 1981–]

*Stein, Bruno, 'UFOs, Hitler and David Bowie', *Creem* (February 1975), pp. 52–5; reprinted as 'Flying saucers, Hitler and David Bowie', *New Musical Express* (22 February 1975), p. 14

Stewart, Tony, 'Heil and farewell', *New Musical Express* (8 May 1976), p. 9

Street, John, *Rebel Rock*, Oxford, Blackwell, 1986

Sutherland, Steve, 'The man who fell back down to earth', *Melody Maker* (26 March 1983), pp. 3+

—— 'Tonight', *Melody Maker* (29 September 1984), p. 28

—— 'Tin Machine: Metal gurus', *Melody Maker* (1 July 1989), pp. 28–30

—— 'Tin Machine: The industrial blues', *Melody Maker* (8 July 1989), pp. 29–30

—— 'David Bowie: A pressing engagement', *Melody Maker* (3 Febraury 1990), pp. 8–9

—— 'Bowie boys keep swinging', *Melody Maker* (24 March 1990), pp. 24–7

—— 'Bowie: Ch-ch-ch-ch-ch-changes', *Melody Maker* (31 March 1990), pp. 14–15

—— 'One day, son, this could be yours . . .', *New Musical Express* (20 March 1993), pp. 28–31

—— 'Alias Smith and Jones', *New Musical Express* (27 March 1993), pp. 12–13

Sweeting, Adam, 'Let's dance', *Melody Maker* (16 April 1983), p. 25

—— 'Absolute beginners', *Melody Maker* (22 March 1986), pp. 23–6

—— 'Role over Bowie', *Observer Magazine* (12 April 1987), pp. 26–9, 31

—— 'Serious twilight', *Guardian* (22 June 1987)

—— 'A tin band wagon hits and runs', *Guardian* (29 June 1989)

—— 'The star who fell to earth', *Guardian* (3 March 1990), supplement, pp. 4–6

—— 'A lad too sane', *Guardian* (22 March 1990)

—— 'White duke, black pudding', *Guardian* (2 April 1993), p. 8

Selective Bibliography

Tamm, Eric, *Brian Eno: His Music and the Vertical Colour of Sound*, Boston, Faber, 1989

—— *Robert Fripp*, London, Faber, 1990

Taylor, Ian, and Wall, Dave, 'Beyond the skinheads – Comments on the emergence and significance of the glamrock cult', in *Working Class Youth Culture*, ed. Geoff Mungham and Geoff Pearson, London, Routledge & Kegan Paul, 1976, pp. 105–23

Taylor, Rogan, *The Death and Resurrection Show*, London, Anthony Blond, 1985

Telford, Raymond, 'Hype and David Bowie's future', *Melody Maker* (28 March 1970), p. 30

Testa, Bart, '"Heroes"', *Rolling Stone* (12 January 1978), p. 56

Thomas, David, 'David Bowie', *The Face* (May 1983), pp. 14–20

Thomas, Dave, 'David Bowie's rarest recordings', *Record Collector* (November 1985), pp. 3–6

*Thomas, Leslie, 'For those beyond the fringe', *Evening News and Star* (2 November 1964), p. 6

Thompson, Dave, *David Bowie: Moonage Daydream*, London, Plexus, 1987

[*Time*], 'Vaudeville rock', *Time* (30 October 1972), pp. 81–2

—— 'It's real love', *Time* (18 January 1993) p. 48

Tiven, J., 'Darling David Bowie', *Stereo Review* (May 1974), p. 82

Tobler, John, and Grundy, Stuart, 'Tony Visconti' in *The Record Producers*, London, BBC Publications, 1982, pp. 168–93

Townley, Ray, 'Lester . . . who?', *Downbeat* (31 January 1974), pp. 11–12

Trakin, Roy, 'Never let me down', *Creem* (August 1987), pp. 14–15

Tremlett, George, *The David Bowie Story*, London, Futura, 1974; New York, Warner, 1975

[*Trouser Press*], 'Bowiewatch '82', *Trouser Press* (4 March 1982), pp. 46+

Truman, J., 'Riffs: Phase IV Bowie damage', *Village Voice* (26 April 1983), p. 64

Tucker, Ken, 'Bowie: Synth pop without the synths', *Rolling Stone* (26 May 1983), pp. 59, 61

Tulich, K., 'Bowie to score Aussie film', *Billboard* (3 March 1989), p. 86

Turner, Steve, 'The scruffy little failure who became David Bowie', *New Musical Express* (18 May 1974), pp. 8–9, 15

Tyler, Andrew, 'Just an old poser', *Disc* (23 September 1972)

Valentine, Penny, 'Bowie coming back to life', *Sounds* (29 January 1972), p. 27

—— 'Letter from Britain: Living up to Bowie', *Creem* (November 1978), pp. 36, 70, 72

—— Gilbert, Jerry, Hayman, Martin, and Peacock, Steve, 'Bowie: Man and the mask', *Sounds* (3 March 1973), pp. 10–11

[*Vanity Fair*], 'David Bowie after the glitter', *Vanity Fair* [US] (May 1983), pp. 72–3

—— 'Portrait', *Vanity Fair* [US] (November 1983), pp. 98–9

Van Matra, Lynn, 'Driven by change, rock's David Bowie turns actor', *Chicago Tribune* (3 August 1980), VI, p. 2

Vare, Ethlie Ann, 'Backstage and beyond with Bowie: An intimate journal of Bowie's 1983 Serious Moonlight tour', *Rock Magazine* (December 1983), pp. 36–41, 48

Venn, Couze, 'Popular music and cultural imperialism', *Media Culture and Society*, 9/3 (July 1987), pp. 384–8

Verlant, Gilles, *David Bowie: Portrait de l'artiste en rock-star*, Paris, Albin Michel, 1981

Waddington, Rick, 'Ziggy the crooner', *Melody Maker* (14 February 1976), p. 13

Wale, Michael, 'David Bowie: Rock and theatre', *Times* (24 January 1973)

Walters, B., 'Music: The new Bruce!', *Village Voice* (5 May 1987), pp. 72+

*Watts, Michael, 'Oh you pretty thing', *Melody Maker* (22 January 1972), pp. 19, 42

*—— 'Bowie: Waiting for the man', *Melody Maker* (1 July 1972), p. 28

—— 'The rise and rise of Ziggy Stardust', *Melody Maker* (19 August 1972), pp. 8–9

—— 'Stranger in a strange land', *Melody Maker* (24 February 1973), pp. 3–4

—— 'Bowie, the darling who put glam into rock', *Melody Maker* (6 October 1973), p. 37

—— 'Bowie's MainMan', *Melody Maker* (18 May 1974), pp. 40–2

—— 'Bowie: The exile returns to messiah's welcome', *Melody Maker* (8 May 1976), p. 8

—— 'Low', *Melody Maker* (22 January 1977)

—— 'Bowie: Funereal in Berlin', *Melody Maker* (29 January 1977), pp. 36, 54

—— 'Bowie today'/'From Brixton to Berlin'/'Confessions of an elitist', *Melody Maker* (18 February 1978), pp. 1, 33–40

—— 'Bowie on Bowie' in *Melody Maker Book of Bowie* [tour souvenir issue], 1978, pp. 19–31

—— 'Earls Court: Station to Station', *Melody Maker* (8 July 1978), p. 13

—— 'When Bowie's bad, he's bad', *Melody Maker* (9 December 1978), p. 9

—— 'Bowie's Lodger: Where new muzik meets Errol Flynn', *Melody Maker* (19 May 1979), p. 13

—— 'Ziggy's rock and role reversal', *Times* (30 May 1983), p. 9

Weitzman, Steve, 'Bowie's saxophone struggle', *Musician* [US] (May 1983), p. 122

Selective Bibliography

Welch, Chris, 'A mixture of Dali, 2001 and the Bee Gees', *Melody Maker* (11 October 1969), p. 22

—— 'Why does David Bowie like dressing up in ladies' clothes?', *Melody Maker* (17 April 1971), p. 22

—— 'Bowie A–Z', *Melody Maker* (12 May 1973)

—— 'Bowie free for all', *Melody Maker* (27 October 1973), p. 3

—— 'Bowie: Myths and mystique', *Melody Maker* (12 March 1977), p. 14

—— 'Bowie and Bolan get it on', *Melody Maker* (17 September 1977), pp. 16, 35

Wenders, Wim, 'Wim Wenders ans Telefon!', *Der Spiegel* (12 April 1993)

White, Timothy, 'Turn and face the strange', *Crawdaddy* (February 1978), pp. 52–5

—— 'David Bowie: A fifteen-year odyssey of image and imagination', *Musician* [US] (May 1983), pp. 52–6, 122; reprinted in *Rock Lives*, London, Omnibus, 1991, pp. 382–402

—— 'Tonight', *Musician* [US] (December 1984), pp. 98–9

—— 'David Bowie: Sound & Vision for 1990', *Musician* [US] (April 1990), p. 7

—— 'Turn and face the strange: David Bowie looks back', *Musician* [US] (July 1990), pp. 7, 60–70

—— and Fricke, David, 'David Bowie', *Musician* [US] (February 1987), p. 31

Wild, David, 'Tin Machine is more than David Bowie's latest invention', *Rolling Stone* (31 October 1991), pp. 75–8, 106

*—— 'Bowie's wedding album', *Rolling Stone* (21 January 1993), p. 14

*Willis, Ellen, 'Bowie's limitations', *New Yorker* (14 October 1972), pp. 171–3

Wykoff, D., 'Box set full of Sound & Vision signifying Bowie', *Billboard* (19 August 1987), p. 57

Young, Charles M., 'Bowie plays himself', *Rolling Stone* (12 January 1978), pp. 11, 13–14

Zanetta, Tony and Edwards, Henry, *Stardust: The Life and Times of David Bowie*, London, Michael Joseph, 1986

Discography

This discography is selective. It does not attempt to detail every extant recording bearing Bowie's name. We have sought instead to list those recordings – singles, original albums, compilations – which are useful in building a comprehensive CD library of Bowie as 'singer-song-writer'. We include only those singles which contain tracks otherwise unavailable in the UK at present, or which differ substantially from the more accessible CD mixes. We do not document Bowie's production and songwriting credits for other artists. Nor do we cover his more recent 'guest appearances' with the likes of Tina Turner and Adrian Belew. For wider coverage of official Bowie recordings, readers should refer to the various *Record Collector* articles listed in the bibliography. Where possible, discs are presented here in logical sequence with the original UK LP catalogue number cited above the current UK CD reissue data.

Early years

1964–6

David Bowie Early On

Liza Jane/Louie go home/I pity the fool*/Take my tip*/That's where my heart is [previously unreleased demo]/I want my baby back [previously unreleased demo]/Bars of the county jail [previously unreleased demo]/You've got a habit of leaving*/Baby loves that way*/I'll follow you [previously unreleased demo]/Glad I've got nobody [previously unreleased demo]/Can't help thinking about me†/And I say to myself/Do anything you say†/Good morning girl†/I dig everything†/I'm not losing sleep†

Rhino R2 70526 (CD)

Although this is an American release, it has been widely available in the UK and is the best collection of Bowie's earliest recordings. Tracks marked * were issued in the UK on a CD EP, *The Manish Boys/*

Discography

Davy Jones & The Lower Third (See For Miles SEACD 1). Tracks marked † were issued in the UK on a short-length CD, *Don't Be Fooled By The Name* (PRT CDPR 04), repackaged by Castle (PYC 6001).

1967

David Bowie

Uncle Arthur/Sell me a coat/Rubber band [version 2]/Love you till Tuesday/There is a happy land/We are hungry men/When I live my dream [version 1]/Little bombardier/Silly boy blue/Come and buy my toys/Join the gang/She's got medals/Maid of Bond Street/Please Mr Gravedigger [version 2]

Deram DML 1007
Deram 800087 2 (CD)

Many other tracks recorded in this period have since appeared on compilation albums. *The David Bowie Collection* (Castle CCSCD 118) contains all the tracks from the Deram album plus 'The laughing gnome', 'The gospel according to Tony Day', 'Did you ever have a dream', 'The London boys', 'Karma man' and 'In the heat of the morning'. An Australian CD (Deram/Polydor 820549 2) contains all the above tracks plus 'Let me sleep beside you'. The video soundtrack album, *Love You Till Tuesday* (Pickwick PWKS 4131P), contains some of this material plus 'Space oddity' [alternative version], 'When I'm five', 'Ching-a-ling' and 'Let me sleep beside you'.

RCA

1969

David Bowie
Man of Words, Man of Music (US) Reissued by RCA as *Space Oddity* (1972)

Space oddity/Unwashed and somewhat slightly dazed/Don't sit down*/Letter to Hermione/Cygnet committee/Janine/An occasional dream/Wild eyed boy from Freecloud/God knows I'm good/ Memory of a free festival
    [Extra tracks on EMI issues only: Conversation piece/Memory of a free festival (Part 1)/(Part 2)]
*Does not appear on RCA issues

Philips SBL 7912
RCA LSP 4813
RCA PD 84813 (CD)
EMI EMC 3571
EMI CDP 791835 2 (CD)

1970

The Man Who Sold The World

The width of a circle/All the madmen/Black country rock/After all/Running gun blues/Saviour machine/She shook me cold/The man who sold the world/The supermen
    [Extra tracks on EMI issues only: Lightning frightening/Holy holy/ Moonage daydream*/Hang on to yourself*]
*Previously issued as by Arnold Corns

Mercury 6338 041
RCA LSP 4816
RCA PD 84654 (CD)
EMI EMC 3573
EMI CDP 791837 2 (CD)

1971

Hunky Dory

Changes/Oh! You pretty things/
Eight line poem/Life on Mars?/
Kooks/Quicksand/Fill your heart/
Andy Warhol/Song for Bob Dylan/
Queen bitch/The Bewlay Brothers

[Extra tracks on EMI issues only:
Bombers/The supermen (alternative
version)/Quicksand (vocal and
guitar only)/The Bewlay Brothers
(alternative version)]

RCA SF 8244
RCA PD 84623 (CD)
EMI EMC 3572
EMI CDP 791843 2 (CD)

1972

*The Rise and Fall of Ziggy Stardust and
The Spiders From Mars*

Five years/Soul love/Moonage
daydream/Starman/It ain't easy/Lady
Stardust/Star/Hang on to yourself/
Ziggy Stardust/Suffragette city/Rock
'n' roll suicide

[Extra tracks on EMI issues only:
John I'm only dancing/Velvet
goldmine/Sweet head/Ziggy
Stardust (demo)/Lady Stardust
(demo)]

RCA SF 8287
RCA PD 84702 (CD)
EMI EMC 3577
EMI CDP 794400 2 (CD)

1973

Aladdin Sane

Watch that man/Aladdin Sane/
Drive-in Saturday/Panic in Detroit/
Cracked actor/Time/The prettiest
star/Let's spend the night together/
The Jean genie/Lady grinning soul

RCA RS 1001
RCA PD 83890 (CD)
EMI EMC 3579
EMI CDP 794768 2 (CD)

Pin-ups

Rosalyn/Here comes the night/I wish
you would/See Emily play/
Everything's alright/I can't explain/
Friday on my mind/Sorrow/Shape of
things/Don't bring me down/
Anyway, anyhow, anywhere?/
Where have all the good times
gone?

[Extra tracks on EMI issues only:
Growin' up/Amsterdam]

RCA RS 1003
RCA PD 84653 (CD)
EMI EMC 3580
EMI CDP 794767 2 (CD)

1974

Diamond Dogs

Future legend/Bewitched/Diamond
dogs/Sweet thing/Candidate/Sweet
thing (reprise)/Rebel rebel/Rock 'n'
roll with me/We are the dead/1984/
Big Brother/Chant of the ever
circling skeletal family

[Extra tracks on EMI issues only:
Dodo/Candidate (demo version)]

RCA APL 1 0576
RCA PD 83889 (CD)
EMI EMC 3584
EMI CDP 795211 2 (CD)

David Live

1984/Rebel rebel/Moonage
daydream/Sweet thing/Changes/
Suffragette city/Aladdin Sane/All the
young dudes/Cracked actor/Rock 'n'
roll with me/Watch that man/Knock
on wood/Diamond dogs/Big Brother/
Width of a circle/The Jean Genie/
Rock 'n' roll suicide

[Extra tracks on EMI issues only:
Band introduction/Here today, gone
tomorrow/Time]

RCA APL2 0771
(not issued on RCA CD)
EMI DBLD 1
EMI CDP 795363 2 (CD)

Discography

1975

Young Americans

Win/Somebody up there likes me/
Can you hear me/Across the
universe/Fame/Fascination/Right/
Young Americans
    [Extra tracks on EMI issues only:
Who can I be now?/It's gonna be
me/John I'm only dancing again]

RCA RS 1006
RCA PD 80998 (CD)
EMI EMC 1021
EMI CDP 796436 2 (CD)

1976

Station to Station

Station to station/Golden years/
Word on a wing/TVC 15/Stay/Wild is
the wind
    [Extra tracks on EMI issues only:
Word on a wing/Stay (both recorded
live 23/3/76)]

RCA APL1 1327
RCA PD 81327 (CD)
EMI EMC 1020
EMI CDP 796435 2 (CD)

1977

Low

Speed of life/Breaking glass/What in
the world/Sound and vision/Always
crashing in the same car/Be my wife/
A new career in a new town/
Warszawa/Art decade/Weeping wall/
Subterraneans
    [Extra tracks on EMI issues only:
Some are/All saints/Sound and
vision (1991 remix)]

RCA PL 12030
RCA PD 89002 (CD)
EMI EMD 1027
EMI CDP 797719 2 (CD)

"Heroes"

Beauty and the beast/Joe the lion/
"Heroes"/Sons of the silent age/

Blackout/V–2 Schneider/Sense of
doubt/Moss garden/Neuköln/The
secret life of Arabia
    [Extra tracks on EMI issues only:
Abdulmajid/Joe the lion (1991
remix)]

RCA PL 12522
RCA PD 83857 (CD)
EMI EMD 1025
EMI CDP 797720 2 (CD)

1978

Stage

Hang on to yourself/Ziggy Stardust/
Five years/Soul love/Star/Station to
station/Fame/TVC 15/Breaking glass/
"Heroes"/What in the world/
Blackout/Beauty and the beast/
Warszawa/Speed of life/Art decade/
Sense of doubt
    [Extra track on EMI issues only:
Alabama song]

RCA PL 02913
RCA PD 89002 (CD)
EMI EMD 1030
EMI CDS 798617 2 (CD)

1979

Lodger

Fantastic voyage/African night
flight/Move on/Yassassin/Red sails/
DJ/Look back in anger/Boys keep
swinging/Repetition/Red money
    [Extra tracks on EMI issues only: I
pray olé/Look back in anger/(new
version recorded 1988)]

RCA BOWLP 1
RCA PD 84234 (CD)
EMI EMD 1026
EMI CDP 797724 2 (CD)

1980

Scary Monsters and Super Creeps

It's no game (Part 1)/Up the hill
backwards/Scary monsters (and
super creeps)/Ashes to ashes/

Fashion/Teenage wildlife/Scream like a baby/Kingdom come/Because you're young/It's no game (Part 2)

[Extra tracks on EMI issues only: Space oddity (7-inch B-side)/Panic in Detroit (previously unreleased version) Crystal Japan (rare Japanese 7-inch A-side)/Alabama song]

RCA BOWLP 2
RCA PD 83647 (CD)
EMI EMD 1029
EMI CDP 799331 2 (CD)

1983

Ziggy Stardust – The Motion Picture

Hang on to yourself/Ziggy Stardust/Watch that man/Medley: Wild eyed boy from Freecloud, All the young dudes, Oh! You pretty things/Moonage daydream/Space oddity/My death/Cracked actor/Time/Width of a circle/Changes/Let's spend the night together/Suffragette city/White light, white heat/Rock 'n' roll suicide

RCA PL 84862
(not issued on RCA CD)
EMI EMD 1037
EMI CDP 780411 2 (CD)

EMI

1983

Let's Dance

Modern love/China girl/Let's dance/Without you/Ricochet/Criminal world/Cat people (putting out fire)/Shake it

EMI (America) AML 3029
EMI (America) CDP 746002 2 (CD)

1984

Tonight

Loving the alien/Don't look down/God only knows/Tonight/Neighbourhood threat/Blue Jean/ Tumble and twirl/I keep forgettin'/Dancing with the big boys

EMI (America) EL 240227 1
EMI (America) CDP 746047 2 (CD)

1987

Never Let Me Down

Day in day out/Time will crawl/Beat of your drum/Never let me down/Zeroes/Glass spider/Shining star (makin' my love)/New York's in love/'87 and cry/Too dizzy/Bang bang

EMI (America) AMLS 3117
EMI (America) CDP 746677 2 (CD)

Savage Records

1993

Black Tie/White Noise

The wedding/You've been around/I feel free/Black tie, white noise/Jump they say/Nite flights/Pallas Athena/Miracle good night/Don't let me down and down/Looking for Lester/I know it's gonna happen someday/The wedding song

[Extra tracks on CD and DCC only: Jump they say (remix)/Lucy can't dance]

Savage Records 74321 13697 2 (CD)

Discography

Uncollected Singles _____

1972

John I'm only dancing/Hang on to yourself
  (Two versions of the A-side were released with this number)

RCA 2263

1974

Rebel rebel (7-inch version)/Lady grinning soul

RCA APBO 0287

Hang on to yourself/Man in the middle
  [Single issued as by Arnold Corns]

Mooncrest MOON 25

1977

Helden/V-2 Schneider (German version of "Heroes")

RCA PB 9168 (import)

1978

Heroes/V-2 Schneider (French version of "Heroes")

RCA PB 9167 (import)

1981

Under pressure (with Queen)/Soul brother (Queen only)

[Issued on Queen CD *Hot Space* (EMI CDP 746215 2)]

EMI 5250

1982

Baal's hymn/Remembering Marie/
Ballad of the adventurers/
The drowned girl/The dirty song

RCA BOW 11

Cat people (putting out fire)/(Paul's theme)
  [Bowie on A-side only.
Soundtrack version issued in the US on CD (MCA MCAD 1498)]

MCA MCA 770

1983

Modern love/Modern love (live)

EMI 158

1985

Dancing in the street (with Mick Jagger)/instrumental

EMI EA 204

1986

Absolute beginners (7-inch version)/Dub mix

Virgin VS 838

1987

Day in day out/Julie

EMI EA 230

Time will crawl/Girls

EMI EA 237

Time will crawl (12-inch limited edition with the B-side sung in Japanese)

EMI 12 EAS 237

1990

Fame 90/(alternative version)
  [Several remixes of this song were issued in alternative formats]

EMI FAME 90

1992

Real cool world/(alternative version)
  [Issued on a CDEP with

Tin Machine ─────────────────────────────

1989

Tin Machine

Heaven's in here/Tin machine/
Prisoner of love/Crack city/I can't
read/Under the god/Amazing/
Working class hero/Bus stop/Pretty
thing/Video crimes/Run/Sacrifice
yourself/Baby can dance

EMI CD791990 2 (CD)

1991

You belong in rock 'n' roll/Amlapura
(single version)
  [CDEP versions contain additional
tracks]

London LON 305
London LONCD 305
London LOCDT 305

Tin Machine II

Baby universal/One shot/You belong
in rock 'n' roll/If there is something/
Amlapura/Betty wrong/You can't
talk/Stateside/Shopping for girls/A
big hurt/Sorry/Goodbye Mr Ed

Other Material ─────────────────────────

1978

Peter and the Wolf

Prokofiev's *Peter and the Wolf*
narrated by Bowie with the
Philadelphia Orchestra conducted
by Eugene Ormandy

RCA RL 12743
RCA RD 82743 (CD)

numerous remixes (Warner
W0127CD)]

Warner W0127

Victory 511216 2 (CD)

Baby universal (remix)/You belong
in rock 'n' roll
  [A limited edition CDEP contains
extra tracks recorded for a BBC
Radio session]

London LON 310
London LOCDT 310

Ruby Trax

[Compilation album containing
unreleased live performance of Go
now (lead vocal not by Bowie)]

Forty NME 40 CD (CD)

1993

Tin Machine Live: Oy Vey, Baby

If there is something/Amazing/I
can't read/Stateside/Under the god/
Goodby Mr Ed/Heaven's in here/
You belong in rock 'n' roll

Victory 828328 2 (CD)

Just a Gigolo (soundtrack)
Bowie's Revolution song

Jambo JAM 1

1982

Bowie Rare

Ragazzo solo, Ragazza sola/'Round
and 'round/Amsterdam/Holy holy/

Discography

Panic in Detroit (live)/Young Americans (US 7-inch version)/ Velvet goldmine/John I'm only dancing (again)/Helden/Moon of Alabama/Crystal Japan

RCA PL 45406

1985

The Falcon and The Snowman (soundtrack)
This is not America

EMI (America) EJ 240305 1
EMI (America) CDP 748411 2 (CD)

1986

Absolute Beginners (soundtrack)
Absolute beginners/That's motivation/Volare

Virgin V 2386
Virgin VD 2514
Virgin CDV 2386 (CD)

Labyrinth (soundtrack)
Underground (opening titles)/Magic dance/Chilly down/As the world falls down/Within you/Underground

EMI (America) AML 3104
EMI (America) CDP 746312 2 (CD)

1987

When the Wind Blows (soundtrack)
When the wind blows

Virgin V 2406
Virgin CDV 2406 (CD)

1989

Sound + Vision
(limited edition box set)
Space oddity (demo)/London bye ta-ta/1984 + Dodo (medley)/After today/It's hard to be a saint in the city/Helden (1989 remix)/John I'm only dancing (live)/Changes (live)/ The supermen (live)/Ashes to ashes (video edit)

[This imported set includes 41 other tracks already available. The live items listed above were recorded at the Boston Music Hall, 1/10/72. The CD version contains three CDs plus one CD video]

Rykodisc RCD 90120/21/22
(also on LP and cassette)

248

Index

Index

Index